OIL AND WORLD POLITICS

OIL AND WORLD POLITICS

The real story of today's conflict zones: Iraq, Afghanistan, Venezuela, Ukraine and more

JOHN FOSTER

JAMES LORIMER & COMPANY LTD., PUBLISHERS
TORONTO

James Lorimer & Company Ltd., Publishers acknowledges funding support from the Ontario Arts Council (OAC), an agency of the Government of Ontario. We acknowledge the support of the Canada Council for the Arts, which last year invested $153 million to bring the arts to Canadians throughout the country. This project has been made possible in part by the Government of Canada and with the support of the Ontario Media Development Corporation.

Cover design: Tyler Cleroux
Cover images: Best Army Photos 2 by Expert Infantry on Flickr, iStock

Library and Archives Canada Cataloguing in Publication

Foster, John, 1934-, author
    Oil and world politics : the real story of today's conflict zones : Iraq, Afghanistan, Venezuela, Ukraine and more / John Foster.

Includes bibliographical references and index.
Issued in print and electronic formats.
ISBN 978-1-4594-1344-3 (softcover).--ISBN 978-1-4594-1345-0 (EPUB)

    1. Petroleum industry and trade--Political aspects. 2. Petroleum industry and trade--Military aspects. 3. Petroleum industry and trade--Economic aspects. 4. World politics--21st century. I. Title.

HD9560.5.F58 2018   338.2'7282   C2018-903543-9
                                               C2018-903544-7

James Lorimer & Company Ltd., Publishers
117 Peter Street, Suite 304
Toronto, ON, Canada
M5V 0M3
www.lorimer.ca

Printed and bound in Canada.

Photo Credits: Business Recorder (Pakistan): p. 100; Cosa Cosa Cosa: p. 118; Cpl Michael Bastien, MARPAC Imaging Services ET2014-7050-03: p. 122; Sarah Sanders, Press Secretary, The White House: p. 246; Sergeant Daren Kraus, Image Tech, TFK Afghanistan, Roto 9: p. 155; Shutterstock: p. 33, 172, 201; U.S. Department of Defesnse: p. 47; U.S. Department of State: p. 75

Map Credits: The following sources were used to create the maps in this book: awesomestories.com, China Daily, BBC, economists-pick-research.hktdc.com, Euractiv, Gazprom, Institute for the Study of War, Inter-State Gas Systems Pakistan, International Energy Agency, marsecreview.com, mediterraneanaffairs.com, noelmaurer.typepad.com, Oil Price.net, reseauinternational.net, Sui Northern Gas Pipelines, US Energy Information Administration, and worldpress.org

To my family, and all those who ask bold questions in search of truth and understanding.

CONTENTS

LIST OF MAPS

FOREWORD

About a decade ago, I was attending a series of lectures on world affairs in Kingston, Ontario. The speakers extolled all the wonderful things Western leaders were doing for the world. I was a bit sceptical whether the non-Western world was as accepting as they insinuated. At one point, the organiser saw me rolling my eyes in the back row. He nabbed me during the coffee break. "So you didn't agree with the speaker?" he asked.

"He speaks from a Western perspective," I replied. "What about the underlying motivations, the Petroleum Game?" To my surprise, he promptly asked me to give a lecture. I equivocated: "I'm an economist; I couldn't do that." On the way home, I told my wife, Millie Morton, about the conversation. She said: "You can do it; I'll help you."

That's how this book began. For a couple of years, we had been struggling to understand the daily news in a small group setting. Why was Afghanistan so important? Why was Iraq invaded and destroyed? The reasons for war didn't make sense. Millie and I had both worked in international development. I have a background in the economics of petroleum. She is a sociologist, skilled in asking probing questions, simplifying complex issues, and finding the essence of the story. She became my ongoing collaborator.

At that time, 21 Canadians had lost their lives in Afghanistan. Official pronouncements about finding bin Laden, promoting democracy and sending girls to school seemed laudable — but were they the real reasons for massive military expenditures? We dug beneath the surface of government pronouncements and newspaper headlines. We read original documents, newspapers from countries around the world, analyses from think-tanks and speeches given by high-level people. Our investigations led us to find a petroleum issue openly discussed in Asia, but rarely mentioned in the West. In Afghanistan, there was a petroleum story — plans for a natural gas pipeline with geopolitical significance.

We worked hard to prepare a presentation that was clear, interesting and entertaining. The talk in November was an uncanny experience. When I began, I could have heard a pin drop. The audience included about 300 retirees from all walks of life, and they, too, wanted to discover what was going on. They asked questions about history, geography and culture. They wanted insights beyond the news in mainstream media.

Three months later, I gave a similar talk to a foreign affairs group in Ottawa, including retired and serving diplomats, civil servants and parliamentarians. The response was equally encouraging. Paul Dewar, MP, Opposition foreign affairs critic, acclaimed the research. He later referred to it in a parliamentary debate on Afghanistan.[1] Then, at the request of the Canadian Centre for Policy Alternatives, I wrote a short paper entitled "A Pipeline through a Troubled Land."[2] It documented long-standing US plans to build a gas pipeline from Turkmenistan, through Afghanistan, to Pakistan and India, and link the four countries together. Shawn McCarthy, energy reporter at the *Globe and Mail*, invited me to an interview in Ottawa. For two and a half hours, he asked detailed questions, admitting he had read all 82 of my endnotes. Later that week (June 19, 2008), my findings became banner headlines in the *Globe and Mail*: "Pipeline Opens New Front in Afghan War."[3]

Since then I've documented petroleum stories in Iraq, Iran, Syria, Ukraine and other parts of the world. Could it just be a coincidence? The patterns from one country to another and the similarities over time suggested otherwise. The evidence of international rivalry over petroleum was overwhelming. The competition showed up periodically in policies, speeches and actions. That's why I call what's going on the Petroleum Game.

Petroleum stories vary from one country to another. They may be about the petroleum resources of a country. Or they may relate to a country's strategic location — as a route for pipelines or a place in close proximity to significant sea routes. Petroleum is only part of the story. Sometimes there are historic animosities, other valuable resources or power-seeking goals. Nevertheless, petroleum deserves public attention. It is a vital resource for all modern economies, a source of enormous wealth and power.

Given the acknowledged connections between petroleum and climate change, understanding petroleum becomes critical to our future on Earth. Many vested interests support petroleum's current role. The links between petroleum and ongoing conflict and misery merit attention, too. This connection is almost as old as the discovery of petroleum itself, but rarely discussed openly as events are unfolding.

I know a bit about conflict. I was a child in London during the Blitz of World War II. I saw the destruction caused by bombs landing close to my home. During the war, Churchill met with his cabinet in underground rooms that are now a museum. In the War Cabinet Rooms, the uniforms on the mannequins, maps stuck on the walls and the secret telephone for transcontinental calls to President Roosevelt evoke a time I remember well. I slept many nights in the bomb shelter my father built in our garden or under the heavy Morrison table where my parents pretended that was a normal thing for a family of five to do.

I visited the War Cabinet Rooms with members of my family a few years ago. Sixty years had passed since World War II. Yet when the 1940s air raid siren sounded in the museum, I also heard the sound of the V-1 — a low throb stealing through the dark sky. I held my breath, waiting for the boom of the landing. My discomfort forced me to leave the museum. The sounds of war still disturbed my well-being. Around the world, millions of others share my experience when they hear drones circling overhead or shells landing nearby.

During the Suez Crisis of 1956, I served in the Royal Navy on the first tank landing craft to arrive in Port Said. Politics were never discussed in the wardroom, so I only learned later what had really happened. After Egypt's President Nasser nationalized the Suez Canal, Britain and France, with Israeli support, planned quietly to take back the canal. An Anglo-French enterprise had run the canal for 87 years. It was a strategic transit route for oil, with two-thirds of Europe's oil passing through it. Britain viewed it as a lifeline to its imperial interests. Eventually the invasion was revealed to be a stitch-up, with only a few people in each country knowing the plan. As sailors, we were pawns in the game.

In this book, my intent is to bring together little-known stories linking petroleum and conflict. From diverse reliable sources (replete with endnotes), I have drawn a big picture of what has been going on in recent years. The book is based on public information and on understandings that evolved during my years as an energy economist with two international banks and two oil companies. Much of my working life was spent bridging cultures. With suitcase and briefcase, I visited more than 35 countries around the world, meeting officials and struggling to understand petroleum. My job was economic analysis.

11

Now, with the experience of a lifetime, I want to share my understandings of both petroleum and conflict. In a world focused on soundbites and crises, the big picture is often obscured. That's why I've included backstories — cultural, geographical and historical information relevant to the situation in 2018. Featured are countries experiencing recent military interventions and their consequences — Afghanistan, Iraq, Libya, Syria. Included also are countries experiencing punishing sanctions or political interference, such as the training of opposition leaders or the funding of rebellion. Each chapter could be a lengthy book, but my goal is to convey the essence of competing narratives while showing how the Petroleum Game is being played in many countries simultaneously.

My challenge has been to ferret out the pieces of a multi-faceted puzzle and fit them together into a coherent story — the world in conflict and the petroleum connection. Power, politics and petroleum go together. It's time to discuss the Petroleum Game openly. This book aims to expand the conversation.

John Foster
Kingston, Ontario, Canada

CHAPTER 1
PETROLEUM AND GEOPOLITICS

"All things are subject to interpretation. Whichever interpretation prevails at a given time is a function of power and not truth."

— Friedrich Nietzsche

Once, during my early years working with British Petroleum (BP) in London, UK, Robert Belgrave, my boss, asked me to accompany him to a lunch meeting. My role, he said, was to serve as a witness. He wanted me to hear and remember everything that was said.

Our invitation came from two men who worked at the American Embassy. We met them at a high-end restaurant and sat at a corner table with white tablecloths and elegant service. One man introduced himself as the US petroleum attaché. He had a relaxed, friendly manner that tended to put me at ease. The other I've always thought of as Mr. X, because he never stated his name or position. He had a crew cut and a wiry, tense appearance. Mr. X came quickly to the point of the meeting and did most of the talking. He was concerned with the actions of BP's Belgian affiliate. He said it had been observed at the port of Antwerp loading lubricant oil into a tanker destined for Cuba. He wanted BP to recall the ship and honour the US embargo on trading with Cuba.

My boss listened carefully, rephrasing what he was hearing to make sure there was no misunderstanding. He had been a seasoned diplomat before joining BP mid-career. His response was polite, but forceful. "BP is subject to UK law, not US law," he said. "The UK has a long-standing policy of trading with Cuba. I suggest you talk to the UK government."

Throughout the meeting, I said almost nothing. I was new to the political and strategic side of BP. Previously I had worked on pricing issues, spending long days doing calculations with a manual calculator. Pricing work had been important, but tedious. Now I was learning that oil was geopolitics, too. I was fascinated by the level of interest shown by the Americans and by Robert Belgrave's diplomatic dealings with them. The UK government continued to ignore American pressure on trade with Cuba.

Oil companies think globally. So do the governments of countries where these companies are headquartered — the United States, Britain, Canada, France, the Netherlands. They follow petroleum closely. Western countries share ideas through the International Energy Agency (IEA). In countries with oil interests, there is a complex relationship between government and oil companies. The relationship varies from country to country.

In developed countries, major oil and gas companies have staff who liaise with governments. They hire public relations firms to tout their companies' positions. They belong to trade associations that act as industry advocates. Large companies may even have staff who are seconded to government. Conversely, companies may hire civil servants and diplomats in mid-career or from early retirement to help in government relations.

The links between oil companies and governments are extensive. In Washington, people move back and forth between private sector firms, think-tanks and political levels of the US Administration. In 2017, President Trump selected ExxonMobil's CEO Rex Tillerson to be his secretary of state. During the period 2001–2008, the association between oil companies and the George W. Bush Administration was patent. The energy industry contributed heavily to the two Bush-Cheney election campaigns, and officials at the highest levels of government had an oil industry background. Former Vice-President Dick Cheney had been CEO of Halliburton — a giant company servicing oilfields worldwide. Condoleezza Rice headed Chevron's public policy program before being named national security adviser and later secretary of state in the Bush Administration. During the same period, Tony Blair headed the UK government, and BP was nicknamed "Blair Petroleum" for its ultra-close governmental links.[1]

When Dick Cheney was CEO of Halliburton, he recognized these links.

In 1999, he told the Institute of Petroleum in London, "Oil is unique in that it is so strategic in nature. We are not talking about soap-flakes ... The Middle East ... is still where the prize ultimately lies."[2]

PETROLEUM: THE MOST IMPORTANT COMMODITY

Petroleum is a source of great wealth — for those who sell it, for those who transport it and for those who transform it for its many uses. As the prime form of modern energy, petroleum is the most valuable commodity in world trade. In 2015, the world fuel trade was about US$3 trillion, 18 per cent of all merchandise exports.[3]

Over the past century, oil has grown in importance throughout the modern world. In some ways, petroleum is simple. It's a jug-and-bottle industry. Some countries have it and want to sell it. Other countries need it and want to buy. Companies send huge tanker fleets to collect it and build pipeline networks to move it from one geographic area to another.

Petroleum itself, however, is complex. It includes a range of hydrocarbons from the heaviest bitumen to the lightest natural gas. All are energy commodities but they have different qualities and differing extraction, refining and transportation requirements. There is a world of difference between Libyan light crude oil and Albertan bituminous oil. Libyan oil is high in gasoline content and low in sulphur; it is simple and cheap to refine. Bituminous oil is heavy, viscous like molasses and high in sulphur and metallic contaminants. It is costly to extract, upgrade and refine into high-value products like gasoline. It is so viscous it must be diluted with lighter oils, such as condensate, before it is shipped by pipeline.

Despite its intricacies, the world supply system works remarkably smoothly. With petroleum as the engine of modern economies, industries and governments want to assure steady supplies. Without it, economies grind to a standstill. Unfettered access to oil and gas markets is vital to all countries, whether large or small, importer or exporter, poor or rich.

Natural gas comprises the lightest hydrocarbons that are gaseous at room temperature — mostly methane but also ethane, propane and butane. It can be found by itself or in association with oil. It was once the world's Cinderella fuel, discounted in price to facilitate its commercialization. Natural gas is now prized for its clean burning and low-sulphur content.

15

Environmentally, it is less air-polluting than liquid fuels. Natural gas is used as fuel in central heating and power generation, and as feedstock in petrochemical and fertilizers manufacturing. In power generation, it allows quick and cheap plant construction (unlike hydro or nuclear plants) and rapid plant start-up to meet peak load demand.[4]

Even with its enormous importance to modern economies, oil production itself is being questioned because of its association with climate change. Most scientists now believe global warming must be slowed if the Earth is to escape catastrophic changes in weather. Ever-worsening storms, drought, flooding and forest fires are being associated with global warming. Economist Gordon Laxer (2016) pointed out Canada's greatest source of emissions is the production of petroleum — especially in Alberta's oil sands — rather than petroleum's use in transportation.[5] According to Environment and Climate Change Canada, the oil and gas sector was responsible for 26 per cent of Canadian greenhouse gases in 2015.[6]

Thus, petroleum is important as the prime form of modern energy and as a source of great wealth. It is important because its continued production and use at current levels portends massive upheavals in societies as climate change progresses. Understanding petroleum — and how integral it is to governments, businesses, diplomacy and international conflicts — is essential to addressing challenges to the planet itself.

THE PETROLEUM GAME

The Petroleum Game is played by governments taking actions to improve their own geopolitical advantage vis-à-vis others. These actions can be covert (undercover actions) or overt (declared policies). They can be diplomatic or military, promoted by a country itself or by proxies. The objective is to gain advantage in power, wealth or politics, typically all three.

The game is as old as the discovery of petroleum. Petroleum — both oil and natural gas — has been a major reason for British, French and US involvement in the Middle East. The Middle East is the world's "energy heartland," the home of vast reservoirs of both oil and gas. Geologically, a vast oil corridor runs north from the Arabian Peninsula, through Iraq and Iran, to the Caspian Sea and beyond. It contains more than half the world's oil reserves. As well, four countries — Russia, Iran, Qatar and Turkmenistan — have half of the world's natural gas. The US has a long-standing interest in this energy heartland, as does the United Kingdom. The black areas shown in Map 1 are giant oil and gas reservoirs, or "elephants" in oil industry terminology, each representing a fortune to countries and companies.

Map 1. The Oil Corridor

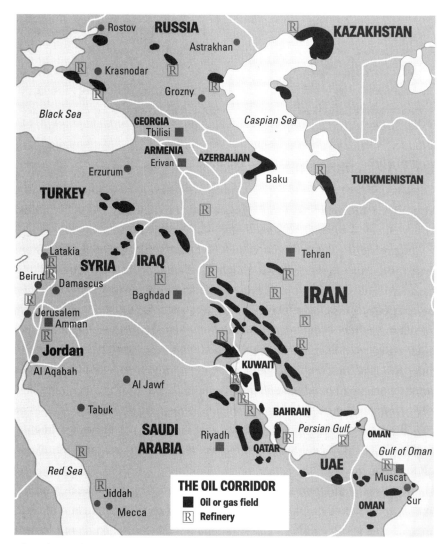

The oil corridor in the Middle East is the world's energy heartland. Each black spot represents a giant oil or gas field — a fortune to countries and companies.

Since petroleum is not evenly distributed around the world, powerful countries want to be sure they have access to markets. Petroleum has been a factor in big power politics, intelligence gathering, regime change efforts and high-level diplomatic discussions. Governments may coordinate their stories. Members of the North Atlantic Treaty Organization (NATO) sing from the same hymn sheet. The reality is this: oil and geopolitics are inseparable.

Control over access to petroleum and its price brings advantage. Consequently, petroleum infiltrates politics and is closely associated with power. Coveting the petroleum of another country is against the rules of international law — yet if it can be accomplished surreptitiously, under the cover of some laudable action, it's a bonanza. Power, politics and petroleum all go together.

DISCOVERING THE PETROLEUM GAME

Discovering the Petroleum Game requires delving into geopolitics. Although countries issue policy statements that may or may not reflect their real intentions, it is through actions that geopolitics emerge.

In considering the various hot spots where conflict or interference were occurring, I have been following themes, events, people. I've puzzled and pondered the narratives promulgated and actions taken by major players in world petroleum. Governmental narratives shed light on the varied views of players or blocs of players. The research was a bit like solving a mystery — seeking cross-fixes on what happened, who participated, when, where, how and why. I learned to do this as an economist with two oil companies and two international banks. My work there encouraged me to understand the world of petroleum not only from a Western perspective but more broadly from the stance of producing and importing countries worldwide. The question has been: what is it like to be in their shoes; and what does that mean?

In following the theme, I sought to understand the thinking behind the conflicts or interventions. I read newspaper and think-tank reports, speeches and policy statements — noting the actions being taken to implement policies. I looked for information on petroleum resources and trade routes. My research began with the conflict in Afghanistan. I discovered differences in the stated reasons for war. In the UK, the emphasis was on eradicating poppies and opium production; in the US, it was about democracy and human rights; in Canada, it was on helping women and sending girls to school. The differences appeared to be based more on what their respective populations would support than anything else. The reasons evolved as the conflict continued, and the differing views in different countries led to further questions.

Rarely mentioned was the planned pipeline from Turkmenistan through Afghanistan to Pakistan and India (TAPI). Though planning had been occurring for several years, the US Department of Energy stopped updating its website information on the project in 2002, shortly after US forces entered Afghanistan. Yet the project was discussed widely in South Asian newspapers. At donor conferences, pipeline plans were discussed — but they were omitted from official communiqués. Why? I followed events. In 2016, US warplanes bombed Syrian troops defending the Deir ez-Zor airport from Islamic State forces. The Pentagon claimed it was an accident. I looked for information on that city. It is a centre for Syria's oilfields. It could have been important in the routing of a proposed gas pipeline from Qatar to Turkey, a project which had US blessing. The besieged city depended on the airport as its lifeline. Was the attack really accidental — or part of a deeper game as various journalists concluded?

Finally, I followed the people. Where were key politicians travelling and who were they meeting? Sometimes officials were forthright in their speeches abroad and quoted by the media of the countries they visited. That was how I discovered Bulgaria's prime minister had adamantly supported a strategic gas pipeline planned from Russia via Bulgaria to Central Europe, but changed his mind just one hour after a visit from Senator John McCain and other US officials. Why?

I found some analysts were credible and consistently reliable, while others were not. Where possible, I followed the money. For example, with no Western reporters able to enter parts of rebel-controlled Syria, Western media relied on organizations called the White Helmets and the Syrian Observatory for Human Rights. I searched for information on the White Helmets and found they were created by a UK private security specialist and former military intelligence officer, James Le Mesurier, and are funded by millions of dollars from the US, Canada, UK and other NATO countries.[7] Were news reports from the White Helmets tailored to suit their sponsors? Were the White Helmets engaged in responsible journalism or public relations? The Syrian Observatory for Human Rights is run from a home in Coventry, England. Its stated aim is to document alleged human rights abuses in Syria.[8] Although it was much quoted by Western media with little cross-checking, the Observatory's sources remained murky.

As I was conducting research, I shared my findings with others in face-to-face dialogues, small group discussions, public speeches and articles for various newspapers and think-tanks. Responses provided cross-fixes from a wide variety of listeners on whether my analysis was solid. Sometimes these exchanges challenged me to dig deeper.

Clearly, in each of the countries discussed, the reasons for conflict are multi-faceted and complex. Nevertheless, the connections to petroleum remain. That is the tale I tell.

BACKSTORY: TWO SHOCKS IN THE 1970S

In 1971, US President Nixon shocked the world by delinking the US dollar from gold. Going off the gold standard eliminated the era of fixed exchange rates. The change was a shock because the US dollar was the world's preferred currency for international transactions, including petroleum. In 1944, the Bretton Woods agreement had established a world financial system in which the United States pegged its currency to gold at US$35 per ounce, and other countries pegged theirs to the US dollar. This system worked well as long as the US ran a strong capital surplus on its balance of payments, but the US gradually had moved into deficit.

The second shock came two years later. During the Arab-Israeli War of October 1973, the Organization of Arab Petroleum Exporting Countries (OAPEC) — a group of 11 Arab countries — imposed an embargo on oil exports to countries supporting Israel.[9] Countries affected were the United States, the Netherlands, Portugal and South Africa. Each had spoken out strongly in favour of Israel. Each had long queues at gasoline stations. Other countries, more circumspect in dealing with Israel and Arab countries, were left untouched. In effect, the OAPEC embargo used oil as a weapon.

The ripple effect of the embargo was widespread. World oil prices quadrupled — from roughly US$3 per barrel to US$12 per barrel. For exporting countries, this was a windfall. For importing countries, the rapid escalation in the cost of oil skewed balance of payments and wrecked government budgets.

Saudi Arabia and other Organization of Petroleum Exporting Countries (OPEC) — a group of 15 nations — experienced a bonanza.[10] The immediate question for Washington was how to recycle these capital surpluses back to Western markets. The United States struck a deal with Saudi Arabia, whereby the Saudis would price oil exports in US dollars, accept only US dollars in payment and invest surplus dollars in US government debt such as US Treasury bills. Other Middle East oil exporters adopted the same practice. That meant oil-importing countries, other than the United States itself, had to acquire US dollars. They stepped up exports of goods and services to the US and were paid in US dollars.

With their immense new wealth, Saudi Arabia, Kuwait, Qatar and United Arab Emirates (UAE) went on a spending binge, nationalizing oil exploration and production and awarding huge construction and arms contracts to Western companies. Their unspent wealth was recycled into London and New York, boosting these financial centres. The UK and United States were quietly content with the windfall.

International oil companies were affected, too. The nationalization of oil exploration and production triggered a fundamental change in the Seven Sisters, the international oil companies operating in the Middle East.[11] Instead of exploring under concession contracts and exporting oil through their own marketing networks, they had to work under contract with OPEC national oil companies and buy oil from them. Their exploration shifted from the Middle East to non-OPEC areas such as the North Sea and Alaska. Their overall emphasis shifted from exploration to international supply and trading.

Globally, countries increasingly used the dollar for non-oil transactions as well. The US expanded the money supply to finance transactions worldwide. As world oil trade grew, so did the supply of US dollars and the amount of US government debt securities. The benefit of the petrodollar system to the United States has been immense. It enabled the US government to make use of an ever-growing mountain of debt.

The two shocks led to a fundamental change in the way all countries addressed petroleum. Around the world, energy security became a watch-word, prolific in mission statements of nations and international organizations. Western countries expressed concerns about vulnerability to Middle East oil disruption or price manipulation.

The International Energy Agency (IEA) was created in 1974 as a direct outcome of the oil embargo. In 2018, it had 29 member countries, including the US, Canada, Japan and most countries in Europe. The International Energy Agency defines energy security as "the uninterrupted availability of energy sources at an affordable price."[12] It publishes an annual energy outlook that is widely used by governments in their planning.

As another consequence of the embargo, the US turned its full searchlight on the world energy scene. It created a Department of Energy and substantially expanded State Department's coverage of international energy issues. Today, the US has literally hundreds of people monitoring world energy — at the Departments of State, Energy and Commerce, the National Security Council, the Pentagon and the Central Intelligence Agency (CIA). No other government matches this scale of coverage.

US diplomat Robin Dunnigan revealed in 2015 that the State Department alone had more than 100 people addressing energy policy.[13] Energy policy is intricately linked with US national security and the energy security of US partners, especially in Europe. With all these Americans following petroleum, every nuance comes under scrutiny.

Both the price of petroleum and the availability of dollars to pay for petroleum have mattered greatly to countries around the world for almost 50 years. Subsequent sections and chapters relate how and why this is changing.

RIVALRIES AND CONFLICTS: US, CHINA AND RUSSIA

The US, China and Russia dominate the world's geopolitics. Each of these powerful countries has its own reasons to be concerned about oil and gas.

The United States is the world's largest consumer of oil, at 19.9 million barrels per day (b/d) in 2017 or 20 per cent of the world's total. The US military alone consumes at least 300,000 b/d, the same as Sweden's total consumption. Oil is vital for American projection of global power. In 2014, with the expansion of fracking, the US became the world's largest oil producer, 13.0 million b/d in 2017. US net oil imports fell to 23 per cent of consumption from their peak of about 60 per cent in 2005. Even so, the US is still the world's second largest net importer of oil in the world, only surpassed (since 2013) by China. Half of US oil imports comes from Canada, which Washington has historically considered a secure source.

Interest in petroleum is embedded into US foreign policy. In his 1980 State of the Union Address, President Carter declared, "An attempt by any outside force to gain control of the Persian Gulf region will be regarded as an assault on the vital interests of the United States of America, and such an assault will be repelled by any means necessary, including military force."[14] That is the so-called Carter Doctrine. The US military's Central Command covers the entire Middle East and Central Asia. Central Command oversees 250,000 US troops plus a similar number of contractors.

Subsequent presidents maintained this policy. After the Soviet Union disintegrated in the early 1990s, the US saw itself as a unipolar nation and petroleum was integrated into new power games. In his 1997 book *The Grand Chessboard*, former US National Security Advisor Zbigniew Brzezinski described America as standing at the centre of an interlocking world, in which power originated ultimately from a single source: Washington, DC.[15] He wrote: "The US controls all the world's seas; its military legions are firmly perched on the western and eastern extremities of Eurasia; they control the Persian Gulf; and American vassals dot the Eurasian continent." Indeed, many observers have compared Washington to ancient Rome, with vassal states paying tribute to the imperial centre.

During George W. Bush's presidency, a senior adviser (reportedly Karl Rove) described the mindset: "We're an empire now, and when we act, we create our own reality. And while you're studying that reality — judiciously, as you will — we'll act again, creating other new realities, which you can study too, and that's how things will sort out. We're history's actors — and you, all of you, will be left to just study what we do."[16] That was the attitude within Washington, DC, as a new millennium unfolded.

The neoconservative backers of George W. Bush put little faith in the multilateral system and worked to paralyze it. They implemented a policy of US global domination through overwhelming power and unilateralism — a unipolar world. Their bible was the Project for the New American Century (PNAC), founded by William Kristol and Richard Kagan.[17] Signatories to its Statement of Principles included Donald Rumsfeld, Jeb Bush, Paul Wolfowitz, Richard Perle, Elliot Abrams and Lewis Libby, all moving into high positions in the George W. Bush Administration. One of PNAC's key reports was *Rebuilding America's Defenses: Strategy, Forces and Resources for a New Century*, published in 2000.[18] It posited, "At present the United States faces no global rival. America's grand strategy should aim to preserve and extend this advantageous position as far into the future as possible."

The Bush Administration introduced the Doctrine of Preemption. The 2006 National Security Strategy stated, "Under long-standing principles of self defense, we do not rule out the use of force before attacks occur, even if uncertainty remains as to the time and place of the enemy's attack."[19] President Obama was more circumspect. The White House dropped Bushisms such as the "global war on terror" in favour of "overseas contingency operations."[20] But it was really more of the same, using the military as the primary tool of asserting US dominance. Drones, special forces and extrajudiciary assassination were preferred rather than rendition and black hole prisons without trial. Dead men tell no tales!

Addressing the US nation in 2013, Obama called America an "exceptional" country.[21] What does this mean? Hillary Clinton defined it as "America's unique and unparalleled ability to be a force for peace and progress, a champion for freedom and opportunity ... When America fails to lead, we leave a vacuum that either causes chaos or other countries or networks rush in to fill the void."[22] This view of US motivations as benign is prevalent in Washington circles and supported by mainstream media. Freedom, democracy and human rights are US motivations even in countries it is bombing. Recurring phrases such as exceptionalism and full spectrum dominance illustrate a mindset. The implicit assumptions are rarely questioned.

In 2013, a day after Obama referred to the US as "exceptional," Russia's President Putin wrote a cautionary article in the *New York Times*, noting the perils of exceptionalism. "There are big countries and small countries, rich and poor, those with long democratic traditions and those still finding their way to democracy ... We are all different, but ... we must not forget that God created us equal."[23] His message was ignored.

In all its dealings, the US regards itself as entitled to a global reach.

Washington insiders used the term "benevolent global hegemony," with energy very much a part of this hegemony. Addressing the UN General Assembly in 2013, President Obama reiterated US Middle East policy. He said, "The United States of America is prepared to use all elements of our power, including military force, to secure our core interests in the region. We will confront external aggression against our allies and partners, as we did in the Gulf War. We will ensure the free flow of energy from the region to the world."[24]

The Gulf States — Saudi Arabia, Kuwait, Qatar and UAE — all have defence arrangements with Washington. Each is an autocratic oligarchy, with a relatively small population and heavy reliance on immigrant labour. They invest huge capital surpluses from petroleum in Western financial markets and buy huge amounts of armaments from Western countries. They are adroit investors of their oil revenues, aided and abetted by the City of London. They invest heavily in other Sunni Muslim countries. Their wealth gives them global clout.

Beyond the Middle East, the US has been active in Eurasia. In *The Grand Chessboard*, Brzezinski wrote, "For America, the chief geopolitical prize is Eurasia ... An enormous concentration of gas and oil ... is located in the region." Washington seeks to draw Central Asia to *its* zone of influence in South Asia, away from Russia and China. Afghanistan is the bridgehead.

The US works closely with the European Union (EU) on energy. The EU has an energy commissioner. The US has a Special Envoy for International Energy Affairs, whose focus under President Obama was on Europe and reducing its reliance on Russian gas.

Over the years, as I visited oil-producing countries and studied the petroleum sector, I found the US embassy always had one or two people who followed petroleum issues. The embassies of other countries had knowledgeable people, too.

Within the trove of US embassy cables revealed by WikiLeaks in 2010, 24,000 — nearly one in ten — referred to oil or natural gas. The Russian state-owned gas company Gazprom featured in 1,800 of them. Reporting this, the McClatchy newspaper chain wrote, "In the cables, US diplomats can be found: pressing oil companies to adjust their policies to match US foreign policy goals; helping US-based oil companies arrange deals on favourable terms; and pressing foreign governments to assist companies that are willing to do the US's bidding."[25] Clearly, petroleum is a preoccupation of US diplomats.

The US and other major powers use their intelligence agencies to collect commercial intelligence. Brazil illustrates what can happen. Its national oil company Petrobras is "a major source of revenue for the government and is developing the biggest oil discoveries of this century ... deep under the Atlantic," according to *The Guardian* newspaper.[26] The discoveries are of interest to American firms and evidently the US National Security Agency (NSA). In 2013, US whistle-blower Edward Snowden revealed the NSA was monitoring phone calls and emails of Petrobras and Brazil's president at that time, Dilma Rousseff.[27]

Further revelations indicated that Canada's Communications Security Establishment was monitoring computers at Brazil's Ministry of Mines and Energy.[28] The US and Canada, along with Britain, Australia and New Zealand, comprise the Five Eyes intelligence-sharing network. US journalist Glenn Greenwald, who helped bring Snowden's findings to light, commented that "the United States does not seem to be interested only in military affairs but also in trade secrets."[29]

Brazil's President Rousseff took specific actions in response to the revelations. She cancelled a state visit to Washington and publicly rebuked the United States at the 2013 United Nations General Assembly.[30] She demanded an explanation from the Canadian government, saying its spying appeared to be a clear case of industrial espionage.[31] During this same period of time, Boeing (a US firm) was competing with a Swedish firm for a major contract for military aircraft. When the Brazilian government made their decision, they awarded the contract to the Swedish firm. At least in this case, insider knowledge gained from espionage was not rewarded.

In short, the US sees itself as entitled to influence countries around the world. As the world's largest consumer of petroleum, it regards petroleum as a vital interest. It forges important diplomatic relationships with producing countries and monitors related issues through its intelligence services. All this adds up to extraordinary US attention to petroleum in its foreign policy. Many of its rivalries and conflicts have a petroleum connection.

* * *

China has a vital interest in petroleum, too. It is the world's second largest oil-consuming nation (12.8 million b/d in 2017) and the world's eighth largest oil producer (3.8 million b/d). In recent years, China's astonishing economic growth has turned it from oil self-sufficiency in 1990 to the world's largest importer in 2017 (9.1 million b/d). China's major source of oil is the Middle East where it has invested heavily in oil exploration and development, particularly in Iran. China trades with Iran and Russia in yuan, rial and rubles, their own currencies rather than petrodollars.

China is concerned about energy security and acutely aware of its vulnerability to blocked sea routes. In 2012, it perceived the US Pivot to East Asia strategy as a China-containment policy. Tankers carrying Middle Eastern oil to China must pass through three narrow waterways or chokepoints — the Strait of Hormuz, Strait of Malacca and South China Sea, all vulnerable to US Navy interference. To reduce its dependence on seaborne imports, China began investing in pipelines to bring oil and gas overland from Russia and Central Asia. In 2016, Russia became China's largest source of imported oil, overtaking Saudi Arabia.

Since 2009, China has built three massive pipelines to bring gas from Turkmenistan to Shanghai — 7,000 kilometres. This was accomplished without wars or drones. Turkmenistan has immense gas reserves, the world's fourth largest. China also partnered with Russia to build a huge gas pipeline from eastern Siberia to China. In 2018, they were planning another from western Siberia. In just a few years, Russia's largest gas customer would become China. The two countries agreed to trade in rubles and yuan — a challenge to the US petrodollar.

China focuses on commercial interests. Through its One Belt One Road initiative, it planned massive infrastructure investments to link trade routes by land and sea to Europe. The initiative was comprehensive, embracing ports, shipping, rail, roads, fibre-optics and more. China recently introduced regular freight train services to Europe. In 2016, the first freight train from China's northeast arrived at a Russian terminal near Moscow. The journey took just nine days across the Trans-Siberian Railway, 20 days less than the traditional sea-and-rail route. In 2017, the first container train

Map 2. Oil and Gas by Sea and Land to China

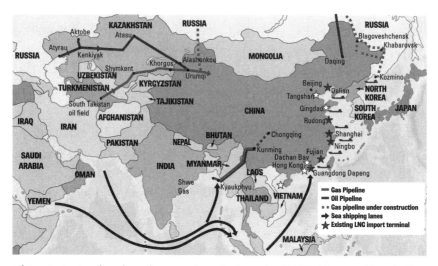

China imports oil and gas by sea primarily from the Middle East, and by pipeline from Russia and Central Asia.

reached London from China after a 12,000-km, 18-day journey through Kazakhstan, Russia, Belarus, Poland, Germany, Belgium and France. The rail service was reportedly cheaper than air transport and faster than sea. London was the fifteenth European city to receive Chinese rail cargo.

China has allocated enormous financial support for these infrastructure projects. In 2015, it created the Asian Infrastructure Investment Bank (AIIB), an alternative to the World Bank. As of March 2018, the AIIB had 64 members and 20 prospective members, not only Asian but also most European and Middle Eastern countries. Canada joined, but the US had not. As well, in 2015, the BRICS states (Brazil, Russia, India, China, South Africa) created the New Development Bank, also an alternative to the World Bank.

All these investments offer China increased security in its exports and imports of all goods, including energy. Railways and pipelines will bind China to other countries for many years to come. China's independence, economic success and its relationships with other countries are intricately linked to its petroleum interests. Concern about access to petroleum makes China attentive to any infringement of its trade routes. China must weigh petroleum carefully in its foreign policy.

Map 3. One Belt One Road

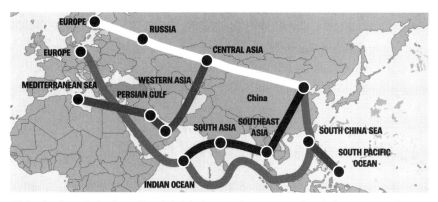

China's One Belt One Road initiative envisages massive infrastructure investments to link trade routes by sea and land to Europe.

* * *

Russia is a giant in the world of petroleum, the world's third largest oil producer (11.2 million b/d in 2017) and the world's largest exporter (overtaking Saudi Arabia as of 2017). For natural gas, Russia is the world's largest exporter by far, and most of its gas goes to Europe. Europe is the world's largest importer of gas. Europe has been using Russian gas since the 1960s. The US has consistently opposed this on grounds of European energy security. Yet the binding of East and West by pipeline helped build openness (Glasnost) and trust. As noted earlier, China, too, has become a major customer for Russian gas.

Russia's oil and gas resources are vital to its economy, providing more than 60 per cent of its export revenues and almost 40 per cent of its government revenue in 2017. Russia partners with Western and Chinese companies to develop its petroleum resources. A major concern is the Turkish Straits (the Dardanelles, Sea of Marmora and Bosphorus) — a narrow waterway connecting the Black Sea with the Mediterranean. This is a strategic route for Russian exports. Russia's only naval port on the Mediterranean Sea, in Syria, is also of vital concern for reasons outlined in later chapters.

Ukraine has been the main transit route for the pipelines bringing Russian gas to Europe. Pipelines matter — for Russia, Ukraine and Europe.

The gas can only go where the pipelines go. Since the dissolution of the Soviet Union, Russia has had pricing and payment problems with Ukraine. These problems have even led to gas not reaching some European countries that depend on it. Recently, Russia made repeated efforts to diversify by planning new export pipelines in joint ventures with Europeans. One new pipeline, Nord Stream, connects with Germany via the Baltic Sea, bypassing Ukraine. Other Russian efforts at joint ventures have been thwarted by the European Commission and the United States. Russia has been subjected to a full-scale demonizing, especially President Putin, during the Obama and Trump Administrations.

Petroleum is of vital interest to Russia's economy. Reliable transit routes on land and sea are critical to getting Russian oil and gas to market. Western demonizing, sanctions and efforts to block pipeline projects interfere with Russia's livelihood. Clearly, petroleum is a key component of Russia's relations with other countries.

The United States, China and Russia have some interests in common and others that diverge. In recent years, conflicts have unfolded in Afghanistan, Iraq, Iran, Libya, Somalia, Syria, Ukraine and Yemen. The narratives presented by Western governments and media emphasize problematic leaders, civil war and refugees. Yet in each country, petroleum plays a role in rivalries and conflicts.

NEW ECONOMIC REALITIES IN THE TWENTY-FIRST CENTURY

The world oil scene has changed dramatically since the turn of the twenty-first century. In 2000, the prevailing wisdom was that petroleum production had peaked and scarcity loomed. The International Energy Agency endorsed this view. Oil companies acted on it, pursuing high-cost projects in the deep offshore, High Arctic, Alberta oil sands, US shale basins and Venezuelan heavy oil belt. High prices for petroleum made such projects worthwhile. Governments acted on the belief, too. Vice-President Cheney chaired the US Energy Task Force in 2001, searching for solutions to petroleum scarcity. President George W. Bush decided to invade Iraq in a quest for control of Iraq's resources. A little more than a decade later, governments and companies began adjusting to a world glut and cheap oil. What happened to completely change conventional wisdom?

Saudi Arabia has been blamed frequently for the oil price collapse in 2014, but the reasons for the collapse can be found largely in the US and Canada. For Washington, heavy dependence on foreign oil imports has been a preoccupation for many years. Until the 1950s, the US was a net oil exporter. From then on, imports grew, peaking in 2005 at about 60 per cent of consumption. Oil consumption kept rising and production kept falling, with no major discoveries after the Alaska North Slope to offset output decline in the lower-48 states. With fracking, Washington's wildest dreams came true.

* * *

Fracking is a new way of extracting oil and gas from previously inaccessible shale basins of low permeability.[32] Fracking operations escalated in the US from about 2008. The leading shale gas-producing basin is Marcellus, straddling Pennsylvania and West Virginia, extending into upstate New York (where there is a moratorium on fracking).[33] The major shale oil-producing

Map 4. US Shale Oil and Gas Basins

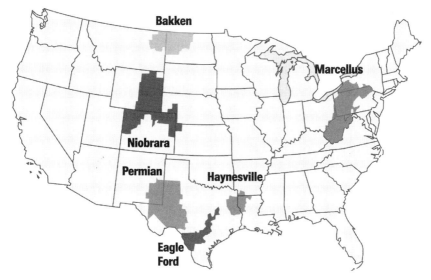

Fracking operations have resulted in remarkable increases in US oil and gas production since 2008.

basins are Eagle Ford and Permian, both in Texas, and Bakken in North Dakota, extending in Canada to Saskatchewan and Manitoba. They produced more than 4.5 million b/d by mid-2015, up from a mere 100,000 b/d in 2007.

Through fracking, the United States has become the world's largest oil producer, leapfrogging Saudi Arabia and Russia as of 2017. US dependence on imported oil declined from a peak of more than 60 per cent of consumption in 2005 to just 23 per cent in 2017.[34] In 2013, President Obama eulogized, "For the first time in nearly two decades, the United States of America now produces more of our own oil here at home than we buy from other countries. That's a tremendous step towards American energy independence."[35]

US liquefied natural gas (LNG) is also entering the world market big-time.[36] The first new LNG export terminal in four decades opened in 2016, and several other projects are under construction or have received federal approval. By 2020, the US could become the world's third largest LNG exporter (after Australia and Qatar), according to the US Energy Information Administration.[37]

Is fracking a panacea for the future? A respected Canadian geoscientist, David Hughes, believes it provides only a temporary respite from the decline in supply from conventional sources. He found startling decreases of 40 per cent or more annually in the productivity of wells in major US shale basins.[38] Companies drill a large number of wells each year to offset these decline rates. Major environmental problems exist too. Massive amounts of water are required for fracking. According to Canadian environmentalist David Suzuki, the disposal of toxic wastewater can contaminate drinking water and harm human health. Pumping wastewater into the ground increases the risk of earthquakes, and gas leakage can even cause tap water to become flammable.[39] Some of these negatives are already occurring.

Canada contributed to the oil glut and the collapse of prices through extraordinary expansion in Alberta's bitumen sands. During ten years, Canada's oil production rose by 1.5 million b/d (47 per cent) to reach 4.8 million b/d in 2017. It became the world's fifth largest producer — after the US, Saudi Arabia, Russia, and Iran.[40] Canada's oil reserves are ranked the world's third largest, after Venezuela and Saudi Arabia. Former Prime Minister Stephen Harper dubbed Canada an "energy superpower."

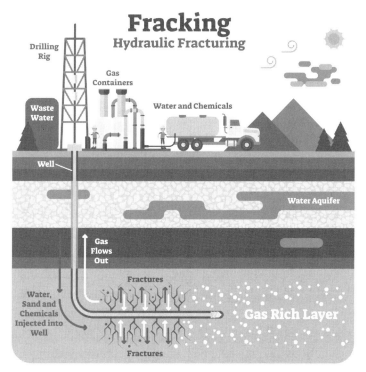

Fracking
Hydraulic Fracturing

Through expansion of the process of fracking, the US became the world's largest oil producer in 2014.

As well, companies have introduced fracking to develop huge shale gas deposits in northeast British Columbia. Various projects are planned to export the gas in liquefied form to Asian markets, though how many of the plans will come to fruition is another matter. Fracking in Canada is controversial. As of June 2018 Western provinces allow it, but Québec, New Brunswick, Nova Scotia and Newfoundland have declared a moratorium on fracking. Ontario is undecided. Canada is the world's third largest producer of conventional natural gas, much of which is exported to the United States but now faces stiff competition from American fracked gas.

The increase in North American oil production hit the world market like a tsunami. In 2015, a pervasive economic slowdown was underway. Previously, Saudi Arabia had acted as the world's traditional swing producer, reducing or raising production as demand changed. This time the Saudis were unwilling to cut output and lose market share. The increase in North American oil production during the preceding eight years (7.0 million b/d) amounted to 60 per cent of Saudi total production in 2015. Other OPEC countries were equally unwilling to cut production. Iraq continued to increase its oil exports. So did Iran, aiming to regain its share of the world market after years of sanctions.

World oil prices collapsed and natural gas prices dropped also. The price of West Texas Intermediate — the North American benchmark crude oil — fell during 2014 and 2015 from over US$100 per barrel to below US$27 in February 2016. It later recovered part way, to about US$70 in June 2018 reflecting the fall in Venezuelan oil exports and renewed US sanctions on Iranian oil exports. The price of Brent Blend, the European benchmark, behaved similarly. But the earlier heady expectations have not returned. As of June 2018, oil industry budgets in North America are slashed; so are production forecasts. The US and Canada have long thought of themselves as price-takers, having to accept prevailing world oil prices, their own transactions not affecting world prices. Not so — they proved to be price-makers.

The 2014 collapse in oil prices created new conditions for countries around the world, wreaking havoc with budgets and requiring changes in existing policies. In some oil-exporting countries, like Venezuela, unrest increased. In contrast, importing countries experienced the benefits of cheaper fuel and advantages to economic growth. Governments and companies were caught unawares. They had not foreseen the 2014 price collapse. How could they be so wrong?

Many factors contribute to the limitations of forecasts. Economists design elaborate models based on regression from the past, but the data may be unreliable or misleading. Sometimes statistics for petroleum production, trade and inventories are secret and must be estimated. Even short-term predictions for the current year can go awry. Predictions for the medium-term (the next five years) are even more difficult. Predicting the long-term (the next ten years or more) requires moving into the dream world. Many factors can affect what happens; the world is a big place; the uncertainties and unknowns are wild.

Most forecasters now use scenarios — a range of possibilities. Shell International pioneered this approach to strategic planning in the 1970s. At the time, their main scenarios were called la Belle Époque (where all goes swimmingly well) and the World in Internal Contradictions (where things go wrong). Scenarios ask "what if?" In contrast, single-point forecasts are misleading. When forecasts use simple sensitivities (high, low, medium), users typically choose the medium, and the sensitivities chosen may not prepare them for the surprises the future will bring.

For public affairs purposes, governments and companies may select just one of several scenarios to illustrate a perception they wish to promulgate. Years ago, on a World Bank economic mission, I arranged a breakfast meeting with the local head of an international oil company operating in Indonesia. I asked how he saw the prospect for Indonesian oil production. He paused: "We have forecasts for everyone — for the general public, tax authorities, international agencies. Which one do you want?" I ended up having to create my own forecast.

In fact, few governments or companies have the expertise or budget to attempt world energy forecasting. Most rely on the International Energy Agency's annual *World Energy Outlook*. For its part, BP does prepare and publish energy perspectives. Its 2017 *Energy Outlook* perceived an abundance of oil to meet demand during the next two decades, with low-cost producers having a competitive edge over higher-cost ones.[41] Most of the world's lowest-cost fields are located in the Middle East and Russia, followed by US fracked oil. BP invested heavily in Russian oil — to its competitive advantage.

* * *

Canada's dilemma related to the nature of its oil resources. Bitumen oil is capital-intensive, requiring long lead-times to bring in new production. In contrast, US fracked oil and gas operations require relatively little capital and have proven resilient to lower prices. The implications of lower world oil prices for Alberta's high-cost bitumen are stark. In a world awash in oil, international companies have been divesting Albertan assets in order to invest in lower-cost oil resources elsewhere. While Canadian-based firms such as Canadian Natural Resources, Cenovus and Suncor remain entrenched, bitumen oil is less profitable for host governments and oil companies alike. Not surprisingly, the oil industry has been lobbying for lower royalties and no carbon taxes.

A major issue has been how to bring Alberta's burgeoning bitumen oil production to market. The benchmark price, Western Canadian Select (a bitumen/diluent blend), is always lower than West Texas Intermediate, reflecting the lower intrinsic worth of bitumen oil. While the differential is typically about US$15 per barrel, as in April 2018, it has from time to time been appreciably higher. The oil industry argued that pipeline constraints were blocking production and depressing the price. To overcome the constraints, six pipeline projects were planned, aiming at export markets south, west and east. All the projects have swirled in environmental controversy.

Map 5. Canadian Oil Pipeline Projects

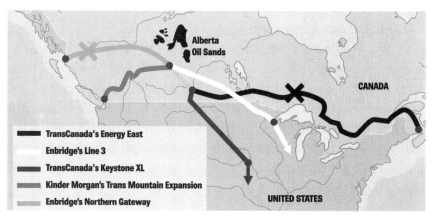

Pipeline projects to bring Alberta's bitumen oil to export markets have swirled in environmental controversy. Two projects (marked with X) were abandoned.

Two projects south were designed to augment oil exports to the United States. TransCanada's Keystone XL pipeline to Nebraska would link to existing pipelines to US Gulf Coast refineries. The project was nixed by President Obama and revived by President Trump. Construction was rescheduled to start in 2019 but protests continued. Enbridge's Line 3 is an existing crude oil pipeline from Edmonton, Alberta, to Superior, Wisconsin, and is part of the company's Mainline System. Enbridge planned to replace Line 3 with new pipe, doubling the line's capacity to 760,000 b/d. It is constructing the Canadian section. It received approval in 2018 for routing through Minnesota, despite strong environmental and Indigenous opposition.

Two projects east were designed to deliver oil to refineries in eastern Canada and one of them (Energy East) to marine export terminals as well. Enbridge completed its 9B Line project in 2015, reversing the existing line's flow eastward from Toronto to Montreal. TransCanada cancelled its Energy East project in 2017. It had envisioned converting an existing line from gas to oil and building additional pipe.

Two projects west envisioned delivering bitumen oil to export terminals in British Columbia. In 2016, Enbridge cancelled its Northern Gateway project to Kitimat, B.C. Kinder Morgan continued its plans to expand the Trans Mountain pipeline system by building a new line to its export terminal at Burnaby, B.C., parallel to the existing line. Burnaby is located within the Greater Vancouver metropolitan area.

Environmental controversy followed all of these projects. British Columbia's concerns related to oil spills during transportation on land and water. Alberta's problem was the impact on local people and wildlife resulting from production pollution, tailing ponds, scarred landscape and contaminated rivers. An underlying concern is the effect of bitumen oil production and consumption on global warming.

In 2018, the Trans Mountain project became mired in an ugly spat between the two provincial governments, with the Government of Canada supporting Alberta. The powerful Albertan oil lobby was pushing for the pipeline. The politics surrounding development of the oil sands run deep.[42] Following a summit meeting of the three governments in April, Prime Minister Justin Trudeau declared, "The Trans Mountain pipeline expansion is a vital strategic interest to Canada. It will be built." In May, the Canadian government agreed to buy the pipeline from Kinder Morgan for $4.5 billion, stating this would enable the expansion to start without further delay.

Is financial assistance a prudent use of taxpayers' money? The primary market for bitumen oil is not overseas but in the United States, where specialized refineries exist that can upgrade and refine it. These refineries were built to process heavy Venezuelan oil but are moving to Canadian bitumen oil. Most other refineries worldwide have not invested in the expensive equipment to process bitumen. Instead, they choose from an abundance of lighter crude oils, which are more desirable in quality and easier to refine.

The business case for the pipeline expansion was based on National

Energy Board forecasts before the oil price collapse in 2014.[43] Most of the existing pipeline's throughput goes directly to Vancouver, B.C., and Washington state refineries. Of 17 crude oil tankers loaded at the Burnaby terminal in 2016, only one cargo went to Asia.[44] How solid are the forecasts for the Asian market? Is the project being promoted for political rather than economic reasons?

In contrast, and despite the pipeline stalemates, bitumen oil has been quietly reaching US markets by rail transit and by de-bottlenecking and expansion of other pipelines. Rail freight has mushroomed for both bitumen and fracked oil. Trains move seamlessly across the US/Canada border, crisscrossing to refineries in either country. Rail offers flexibility, more than pipelines, but is more costly.

The oil train disaster at Lac-Mégantic, Québec in 2013 put the spotlight on safety of oil-by-rail. The runaway train devastated the town centre with much loss of life. Fracked oil is light, volatile and explosive. The fracked oil originated from North Dakota and was on its way to a New Brunswick refinery. In contrast, bitumen oil is heavy like treacle, relatively stable but the devil to clean up. Prodded by the disaster, governments in both countries promulgated new safety regulations for oil-by-rail.[45]

LOOKING TO THE FUTURE

A perpetual concern derives from the reality that petroleum is a finite resource. Its production will peak someday and gradually decline. But when exactly will this happen? Many estimates have unfolded since US geologist M. King Hubbert developed the concept in the 1950s. Since 2002, the Association for the Study of Peak Oil and Gas, a network of scientists and researchers, has organized annual international conferences on the issue. Estimates of when oil will peak continue to shift into the future.

In part, oil production is a question of investment. Constant new investment is needed to offset the natural decline in reservoir production. In 1978, I visited Trinidad and Tobago on a World Bank economic mission. The nation's proven oil reserves were estimated enough to last seven years. Did the nation run out of oil in 1985? No, there were still seven years of reserves, as oil companies kept investing in field development. By 2014, the country had 20 years of proven reserves.

A fascinating documentary, *A Crude Awakening: The Oil Crash* (2006), has striking shots of fields exhausted and abandoned.[46] Many such fields exist, but the speed of exhaustion varies enormously. Driving south on Route 219 through Pennsylvania, I passed the refinery in Bradford and came to the Custer City Oil Museum — with its abandoned derricks and nodding pumpjacks. The curator told me the field first started production in 1871 and is still supplying crude oil to a local refinery making high quality lubricants.

Global warming is a threat to the planet itself. This was vividly illustrated in former Vice-President Al Gore's films *An Inconvenient Truth* (2006) and *An Inconvenient Sequel: Truth to Power* (2017). Climate change also leads to conflict and war, as people emigrate en masse to escape natural disasters and clash with other people unwilling to accept massive immigration. In 2016, the Pentagon ordered its officials to start incorporating climate change into every major consideration, from weapons testing to preparing troops for war.[47]

Even with carbon taxes, green technologies and conservation, petroleum is likely to be around for a long time. Petroleum is essential to modern economies. It generates great wealth for governments and companies alike, making them reluctant to address environmental concerns. Producing countries have little incentive to cut back on petroleum output. Transportation systems and city layouts are very much based on petroleum-driven vehicles; and municipalities have little inducement to make radical policy changes. National governments are good at rhetoric and weak on action, except in times of emergency. Whether results will come soon enough to save the planet is a moot question, the more so since 2017 when the US Administration pulled out of the Paris Agreement on climate change. Other countries fortunately remain committed.

The challenge is how to meet the world's increasing demand for energy while reducing carbon emissions. Petroleum is still essential to modern economies. Its close association with wealth, power and politics is very difficult to change. Climate change intrudes on economies through ever-worsening storms, floods, fires, droughts and famines. Further global economic and environmental upheaval is anticipated. Petroleum is a part of the problem with no easy answers.[48] Meanwhile, conflicts relating to petroleum continue, suggesting a mindset paying little attention to the connection between petroleum and climate change.

CHAPTER 2
IRAQ — A QUEST FOR CONTROL

"Of course it's about oil. Oil fuels a lot of geopolitical moves."

—US General Abizaid (retired), speaking in 2007
about the Iraq War[1]

On March 20, 2003, a coalition of US-led forces descended on Baghdad. In preceding months, leaders had avoided talking about Iraq's enormous petroleum resources. They asserted Iraq was dangerously close to acquiring weapons capable of attacking the West. The assertion turned out to be rubbish — there were no weapons of mass destruction (WMD). Why then did the United States and the United Kingdom initiate a war with Iraq?

Since 2007, several Washington insiders, including former Head of US Central Command General Abizaid and ex-chairman of the Federal Reserve Alan Greenspan, have agreed petroleum was a key reason for the war. In his book *The Age of Turbulence*, Greenspan writes, "I am saddened that it is politically inconvenient to acknowledge what everyone knows: The Iraq war is largely about oil."[2] That same year, Senator Hillary Clinton spoke of US "vital national security interests in Iraq," noting Iraq is located "in the heart of the oil region."[3]

The call for invasion was highly controversial in Canada, as in the United States and Britain. In early 2003, the Canadian Department of Foreign Affairs and International Trade set up a hotline inviting the public to call in and express their views for or against Canada's participation. Impressed by this initiative, my wife and I both did so. To our surprise, we each spoke with a senior official and not, as I'd expected, a public relations firm. Bill Graham was the Liberal foreign minister at the time. In his 2016 book *The Call of the World — A Political Memoir*, he wrote the calls came in eight to two against participating in any invasion, and he fielded some of them himself. With no UN Security Council Resolution underpinning the invasion, Prime Minister Jean Chrétien ruled against Canadian participation. But the US and Britain ignored widespread protests and pushed ahead with the invasion.

IRAQ'S IMPORTANCE

Iraq means "deep roots." The area it occupies today has ancient significance going back before biblical days. Iraq is slightly larger than California and has a population of more than 37 million people, with almost 70 per cent living in urban areas. Prior to the invasion, it was a modern country with municipal services, telecommunications, schools, universities, hospitals and museums.

Iraq's petroleum is of crucial importance to the nation, constituting 95 per cent of its export earnings. Its oil has been a vital commodity in world trade for decades. According to BP's 2018 *Statistical Review*, Iraq's proven oil reserves are the world's fifth largest — after Venezuela, Saudi Arabia, Canada and Iran. In 2017, Iraq's oil production averaged 4.5 million b/d, the world's sixth largest.[4] Oil dominates Iraq's economy and has the potential to rival the production of Saudi Arabia.

THE 2003 INVASION AND PETROLEUM

Indications of the Bush administration's interest in petroleum came just two weeks after George W. Bush became president of the United States in January 2001. One of his first actions was to create an Energy Task Force headed by Vice-President Dick Cheney. US oil imports had recently generated concern by exceeding 50 per cent of consumption.

Little was disclosed about who would attend Energy Task Force meetings or what the focus of their deliberations would be. Despite numerous inquiries from reporters, details about the task force remained a mystery for months. According to the *Washington Post*, the task force held 40 or more meetings with energy firms but would not disclose who attended or what they discussed.[5]

In May 2001, after four months of deliberations, the Energy Task Force published an anodyne report.[6] Stating that America faced "the most serious energy shortage since the oil embargoes of the 1970s," the report envisioned a long-term strategy to promote dependable energy and recommended a lengthy list of measures to increase energy efficiency, develop domestic oil and gas resources and stimulate renewable energy. It was more circumspect on imported oil. Affirming that the Persian Gulf region "will remain vital to US interests," and "Middle East oil producers will remain central to world oil security," it recommended "the President support initiatives by Saudi Arabia, Kuwait, Algeria, Qatar, the UAE, and other suppliers to open up areas of their energy sectors to foreign investment." Conspicuously missing in the 169-page report were the words "Iraq" and "Iran."

Cheney kept the task force's records under wraps, insisting on executive privilege. The non-governmental organization (NGO) Judicial Watch managed to obtain some documents under the *Freedom of Information Act*. After a ruling by the US Court for the District of Columbia, the Commerce Department was forced to release documents prepared for the task force, including a map of Iraqi oilfields, pipelines, refineries and terminals; two charts detailing Iraqi oil and gas projects; and a list of Foreign Suitors for Iraqi Oilfield Contracts.[7] It released similar documents for Saudi Arabia and UAE.[8]

After the 9/11 attacks, rumours began surfacing about US government interest in Iraq. In December 2001, the US State Department launched a Future of Iraq Project. The project included an Oil and Energy Working Group that proposed an "oil policy for a liberated Iraq."[9] The group envisaged a new petroleum law and regulations to decentralize the Iraq National Oil Company and open the sector to international oil companies. Clearly, the US was thinking about Iraq's oil before the invasion.

In May 2005, a memorandum — dubbed the Downing Street Memo — was leaked to the British press and became instant news in the UK.[10] It minuted a secret meeting in July 2002 at which top-level UK officials briefed Prime Minister Tony Blair on Washington's build-up to war. Attendees were told President George W. Bush intended to remove Saddam Hussein, Iraq's leader, through military action, and "the intelligence and facts were being fixed around the policy."

Two weeks elapsed before the North American media gave minor coverage

Map 6. Iraq: Locations of Petroleum Facilities

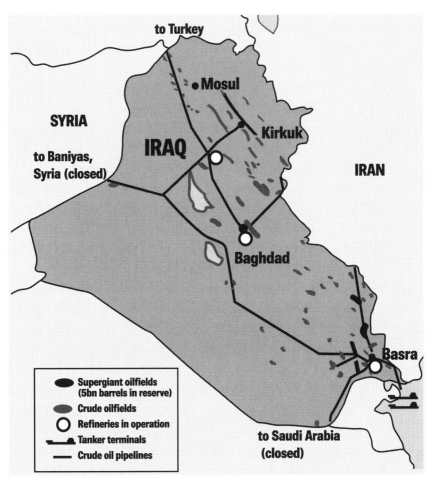

to Turkey

•Mosul

SYRIA

Kirkuk

IRAQ

to Baniyas,
Syria (closed)

IRAN

Baghdad

Basra

**Supergiant oilfields
(5bn barrels in reserve)**

Crude oilfields

O **Refineries in operation**

Tanker terminals

Crude oil pipelines

to Saudi Arabia
(closed)

Iraq's oil is of crucial importance to the nation — and vital to world trade. It has potential to rival the production of oil by Saudi Arabia.

to the memo. Eight months later, the *New York Times*, shamed by Internet bloggers, gave more detailed reporting.[11] During those eight months, the US Administration sought to influence public opinion by offering many statements in favour of invasion and occupation. For instance:

• National Security Advisor Condoleezza Rice (CNN, September 8, 2002): "The problem here is that there will always be some uncertainty about how quickly Saddam can acquire nuclear weapons. But we don't want the smoking gun to be a mushroom cloud."[12]

- Secretary of State Colin Powell (UN Security Council, February 5, 2003): "Saddam Hussein is very much focussed on putting in place the key missing piece from his nuclear weapons program, the ability to produce fissile material."[13]
- President George W. Bush (Dearborn, Michigan, October 14, 2002): "This is a man [Saddam] that we know has had connections with al Qaeda. This is a man who, in my judgment, would like to use al Qaeda as a forward army."
- President George W. Bush (*Associated Press*, January 21, 2003): "He [Saddam] has weapons of mass destruction, the world's deadliest weapons which pose a direct threat to the United States, our citizens and our friends and allies."[14]

For its part, on September 24, 2002, the UK Government published the September Dossier alleging that Iraq possessed weapons of mass destruction, including chemical and biological weapons, and had reconstituted its nuclear weapons program.[15] In the foreword, Prime Minister Tony Blair wrote, "The document discloses that his [Saddam's] military planning allows for some of the WMD to be ready within 45 minutes of an order to use them." The British newspaper *The Sun* carried the headline "Brits 45 mins from doom."

British journalist Greg Muttitt obtained a treasure trove of documents under the UK *Freedom of Information Act*. Even before the war started, the Foreign Office maintained that Shell and BP had to have a long-term stake in Iraq, and was "determined to get a fair slice of the action for UK companies in a post-Saddam Iraq." Muttitt describes this in his 2011 book on Britain's participation in the war, *Fuel on the Fire*.[16]

In 2007, four years after the Iraq war began, Australia's defence minister triggered a political storm in Canberra when he said Iraq was "an important supplier of energy, oil in particular, to the rest of the world, and Australians ... need to think what would happen if there were a premature withdrawal from Iraq."[17] Prime Minister John Howard backed away: "We are not there because of oil and we didn't go there because of oil. The reason we remain there is that we want to give the people of Iraq a possibility of embracing democracy." He refrained from mentioning that wars for the purpose of getting resources like petroleum are illegal under the UN Charter.

Obviously, motivation is hard to pinpoint and leaders are reluctant to enumerate all the reasons for military actions. Petroleum may be only part of the motivation, but its role is documented in the Energy Task Force, the Future of Iraq Project and other documents. Further evidence emerged during the invasion itself.

In the March 2003 invasion, US forces and a coalition of willing countries seized Iraq's major oilfields and refineries. The Oil Ministry in Baghdad was protected. Left unguarded were government ministries, hospitals and museums. They were promptly looted and burned. Archaeological sites were left unprotected, and there was massive looting.

The National Museum in Baghdad, one of the world's cultural treasures, contained precious artifacts from the ancient Mesopotamian civilization (5000–3500 BCE). Prior to the 2003 war, antiquities experts beseeched the Pentagon and UK government to ensure the museum's safety from war and looting. Notwithstanding, it was ransacked in a three-day rampage (April 10–12) during the invasion. Staff returning on April 13 managed to foil further plunder until US troops arrived on April 16. When quizzed in Washington, General Myers, chairman of the Joint Chiefs of Staff, said, "When some of that looting was going on, people were being killed, people were being wounded. It's as much as anything else a matter of priorities."[18] Defence Secretary Donald Rumsfeld added, "Stuff happens." Since then, many artifacts have been returned, but many others remain missing. With what remained, the museum was refurbished and officially reopened in 2015.

Attention to petroleum persisted as the years of occupation continued. For three years, Iraq was governed by a series of temporary authorities until the first government took office in May 2006. First came the Coalition Provisional Authority, reporting directly to the US Secretary of Defense; next the Iraqi Interim Government; and then the Iraqi Transitional Government. During this time, American advisers were entrenched within the Iraqi bureaucracy.

During the 2003 invasion, Baghdad's National Museum became a scene of destruction. Precious artifacts were looted.

In December 2005, the Iraqi Transitional Government gave an undertaking to the International Monetary Fund (IMF) to draft a new oil law within 12 months promoting foreign investment in the oil sector. As a result, the US Agency for International Development (USAID) contracted the US consulting firm BearingPoint (KPMG) to draft the law. The draft built upon the ideas in the Future of Iraq Project undertaken in Washington before the war began, with a view to decentralizing the Iraq National Oil Company and opening the sector to foreign oil companies through production-sharing contracts. What happened in subsequent months raises questions about who wanted the law in the first place — Iraq or the United States.

A draft of the proposed oil law was presented to the US government and oil companies in July 2006. Two months later, the International Money Fund and World Bank likewise received a draft copy. The Iraqi cabinet had to wait until January 2007 to receive a revised draft. Members of the Iraq Parliament saw it for the first time in July 2007. The bill faced severe opposition and stalled.[19]

The US Administration proposed benchmarks, including enactment of the oil law, to assess Iraqi government performance. US Congress adopted these benchmarks in a supplemental bill to fund the war. Despite enormous US pressure, the draft remained in limbo.

Investigative journalists, such as Antonia Juhasz at the *New York Times*[20] and Greg Muttitt in *The Independent*,[21] expressed concern about this "Made in USA" draft law. Most of Iraq's known oilfields and all its undiscovered fields would be opened up to foreign investors under contractual terms far more in their favour than those in other Middle East countries.

The draft law proposed production-sharing agreements rather than service agreements as the *modus operandi* for foreign oil companies. A major difference is that production-sharing agreements allow oil companies to share in the profits,[22] while service contracts are simply based on a fee for providing a service.[23] Service contracts are less attractive to oil companies but are preferred by governments in countries like Iraq where prolific resources are proven and national expertise is available.

In 2008, the Oil Ministry offered short-term contracts without competitive bidding to four major oil companies: BP, ExxonMobil, Shell and Total.[24] Iraqi protests led the Iraqi Oil Ministry to cancel the original offer and initiate two rounds of competitive bidding in 2009. They awarded 12 long-term service contracts for 14 fields, mostly in the Shia south. The successful companies came from a wide range of countries: Angola, Britain, China, France, Italy, Korea, the Netherlands, Japan, Malaysia, Russia, Turkey, the United States.

Texan oilman T. Boone Pickens articulated one American point of view when he complained to the US Congress: "They're opening them [oilfields] up to other companies all over the world ... We're entitled to it. Heck, we even lost 5,000 of our people; 65,000 injured; and a trillion, five hundred billion dollars."[25]

With new investment, Iraq's oil production surged dramatically from 2.5 million b/d in 2009 to 4.5 million b/d in 2017. The Oil Ministry's long-term target was 12 million b/d,[26] later reduced to 8–9 million b/d.[27] If achieved, such an increase would be stunning, an extraordinary escalation after severe setbacks from the various wars since 1980. These wars and earlier interactions between Western countries and Iraq form important backstories to what is going on today.

BACKSTORY: THE WEST AND IRAQ'S OIL

Western intervention to control Iraq's oil goes back many decades. In 1912, when the area was part of the Ottoman Empire, European investors formed the Turkish Petroleum Company (TPC) to explore for oil in Mesopotamia. Shareholders were the Anglo-Persian Oil Company (BP's predecessor), Deutsche Bank, Shell and the entrepreneur Calouste Gulbenkian. Mr. Gulbenkian was the fixer who brought the various parties together. He held five per cent of the stock and was dubbed Mr. Five Percent. The Ottoman government's promised concession went on hold when World War I broke out.

After World War I, Iraq was carved out of the Ottoman Empire.[28] At the 1920 San Remo Conference, France received a League of Nations mandate over Syria and Lebanon, and Britain, a mandate for Iraq and Palestine. The French government acquired Deutsche Bank's shareholding in TPC as war reparations and assigned it in 1924 to the newly formed Compagnie Française des Pétroles (CFP, later renamed Total).

Britain's Foreign Minister Lord Curzon alleged the influence of oil over British policy was "nil."[29] Even so, in 1918 Sir Maurice Hankey, Secretary of the War Cabinet, counselled Lord Curzon's predecessor, Arthur Balfour:

> Oil in the next war will occupy the place of coal in the present war, or at least a parallel place to coal. The only big potential supply that we can get under British control is the Persian and Mesopotamian supply ... Control over these oil supplies becomes a first-class British war aim.[30]

Under the mandate for Iraq, Britain imposed a Hashemite monarchy, aided by British advisers and military forces. The mandate lasted until 1932, when Britain granted independence to Iraq but retained military bases and transit rights. The British stayed four decades, until 1958, when a military coup overthrew the monarchy.

In 1925, Iraq signed a 75-year exclusive concession with the Turkish Petroleum Company to explore for and produce oil throughout Iraq. The consortium found prolific oil two years later in northern Iraq near Kirkuk. At the time, no American company had a foothold in the Middle East. The US State Department was pushing hard for an "Open Door Policy" that would allow them into the region. In 1928, after years of wrangling, the Anglo-Persian Oil Company ceded half of its 47.5 per cent holding to Esso and Mobil. This resolved the ownership of TPC, with four shareholders each owning 23.75 per cent — Anglo-Persian Oil Company, Shell, CFP and Near East Development Corporation (Esso and Mobil) — and Mr. Gulbenkian owning 5 per cent. All shareholders were bound by the Red Line Agreement, prohibiting them from independently seeking oil interests anywhere in the former Ottoman Empire. The Red Line area included Turkey, Iraq and the Arabian Peninsula, but excluded Kuwait as a British preserve. In 1929, TPC was renamed the Iraq Petroleum Company (IPC).

Other American companies were free from the restrictions of the Red Line Agreement because they were not IPC shareholders. American companies (later renamed Aramco) discovered prolific oil in Saudi Arabia (1938) and were joined by Esso and Mobil (IPC shareholders) eight years later. Subsequently, the US government persuaded the other IPC shareholders to modify the Red Line to exclude Saudi Arabia, Bahrain, Egypt, Israel, western Jordan and Yemen.[31]

With a head office in the City of London, the IPC retained its monopoly of exploration and development in Iraq until 1961, when the revolutionary government under General Qasim nationalized 99.5 per cent of the concession area. IPC had neglected exploration, focusing only on oilfields already producing in the concession area. It was allowed to retain ownership of the producing oilfields but lost the rest of its concession area. In 1966, Iraq created the Iraq National Oil Company to operate the nation's oil industry and, in 1971, nationalized the remaining 0.5 per cent. Iraqis knew how to operate their own oilfields.

After the nationalization, oil production increased by leaps and bounds, from 1.4 million b/d in 1966 to 3.5 million b/d in 1979. It fuelled a dramatic upsurge in economic prosperity. Then Iraq initiated a war with Iran. During the Iran-Iraq War (1980–1988), Iraq's southern export facilities were destroyed and it was forced to close its pipeline across Syria. Iraq's oil output sank below 1 million b/d in the early 1980s.

Two years later came the First Gulf War (1990–1991), triggered by Iraq's invasion of Kuwait. Since the days of the Ottoman Empire, Iraq had claimed Kuwait was historically part of Mesopotamia. Eight days before the invasion, US Ambassador to Iraq April Glaspie called on President Saddam Hussein. According to one transcript, she said, "We have no opinion on your Arab-Arab conflicts, such as your dispute with Kuwait. Secretary Baker has directed me to emphasize the instruction, first given to Iraq in the 1960s, that the Kuwait issue is not associated with America."[32] Iraq saw this as a green light to invade Kuwait. It was deceived. The US responded by ruthlessly annihilating the invading Iraqi army.

Subsequently, the UN imposed a financial and trade embargo on Iraq, resulting in widespread starvation, disease and malnutrition. With oil output restricted to a mere 500,000 b/d, Iraq lacked the foreign exchange to import food and other essentials. By way of humanitarian relief, in 1995 the United Nations initiated an Oil for Food Program, funded from Iraq's oil exports, and oil production rose to about 2.5 million b/d.

In 1996, the CBS program *60 Minutes* interviewed US Secretary of State Madeleine Albright. One of the questions and her response are worth noting. The question: "We have heard that half a million children have died [in Iraq]. Is the price worth it?" Her response: "I think this is a very hard choice, but the price — we think the price is worth it."[33] The UN embargo lasted until 2004, after Saddam Hussein was ejected from power.

ONGOING CONFLICT AND PETROLEUM

For Iraqis, the cost of the 2003 war was the destruction of a nation. Infrastructure was devastated, thousands of Iraqis were killed, millions fled as refugees. What manner of liberation was this? As Andrew Bacevich detailed in his book *America's War for the Greater Middle East: A Military History*, the conduct of the war was shameful. Many American decisions were made on the basis of ignorance and hubris.[34]

In 2004, photos came to light of US troops humiliating and torturing Iraqi detainees at the Abu Ghraib prison in Baghdad. The graphic images shocked the world. Defense Secretary Rumsfeld blamed "a few bad apples," but it became clear the widespread torture of detainees at Abu Ghraib, Guantánamo and elsewhere was a coordinated program originating from the upper echelons of the Bush Administration.

Then came the 2004 US assault against the insurgency in Fallujah, 65 kilometres west of Baghdad. US forces destroyed the city to save it, with many civilians killed and others suffering long-term effects — subsequent birth defects and cancer from the widespread use of depleted uranium and phosphorus. Al Jazeera had a TV crew in Fallujah filming the atrocity live. President Bush was upset with Al Jazeera reporting. He wanted to bomb Al Jazeera's headquarters in Qatar and put it out of business, but Prime Minister Blair talked him out of it. Their conversation was recorded in a UK Cabinet memo leaked to the *Daily Mirror* newspaper. The memo was suppressed, and two British officials were jailed for the leak.[35]

A few years later, WikiLeaks published a myriad of US military and diplomatic documents apparently supplied by US Private Chelsea Manning. They included the horrific video of a US army helicopter hovering over a Baghdad square in 2007, the crew gloating as they machine-gunned a group of civilians and two *Reuters* correspondents. The video went viral and the event became known as the Nisour Square massacre; 14 civilians died and 17 were wounded, none of them insurgents. A case against the helicopter crew was thrown out in 2009, then re-tried in 2015. Three members of the crew received 30-year sentences; the fourth received a life sentence. Manning was sentenced to 35 years in military jail for leaking the files. President Obama, in his last days in office, commuted Manning's sentence to just over seven years, and she was released from prison in May 2017.

Britain took part in the invasion and occupation of Iraq despite the largest public protests and demonstrations in British history. Two Cabinet ministers — Robin Cook and later Clare Short — resigned in opposition to the invasion. So did the Foreign Office's deputy legal adviser, Elizabeth Wilmshurst. She found the invasion to be illegal without a second UN Security Council resolution. (The first was Resolution 678 authorizing the 1990 Iraq War.) The Liberal Democrats also insisted on a new UN resolution, but the governing Labour Party, led by Tony Blair, was supported by the official opposition Conservative Party. Britain went to war.

The Iraq War rocked the British nation, shattering public trust in the political establishment. The aftermath continued long after the war concluded. In 2009, to assuage continuing discontent, Prime Minister Gordon Brown established a public inquiry on Britain's role in the Iraq War. Sir John Chilcot chaired the inquiry. The long-awaited *Chilcot Report* was finally published seven years later, in July 2016.[36] The report, 2.6 million words long, examined the years 2001 to 2009 embracing the run-up to the conflict in Iraq, the military action and its aftermath. The report was highly critical of Blair's decision to commit British troops to the 2003 invasion. Peaceful options for disarmament had not been exhausted; military action was not a last resort; Blair deliberately exaggerated the threat posed by Saddam Hussein; the latter posed no imminent threat; and UK intelligence agencies produced flawed information.[37]

The occupation of Iraq fared badly. By mid-2004, the US and its allies in Iraq controlled only islands of territory and were facing full-scale rebellions by both Sunni and Shia Iraqis.[38] Shia and Sunni were fighting each other, too. Baghdad sank into inter-ethnic strife. Although it had been an integrated city before the war, it became a Shia city with Sunni enclaves.

The US-led coalition forces remained in Iraq until 2011. Iraq's Prime Minister Nuri al-Maliki gave notice under the US/Iraq Status of Forces Agreement, and the US reluctantly complied. It left behind a huge new embassy covering 104 acres, almost as big as Vatican City, and a vast network of empty bases. Other coalition forces left, too.

By then, Sunni dissatisfaction was boiling over. They had lost much of their voice in government. The Coalition Provisional Authority had thrown many Sunni out of the civil service and military in its De-Baathification program. Their Sunni leader Saddam Hussein was hanged in what looked more like victor's justice than a fair trial. Saddam's demise also put a convenient end to plans to sell Iraqi oil for euros instead of petrodollars — a potential threat to US financial hegemony. Many Sunni had been forced to leave their homes in the south. Unemployment was rife. The stage was set for the rise of the jihadist Islamic State in the Sunni north. Islamic State expanded rapidly in 2014, acquiring territory straddling Iraq and Syria and aiming to create a state governed by Islamic law. It became notorious for its brutal abductions and killings. Wealthy individuals in the Gulf Arab States, especially Kuwait and Saudi Arabia, provided funding, which was augmented by oil revenue in areas captured. The story is detailed in Patrick Cockburn's 2015 book *The Rise of the Islamic State*.[39]

For their part, the Kurds living in Iraq's northeast saw an opportunity to obtain greater autonomy. Iraq in effect split asunder into three parts — the Shia south, Sunni north (Islamic State), and Kurdish northeast — each

Map 7. Who Controlled Iraq, 2016 and 2018

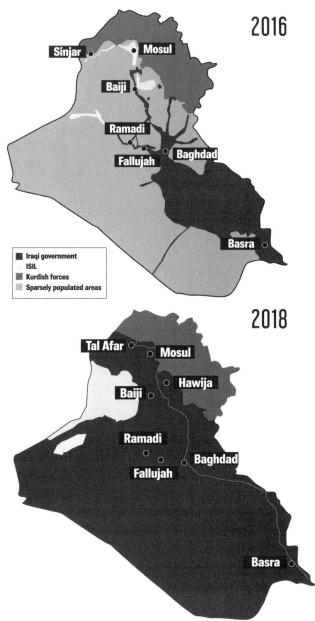

In 2014, Iraq de facto split into three parts — Shia south, Sunni north (Islamic State) and Kurdish northeast. By late 2017, Islamic State had lost much of its territorial gains and oil and gas fields.

controlling its own oilfields. By far the bulk of Iraq's oil production was from government-controlled fields in the Shia south, unaffected by the conflict with Islamic State to the north.[40] In December 2016, southern output reached 3.5 million b/d, approaching that of Iran, UAE and Canada.

In the Sunni north, Islamic State smuggled part of the oil by road to Turkey. Turkish President Erdoğan's own family was involved in the trade (described in Chapter 3). In the semi-autonomous northeast, the Kurdistan Regional Government (KRG) enacted its own petroleum legislation in 2007 and signed deals with exploration companies large and small. Its oilfields produced about 600,000 b/d, much of which was exported via Turkey.[41] The regional capital, Erbil, was a boom oil city until the 2014 oil price collapse. In the years following, the KRG struggled financially.

When Iraqi forces fled northern Iraq in July 2014, Kurdish forces seized Kirkuk, a multi-ethnic city with a giant oilfield. It was producing about 150,000 b/d but was capable of producing four or five times as much if rehabilitated.[42] The KRG exported oil from Kirkuk and Kurdish fields via a new pipeline to the Turkish port of Ceyhan. The Iraqi government regarded these exports as illegal and threatened to sue buyers. To avoid detection, the KRG transferred the oil between ships offshore Malta and also used decoy ships.[43]

When Islamic State threatened the Kurdish northeast and Shia south in August 2014, US forces returned to provide air and ground support to both the Iraqi and Kurdish regional governments. Canadian, British and other special forces were despatched to Iraqi Kurdistan, where Israeli advisers were also numerous. Iran began providing military assistance to Iraqi forces and Shia militias.

Canada sent nine aircraft to join coalition air strikes against Islamic State in Iraq as well as special forces to train Iraqi and Kurdish military. As Leader of the Opposition in 2003, Stephen Harper had strongly advocated Canadian participation in the Iraq invasion. In 2014, he was prime minister and keen to come aboard the coalition. He obtained parliamentary approval, the Conservatives holding a majority of seats. Upon change of government in October 2015, Liberal Prime Minister Justin Trudeau announced plans to withdraw the fighter aircraft but retain surveillance, transport and refuelling aircraft. He tripled the number of military trainers to 600.

Iraqi government forces moved against Islamic State, recapturing Tikrit in 2015, Ramadi and Fallujah in 2016 and Mosul in 2017. Mosul is Iraq's second largest city, with 2 million inhabitants. The recapture of these cities came at a high cost. They were much destroyed by air strikes and shellfire, and many of their citizens fled or were killed or injured. By late 2017, Islamic State had lost much of its territorial gains and oil and gas fields.

Iraqi Kurdistan became in all but name an American protectorate. Confident of US backing, KRG President Barzani held an independence referendum in September 2017 which endorsed full separation from Iraq. He received a surprise. The Iraqi government imposed a no-fly zone on Iraqi Kurdistan, paralysing international flights to Erbil. It swiftly wrested Kirkuk from Kurdish control and moved to reactivate the former oil pipeline from Kirkuk to Ceyhan, bypassing the Kurdish northeast. (It had regained control of the pipeline from Islamic State.) Iraq's neighbours, Iran and Turkey, strongly opposed to independence for their own Kurdish minorities, backed Baghdad. Iran stopped importing and exporting refined oil products to Iraqi Kurdistan. Turkey threatened to cut off the crude oil pipeline from KRG fields to Ceyhan. The loss of oil earnings was a major blow to KRG's aspirations.

Washington seemed to be taken off balance. It had some 10,000 US troops in Iraq, supporting both the Baghdad and Erbil governments. Its evident intent to balkanize Iraq looked to be in disarray. Ottawa suspended the training of Iraqi and Kurdish troops, to avoid its trainers being ensnared in a prospective showdown between the two forces, though Canadian troops continued other operations in Iraq — helicopters, a military hospital and intelligence-gathering.[44]

In 2018, it remained unclear how the divisions within Iraq would be resolved. The omens were not bright. Saddam had been a merciless dictator but, prior to the wars and the UN embargo, Iraq had a high standard of living, excellent education and health care. During the 2003 invasion and subsequent occupation, the coalition made decisions in ignorance of Iraq's culture and people. Infrastructure was devastated, many thousands were killed on both sides, millions fled as refugees. Abu Ghraib was a torturous stain.

Petroleum was part of the decision to invade and became an issue in ongoing fighting. According to BP's *Statistical Review*, Iraq's reserves ranked third in the world at end of 2003 (after Saudi Arabia and Iran). Iraq was a prize. But the quest for control failed. The new Iraqi government resisted opening Iraq's oil to foreign ownership. The Western invasion in 2003 was preceded by numerous Middle East interventions in the twentieth century — all attentive to oil. These interventions and their legacies have contributed to an atmosphere of enormous Iraqi mistrust of Western countries. This mistrust extends into Western countries themselves, where many citizens remain aware of the bloodshed and treasure spent for an unnecessary war.

CHAPTER 3
SYRIA — A TALE OF TWO PIPELINES

"Syria has become the great tragedy of this century."

—António Guterres, UN High Commission for Refugees

Through the years, leaders have seldom mentioned petroleum in connection with Syria. Conflict has been ostensibly about human rights, democracy and the actions of Syria's President Bashar al-Assad. Compared to other Middle Eastern countries, Syria's oil and gas fields are minor, but its geographic location figures in two proposed gas pipelines. Each originates in the Persian Gulf and would pass through Syria on its way to European destinations. Countries supporting either proposal are rivals in the geopolitics of the region.

SYRIA'S IMPORTANCE

Syria's location at the eastern end of the Mediterranean Sea places it at a crossroads between the Middle East and Europe. What happens in Syria has the potential to spill over into other countries. Conversely, what happens in bordering countries (Turkey, Iraq, Jordan, Lebanon and Israel) affects Syria, too.

In many ways the Mediterranean is a virtual preserve of NATO countries. In 1971, the Soviet Union established a naval base at Tartus in Syria, the only Soviet naval facility on the Mediterranean Sea. After the collapse of the Soviet Union, Russia retained the naval base, added an air force base in 2015 near Latakia and continued to support Syria. NATO countries regard these bases as a challenge.

Syria has proven oil reserves of only 2.5 billion barrels, located primarily near the Iraq border and along the Euphrates River. (For comparison, Saudi Arabia has 268 billion barrels of oil reserves.) For natural gas, Syria ranks forty-third in the world, with 240 billion cubic metres of proven reserves. Shale reserves and offshore potential also exist. Though relatively small in Middle Eastern terms, oil and gas are important to the Syrian economy. With exploration and development, further potential exists.

The Syrians are a diverse people, ethnically and religiously. The majority are Sunni Arab (60 per cent or so) but minorities are significant — Alawites (a Shia offshoot), Kurds, Christians, Druze and other groups. Under President Bashar al-Assad — and his father Hafez al-Assad before him — Alawites were allowed advantages. Elements of dissension existed, yet Syria experienced relative harmony. Although demonized by the West, Assad retained strong support from Syria's merchant class and powerful military since the war's inception.

Geopolitically, Syria is aligned with Iran, Iraq and Lebanon. Some analysts refer to a "Shia Crescent" — a half-moon shaped region linking people of these four countries. The term is technically incorrect as the Syrians are 60 per cent Sunni and the government is secular. However, the four countries have become strategically united against pressures from the US, Britain, France, Israel, Saudi Arabia and other Gulf States. Syria and Iran are strategic allies, both supportive of the Lebanese militant group and political party Hezbollah. The US and Israel have historically sought to bring Iran and Hezbollah to heel and have perceived Syria as a weak link in the chain.

Most Syrians live along the Mediterranean coastal plain or along the Euphrates River. The river flows from Turkey through eastern Syria to Iraq — thence the Persian Gulf. Syrian Kurds live mostly in the northeast and along part of the border with Turkey. Syria's capital, Damascus, and its main commercial city, Aleppo, are two of the world's most ancient cities. Syria's population is about 17 million, of whom roughly 6 million are internally displaced and 5 million are refugees abroad.

Until 2011, Syria cooperated with the United States in the Global War on Terror. Syria was one of the CIA's most common destinations for suspects under its Extraordinary Rendition program.[1] For example, after Canadian

Maher Arar was arrested in 2002 on false suspicion of terrorist connections while transiting through New York, US officials rendered him to Syria for torture. Later, the Government of Canada obtained his release and paid him $10 million in compensation for his ordeal.

WESTERN INTERVENTION AND PIPELINE RIVALRY

When two pipeline schemes are proposed and only one is likely to be built, the stage is set for enormous rivalry. That was the situation affecting Syria. Both Qatar and Iran proposed schemes to bring natural gas from the Persian Gulf to Europe, an engineering feat that as of 2018 had never been done before. Each scheme was strategic, huge and would pass through Syria. With each scheme, some countries would earn transit revenue from having the pipeline within their country and other countries would earn nothing. Geopolitically, big powers were aligned with regional allies associated with each scheme.

Building a pipeline is enormously expensive and can only be accomplished when many factors come together to make it geographically and economically feasible. Needed are a willing seller, willing buyers, cooperation among all countries along the proposed route and a market price high enough to encourage risk-taking. Investments are huge and pipelines last decades, binding countries together and generating profits.

Each proposed pipeline would tap the world's largest gas reservoir, which lies in the Persian Gulf and is divided between Qatar (North Dome field) and Iran (South Pars field). Qatar has the world's third largest gas reserves and is the world's largest exporter of liquefied natural gas (LNG). According to BP's *2018 Statistical Review*, Iran has the world's second largest gas reserves but thus far exports nothing as LNG. The two countries' gas exports by pipeline are limited to neighbouring countries: Qatar to UAE, and Iran to Iraq and Turkey. Further afield is the tempting European gas market, supplied from the North Sea (Britain, Netherlands, Norway) and Russia, and to some extent from Algeria, Libya and Nigeria. In earlier decades, experts believed a pipeline from the Persian Gulf to Europe was economically infeasible — out of the question. A combination of declining production from North Sea fields, increasing reliance on Russian gas and higher energy prices (pre-2014) changed the equation. Strategists in

Brussels and Washington gave serious consideration to moving gas from the Middle East to Europe.

An early initiative was a 2006 plan to extend the Arab Gas Pipeline from Syria to Turkey. The pipeline already brought Egyptian gas via Jordan as far north as Syria and Lebanon. In March 2006, the energy ministers of Egypt, Jordan, Syria, Lebanon and Turkey agreed to extend it to Turkey.[2] This fitted Turkey's strategy of becoming a regional gas hub. In the previous five years, it had begun importing gas by pipeline from Iran, Russia and Azerbaijan for its internal market. The Russian firm Stroytransgaz was contracted to build the 63-km section from Aleppo, Syria, to Kilis, Turkey. For unknown reasons, the contract was annulled in early 2009, and the extension failed to materialize.

In May 2009, President Assad unfurled his so-called Four Seas strategy at a meeting with Turkey's President Abdullah Gül.[3] He envisaged Syria, Turkey, Iraq and Iran uniting as a bloc to create a global crossroads for trade, connecting the Mediterranean Sea, Black Sea, Caspian Sea and Persian Gulf. It was an amicable meeting. Assad travelled through the region promoting this strategy. His vision never materialized.

The same year, Qatar announced its proposal for a gas pipeline from the Persian Gulf to Europe. The Emir of Qatar, Sheikh Hamad bin Khalifa Al Thani, met with Turkey's President Gül and Prime Minister Erdoğan and afterward told media, "We are eager to have a gas pipeline from Qatar to Turkey ... A working group will be set up that will come up with concrete results in the shortest possible time."[4] The pipeline route would traverse Saudi Arabia, Jordan and Syria to Turkey. There it would link into the Southern Gas Corridor, a pipeline system being built with EU and US support to bring gas from Azerbaijan to Europe, bypassing Russia. Qatar is an ally of the United States and hosts the operational headquarters of US Central Command. The Qatar scheme had American blessing — the gas was not Iranian and could displace Russian gas to Europe. Turkey wanted it, too, because it offered transit revenue.

Map 8. Pipeline Projects Through Syria

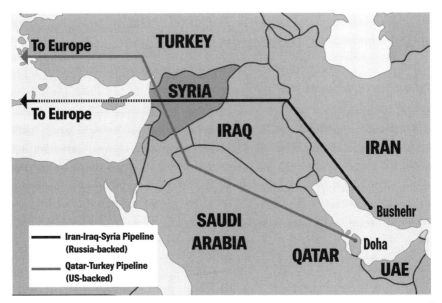

In 2009, Qatar proposed a gas pipeline to Europe via Saudi Arabia, Syria and Turkey. In 2011, Iran proposed a rival line via Iraq and Syria, bypassing Turkey. Both proposals would tap the world's largest gas reservoir located in the Persian Gulf.

To Turkey's annoyance, President Assad rejected the Qatar proposal, favouring a rival pipeline from Iran. Announced in early 2011, it would traverse Iraq to Syria, and possibly Lebanon. From there, it could extend under the Mediterranean to Greece and beyond. It would bypass Turkey. In July 2011, the oil ministers of Iran, Iraq and Syria signed a memorandum of understanding to build the pipeline.[5] By then, unrest in Syria was underway. Qatar became a big-time financier of the unrest. Between 2011 and 2013, it spent upwards of US$3 billion supporting Syrian rebels, far exceeding any other government.[6] Even earlier, US and British covert forces had been operating in Syria.[7]

* * *

The initial demonstrations in 2011 were peaceful calls for government reforms. One concern was higher food prices resulting from drought conditions. In March 2011, the unrest turned violent. When police and demonstrators clashed in the southern city of Daraa, the Assad government cracked down. Western leaders claimed the crackdown was brutal and condemned the violence. They called on the Syrian government to allow demonstrations to take place peacefully. However, according to Israeli media, seven police as well as four demonstrators were killed.[8] Some protesters were armed and not exactly peaceful.

In coming weeks, violent protests spread to other cities — Banias, Homs and suburbs of Damascus. Western media highlighted heavy casualties at the hands of Syrian authorities, and Western leaders issued stern warnings. In July 2011, pro-government protesters attacked the US and French embassies in Damascus. US Secretary of State Hillary Clinton warned: "President Assad is not indispensable, and we have absolutely nothing invested in him remaining in power."[9]

The clarion call sounded for regime change. In August, President Barack Obama proclaimed: "The future of Syria must be determined by its people, but President Bashar al-Assad is standing in their way ... He is imprisoning, torturing, and slaughtering his own people ... For the sake of the Syrian people, the time has come for President Assad to step aside."[10] The EU's foreign affairs chief, Catherine Ashton, asserted "the complete loss of Bashar al-Assad's legitimacy in the eyes of the Syrian people and the necessity for him to step aside."[11]

This was just one month after Iran, Iraq and Syria signed the Memorandum of Understanding for their pipeline. Western leaders and media failed to refer to pipelines, but began placing sanctions on Syria. The US imposed trade and investment sanctions, including bans on petroleum exports from Syria and petroleum investment in Syria. The EU followed suit on September 2.[12] Canada came onboard the following month.

In October, the US pushed the envelope further. It attempted to have the UN Security Council impose worldwide sanctions on Syria. It was thwarted by Russian and Chinese vetos. Earlier in 2011, Russia and China had abstained on a Security Council resolution imposing a no-fly zone on Libya. After Western countries reinterpreted the Libyan resolution as legal cover for a destructive bombing campaign and regime change, Russia and China indicated they would not be fooled again. They prevented the imposition of UN sanctions on Syria.

Western sanctions had a significant effect. Two major oil companies, Shell and Total, declared *force majeure* and suspended Syrian operations; Chinese and Indian partners followed suit. All had been working in joint ventures with Syria's state-owned General Petroleum Company. The ban was a major blow to the economy, as oil exports had been a significant contributor to Syria's exchange earnings and government revenue. Just before the war, oil production had averaged about 400,000 b/d, enough to supply the local market and allow exports of about 130,000 b/d. To meet the shortfall, Syria began importing oil from Iran.[13]

The Syrian uprising grew into a full-fledged internal war with horrendous casualties on both sides. In 2012, the pendulum was swinging in the rebels' favour, yet the Syrian army held firm and President Assad remained in office. In 2013, the pendulum appeared to swing back in his favour.

The official narrative presented by Western leaders and media claimed Assad was a "Bad Guy" who attacked civilians indiscriminately. In fact, both rebels and government forces were responsible for civilian deaths. Omitted from the narrative were admissions of Western support for Sunni extremist groups. In 2013, leaked emails from the private US intelligence firm Stratfor indicated that the US and the UK had been training Syrian opposition forces since 2011 with the aim of bringing an end to the Assad regime from within.[14]

Qatar's former prime minister, Hamad bin Jassim bin Jaber Al Thani, oversaw his country's operation in Syria until 2013. In 2017, he told media that Qatar and Saudi Arabia had been financing Syrian rebels from the beginning. Everything sent to Syria was distributed via the Turks and US forces.[15] He told US commentator Charlie Rose that Qatar, Saudi Arabia, UAE, the United States and other allies worked together since the beginning through two operation rooms located in Jordan and Turkey.[16] *Middle East Eye* confirmed that Saudi Arabia was supporting rebels in southern Syria through the CIA operations room in Jordan, while Qatar and Turkey were focusing on the north.[17]

Strategies to stir up chaos were envisioned in a publicly available report prepared for the US Army in 2008 — *Unfolding the Future of the Long War*. Recognizing the importance of protecting access to oil supplies in the Middle East, the report outlined several strategy options that might be to

American advantage. These included pitting Sunni and Shia against one another to create internal chaos, using covert action to support certain rebels against others and promoting information (i.e., disinformation) operations. One scenario was to take the side of conservative Sunni regimes such as Saudi Arabia, Egypt and Pakistan against Shia regimes, in order to limit Iranian power and influence.[18]

In 2011, when the various countries — within and outside the region — became involved in the Syrian conflict, it was in pursuit of their own interest or those of allies. The stakes were high, with each country seeking any advantage possible. Concerns about access to petroleum and rivalry between the two proposed pipelines were part of that conflict. Between 2011 and 2013, Western involvement expanded and intensified the rebellion through the arming of rebels, coercive diplomacy and false-flag operations. Three actions, discussed below, provide evidence of Western interference. The first was the movement of weapons to Syria to arm rebels. The second, less well-known, was an effort of coercive diplomacy. The third was false-flag operations — rebel chemical attacks to implicate Assad.

* * *

The first action was a so-called ratline to move weapons from the US consulate in Benghazi, Libya, to Turkey.[19] Investigative journalist Seymour Hersh revealed the ratline's existence in an article for the *London Review of Books* in April 2014.[20] The Turkish intelligence service supplied the weaponry to Syrian rebels — mostly Islamic State and al-Nusra Front (also known as al-Qaeda in Syria, rebranded as al-Sham in 2016). The CIA had been running the ratline from early 2012 until rebels in Libya attacked the consulate, torching the building and killing the US ambassador and three other men. The high quality of weaponry, including portable surface-to-air missile launchers, alarmed the US Joint Chiefs of Staff. Hersh observed: "Washington abruptly ended the CIA's role in the transfer of arms from Libya after the attack on the consulate, but the ratline kept going." Arms flowed in from Bulgaria and elsewhere. In effect, while the US claimed publicly to be fighting Islamic State, it was supplying them with powerful weapons.

Hersh is a respected investigative journalist with a track record of uncovering deeply held government secrets. He exposed the Mai Lai massacre during the Vietnam War, the US military's torture of Iraqi detainees at Abu Ghraib in 2004 and the killing of Osama bin Laden.

More evidence emerged in 2014 of Turkey's covert supply of arms to Syrian rebels. Early that year, the Turkish gendarmerie stopped and searched a convoy of trucks near the Syrian border and found weapons and ammunition. The truck belonged to the Turkish intelligence service and, following the intervention of government officials, was granted safe passage into Syria. The government arrested the prosecutor and gendarmerie who had stopped the convoy and alleged the trucks contained humanitarian aid. However, in May 2015, the Turkish newspaper *Cumhuriyet Daily* published a video showing the truck was indeed loaded with arms. The revelations caused a political storm. A Turkish court sentenced the newspaper's editor-in-chief and Ankara bureau chief to five years in jail for revealing state secrets.[21]

Despite all the evidence, Western leaders still avoided mentioning their own role in supplying rebels with weapons. In 2016, the US Congressional Select Committee on Benghazi issued an 800-page report on the events surrounding the attack on the Libyan consulate.[22] Missing was any mention of the consulate's role as a CIA base for covertly funnelling weapons from Libya to Turkey.

A US Defense Intelligence Agency document shed some light on Washington's thinking. The secret document from 2012 was declassified and released in 2015 under a *Freedom of Information Act* court order obtained by the NGO Judicial Watch.[23] The document noted opposition forces were trying to control Syria's eastern region adjacent to Iraq. Western countries, Gulf States and Turkey were supporting these efforts. It asserted: "If the situation unravels, there is the possibility of establishing a declared or undeclared Salafist Principality[24] in eastern Syria [Hasakah and Deir ez-Zor], and this is exactly what the Supporting Powers to the Opposition want, in order to isolate the Syrian Regime."[25] The document clearly supported breaking up Syria as a nation. The eastern region has oil and gas fields providing fuel to western Syria, where most of Syria's population lives.

* * *

The second action, in July 2013, offers insights into coercive diplomacy and geopolitical manoeuvring. Saudi Arabia's intelligence chief, Prince Bandar bin Sultan, flew to Moscow to ask President Putin to end Russian support for President Assad in Syria. In return, he would ensure that natural gas from the Persian Gulf would not threaten Russia's position as the main gas supplier to Europe. Also, Prince Bandar claimed he had control over Chechen rebels and could guarantee there would be no violence from them at the upcoming 2014 Sochi Winter Olympics. It was a stormy meeting. Bandar wanted the meeting to be secret, but Putin rejected confidentiality — and a memo of issues discussed turned up in the press.[26] It stated Bandar was looking for a unified Russian-Saudi petroleum strategy and had American backing for negotiations. Putin rejected Bandar's proposal and insisted Russia's stance on Assad would never change. Bandar then warned military actions were likely."[27]

Could Bandar have carried through on his promises if Putin had accepted them? While it is impossible to know the answer, Bandar was for years the supreme insider. He had been the Saudi Ambassador to the United States at the time of 9/11 and was a close friend of President George W. Bush. The US has had a special relationship with Saudi Arabia since 1945. Prince Bandar retired from government in 2015 when King Salman came to power.

* * *

The third action was the August 2013 chemical attack on civilians in Ghouta, near Damascus. It occurred just as UN experts were arriving in the city to investigate an earlier attack. They visited the area and found evidence of sarin gas, but did not attribute blame to either side.[28] Western leaders blamed President Assad immediately, without presenting any concrete evidence other than the fact that Assad had chemical weapons. Washington endorsed videos and photos uploaded by rebels on the Internet — grisly scenes of gassed children stretched out on the floor. On August 26, US Secretary of State John Kerry said the Syrian government must be held accountable.[29] Nine days later, Kerry released a US government assessment, which claimed with "high confidence" the Syrian government was behind the attack. Kerry called President Assad a "thug and a murderer,"[30] and the US prepared for an attack on Syria.[31]

What happened next was extraordinary. On September 13, Secretary Kerry met in Switzerland with Russian Foreign Minister Sergey Lavrov and brokered a negotiated solution to the crisis. The US, Russia and Syria agreed to a framework for the elimination of Syrian chemical weapons under international supervision. "The United States and Russia have long agreed that there is no military solution to the conflict in Syria," Kerry said. "We must find a political solution through diplomacy."[32]

On September 24, President Obama told the UN General Assembly the Assad regime had used such weapons on August 21. Rockets with large quantities of sarin gas were fired at civilians "from a regime-controlled neighbourhood and landed in opposition neighbourhoods."[33] Around the world, few questioned Washington's assessment. The conclusion that President Assad had attacked his own citizens with chemical weapons received widespread media attention. Yet the findings were called into question by one nun who understood the local culture.

Mother Agnes Mariam de la Croix visited the area where the attack took place and looked closely at the widely released videos and photos. Where were the parents? She knew mothers would have been near their children at the time of the attack. Further, the images showed one child wearing a red shirt in photos taken at different locations. If the photos were accurate, the body had been moved. For other victims, there were similar anomalies. The photos appeared to have been staged. She reported this to the UN.[34]

Further evidence came from a study by rocket experts Richard Lloyd and Theodore Postol at the Massachusetts Institute of Technology.[35] Their assessment of the rocket range concluded the rockets used had a range of only two kilometres and must have been fired from rebel ground, not from areas under government control eight kilometres away.

Later that year, US journalist Seymour Hersh reported that US Intelligence knew months earlier the al-Nusra rebel group had a chemical weapons expert in the area. Hersh accused the White House of cherry-picking the evidence to justify a strike against Assad. He said the rebels were responsible for the attack — a false flag to force Washington to bomb Damascus. Hersh's exposé was published in the *London Review of Books* in December 2013.[36]

Hersh revealed more. The previous year, President Obama had set a red line. If the Syrian government moved or used chemical weapons, he would consider US military involvement. According to Hersh, Turkish intelligence began working with al-Nusra rebels to carry out a covert chemical attack that would push Obama over the red line. US intelligence became aware of these efforts in the spring of 2013. Even so, President Obama was ready to authorize a bombing campaign in September to punish the Syrian government for allegedly crossing the red line. The Joint Chiefs of Staff, chaired by General Martin Dempsey, strongly advised against the campaign. They had learned from British intelligence the sarin samples recovered by the UN fact-finding mission did not match sarin held by the Syrian army. Obama threw the decision to Congress, which negated the campaign. Lavrov's meeting with Kerry helped Washington save face. Over several months, the Syrian chemical arsenal was dismantled and removed. The Assad government remained and the conflict continued.

In 2015, further evidence emerged regarding rebel use of sarin. A Turkish MP, Eren Erdem, accused Turkish businessmen of supplying Islamic State rebels with sarin gas. He said, "All basic materials are purchased from Europe ... Western sources know very well who carried out the sarin gas attack in Syria."[37] He pointed to a Turkish court investigation in 2013. Five Turkish citizens and a Syrian had been arrested for procuring chemical agents for Islamist groups in Syria. With an abrupt change of public prosecutor, all those arrested were released a week later. For his revelations, Erdem himself faced treason charges. His exposé indicated the chemical attacks were false-flag events designed to discredit the Assad government and increase international pressure for regime change.

The geopolitics of the Syrian conflict are immense. So is the gap between what's really going on and what leaders claim. Individual countries supported the rebellion in Syria while claiming to seek an end to the conflict. Before offering further discussion of the ongoing conflict, earlier interventions in Syria merit attention.

THE BACKSTORY

The same countries involved in Syria at the outset of the civil war were involved there a century ago. Syria, like Iraq, is a country created by the French and British in their carve-up of the Ottoman Empire after World War I. In 1920, the San Remo Conference placed Syria and Lebanon under a French mandate and Iraq and Palestine under British control. In 1940, Syria came under the control of the Axis powers after France fell to German forces. In 1941, British and Free French troops entered and occupied Syria. In 1944, the United States and Soviet Union recognized Syria and Lebanon as sovereign states, as did Britain in 1945. Syria became a charter member of the UN; and in 1946, after violent clashes in Damascus and Aleppo, France complied with a UN resolution to withdraw from Syria.

After the Arab Socialist Ba'ath Party was formed in 1947, Syria experienced a decade with several military coups and, for three short years (1958–1961), a merger with Nasser's Egypt to form the United Arab Republic. President Hafez al-Assad came to power in 1971 and governed Syria for 30 years. His son Bashar al-Assad followed in 2000 after his father's death. The early elections were one-candidate elections. In 2012, the constitution was amended to allow contested presidential elections, which were held in 2014. An international delegation from more than 30 countries endorsed the election, though the US, EU and Gulf Cooperation Council called it illegitimate. The voting took place in areas under government control, basically the Mediterranean coastal plain and mountains where most Syrians live. There was no voting in areas under rebel or Kurdish control.

Syria's relations with Israel, its southern neighbour, have been stormy. They have fought three major wars: the 1948 Arab–Israeli War, the 1967 Six-Day War, and the 1973 Arab-Israeli War. Both countries intervened in the Lebanese civil war. The Syrian army occupied the northern part of Lebanon from 1976 to 2005. It withdrew after the assassination of Lebanon's former Prime Minister Rafik Hariri, which the West blamed on Syria. Israel occupied southern Lebanon from 1982 to 2000, until forced out by Hezbollah. Israel has conducted numerous air strikes over Syria, including the 2007 destruction of an alleged nuclear reactor facility. Syria has not recognized the State of Israel.

Neoconservatives in Washington have pushed for regime change in

Damascus for two decades. A much-cited example is their 1996 policy document prepared for Israeli Prime Minister Benjamin Netanyahu, *A Clean Break: A New Strategy for Securing the Realm*.[38] The report advocated an aggressive Middle East policy, weakening Syria through proxy warfare. It intimated that Syria possessed weapons of mass destruction. It pushed for the removal of Saddam Hussein from power in Iraq. Several of the report's authors — Richard Perle, Douglas Feith, David Wurmser — later held senior positions in the George W. Bush Administration. They remained influential intellectuals in Washington throughout the Obama Administration, often criticizing his decisions.

ONGOING CONFLICT AND PETROLEUM

The Syrian war dragged on, with many actions and counteractions receiving Western media attention. Petroleum and pipelines were rarely mentioned. By May of 2015, the fifth year of the war, Islamic State controlled almost 50 per cent of Syria's land mass, including areas producing oil and gas.[39] It was the most successful of the rebel groups. Some rebels from other groups joined it, bringing weapons and ammunition with them. Another prominent rebel group was al-Nusra Front, but there were many others, operating under various names. Sometimes a group changed its name, making identification and goals even more unclear. The boundaries between the various rebel groups remained murky.

After taking control of an area, Islamic State operated like a mini-state. They secured water, flour and petroleum resources; instigated a simple system of taxation; and set up ministries and law courts. The local population became dependent on Islamic State for their survival and cooperated. Its goal was to establish a mini-caliphate with a religious and political leader who was absolute.[40]

Support for rebels came from numerous sources. Wealthy individuals in the Gulf States supported extremist Islamic groups. Qatar and Saudi Arabia funded groups representing Sunni political Islam. Turkey was lax on border enforcement, allowing weapons and money to flow freely. The United States provided weapons and admitted support for the Syrian Kurds and for "moderate" rebels, however they be defined. The Syrian Kurds aimed to consolidate their regional autonomy in the northeast and repulse Islamic

State encroachment. In this, they were assisted by US, British,[41] French[42] and German[43] special forces. Against this mix of immense outside support, Syrian forces were fighting a losing battle in 2015.

* * *

Russia began support for Syria in 2015, at the request of President Assad. In September, Russia launched an air campaign in support of the Syrian army in northwestern Syria. Targets included not only Islamic State but also rebels of al-Nusra Front and the Army of Conquest. The United States expressed annoyance that rebels it supported were being attacked, rebels it claimed were moderate. Russia asserted the boundaries between rebel groups were ill-defined.

Several dramatic events followed tit-for-tat. First, Islamic State struck back against Russia, claiming responsibility for a bomb onboard a Metrojet charter that crashed in October 2015. The jet, with 224 people on board, was on its way to St. Petersburg when it crashed in the Sinai desert. Most of those who died were Russians. In response, Russia increased its air strikes in Syria, pulverizing the supply of arms, equipment and rebels flowing south into Syria. It disrupted and destroyed convoys of oil trucks moving to Turkey from Islamic State-controlled installations in Syria.

Next, Islamic State claimed responsibility for attacks killing 130 people in Paris. In retaliation, the French started air strikes, operating from the UAE and Jordan.[44] So did the British, operating from Turkey's Incirlik airbase.[45] German planes launched so-called intelligence extraction missions, providing information to other coalition members on potential targets.

Two days after the Paris attacks, Presidents Putin and Obama met face-to-face on the sidelines of a G20 conference in Turkey. President Putin brought satellite photos from the Russian defence ministry, showing long lines of oil trucks moving from an Islamic State-controlled installation to the Turkish border.[46] The photos were released at a briefing event in Moscow.[47] Russia claimed it had proof Turkey's President Erdoğan and his family were involved, a charge he denied vehemently.[48] The oil traffic was extensive, though hard to measure as most fields were in Islamic State and

Kurdish hands.[49] The United States had satellites monitoring activities in Syria and must have known.

Within days of the oil trade becoming public, Turkey lashed out against Russia. A Turkish Air Force fighter jet shot down a Russian Sukhoi Su-24 aircraft allegedly 17 seconds in Turkish airspace. Putin said it was a deliberate ambush, that Turkey was guarding oil routes. Russia imposed sanctions on tourism, trade and investment with Turkey. The sanctions included a huge gas pipeline project, Turkish Stream, planned to bring gas from Russia via Turkey to Europe. That project and its geopolitics are discussed in Chapter 8.

With the Syrian conflict in stalemate and the Syrian army regaining territory, Russia and Western countries intimated interest in peace negotiations. In December 2015, the UN Security Council unanimously passed a resolution endorsing a transitional plan for Syria and the UN Secretary-General initiated negotiations in early 2016 between the Syrian government and opposition on a political transition to inclusive and non-sectarian governance. The problem was which opposition groups should participate in the negotiations. Some, which Western leaders maintained were moderate, were invited and others, including Syrian Kurds, were excluded. A two-day conference failed to achieve agreement among participants.

Meanwhile, a refugee crisis was unfolding in countries near Syria and in Europe. Before 2015, Syria's neighbours — Lebanon, Jordan, Turkey — had accepted more than 3 million refugees. In mid-2015, Turkey opened the floodgates, allowing a deluge of refugees in Turkey to flee to Europe. A crisis developed in the European Union, with one member country pitted against another in accepting the refugees. Germany admitted the most. Some countries simply refused to admit refugees and built fences against them. Europe was desperate to staunch the flood of refugees — from Syria as well as Libya and Afghanistan. In early 2016, the EU paid Turkey €3 billion to close the gates and keep refugees in Turkey. Even so, the wars in Afghanistan, Iraq, Libya and Somalia continued to produce a flood of refugees into Europe.

For its part, Canada admitted 46,700 refugees in 2016, its largest single-year number in nearly four decades. The number comprised refugees resettled by federal, provincial and municipal governments; NGOs; and private sponsors. Most refugees came from Syria (33,200), the next four countries being Eritrea, Iraq, Congo and Afghanistan. The federal government itself resettled more than

25,000 Syrian refugees from Syria, fulfilling a Liberal election promise. In contrast, the US admitted just 12,500 Syrian refugees in fiscal year 2016.

Turkey hit the headlines again in July 2016 when a military faction attempted a coup, taking over the Istanbul airport and moving through the city. President Erdoğan survived the attempt, declared a state of emergency and cracked down hard on any opposition by firing thousands from their jobs and exerting control over the media. He blamed an elderly opponent, Fethullah Gülen, for masterminding the coup and called for his extradition from the United States. Relations between Turkey and the US became strained. Western leaders accused Erdoğan of draconian human rights violations. Erdoğan accused US generals of aiding the coup plotters. Russia saw an opportunity. Presidents Erdoğan and Putin met in August to mend fences and end trade and tourism sanctions, which had badly damaged the Turkish economy. The two leaders also agreed to resume planning of Turkish Stream, the pipeline to bring Russian gas to Europe via Turkey. Washington was lobbying in Europe to kill the project.

In August 2016, Turkey faced another challenge. Syrian Kurdish forces (YPG), supported by US and European special forces, crossed west over the Euphrates River and captured the strategic town of Manbij from Islamic State. They aimed to link their western and eastern communities along the Turkish border. This was a red line for Turkey. It regards the YPG as an extension of the PKK, a Kurdish group in Turkey seeking autonomy since the 1980s which Turkey has been fighting bitterly to prevent. Turkish forces crossed the border and stopped the YPG's westward advance.

* * *

Syria's campaign to regain its oil and gas fields began in 2016. Russia, Iran and Hezbollah provided support. At the time, Islamic State controlled the ancient city of Palmyra and its adjacent gas fields, so important to Syria's economy. As well as its archaeological sites dating to the second millennium BCE, Palmyra is a key centre for gas production and phosphate mining. Fields in the region generate half of Syria's gas production. The city is the transit hub for gas pipelines linking fields in the east (Deir ez-Zor) and Kurdish northeast (Hasakah) to western Syria, where much of the

Delegations led by US Secretary of State John Kerry and Russian Foreign Minister Sergey Lavrov held meetings on Syria in September 2016 in Geneva.

population resides.[50] It straddles the dormant pipeline route from Iraq's Kirkuk oilfield to Syria's Mediterranean port of Baniyas, and is also a potential transit route for the Iranian or Qatari gas pipeline if either come to be realized.[51] The city changed hands more than once in 2016 and was finally regained by government forces (Syrian Arab Army) in March 2017. From a Syrian viewpoint, the petroleum resources were crucial to the restoration of a viable economy.

In 2016, government forces regained control of Aleppo, Syria's second largest city. They had always held West Aleppo. They now battled for control of East Aleppo, supported by Russian air cover. In the West, leaders decried the attacks, accusing Syria and Russia of striking hospitals and killing many civilians. The truth was difficult to determine, as Western reporters were not in Aleppo. Information came primarily from the White Helmets, a Syrian civil defence group established in 2013 to operate exclusively in rebel territory. They had received millions of dollars from Britain, Canada, Denmark, Germany, the Netherlands, the United States — all NATO countries. Many of their unverified reports during the siege of East

Aleppo appeared questionable but were widely featured in Western media. By December 2016, the whole city was finally under Syrian control.

Meanwhile, peace negotiations pottered along. In September 2016, Secretary Kerry and Foreign Minister Lavrov met in Geneva to hammer out a ceasefire. Again the issue was which rebel groups were moderate and which were jihadis.[52] Russia accused the US of failing to constrain rebel groups. The agreement was quickly broken. Barely a week into the ceasefire, US, British, Danish and Australian warplanes carried out four air strikes on a Syrian army position defending the Deir ez-Zor airport in eastern Syria. The attack killed 62 Syrian soldiers and wounded more than a hundred. Seven minutes later, Islamic State forces rushed in, seeking to overrun the army positions but were repulsed. The US claimed the aerial attack was a mistake, but there was more to the story.[53]

Deir ez-Zor, located beside the Euphrates, was then one of the few eastern cities remaining in government hands. It was besieged by Islamic State and depended on the airport for food and essential supplies. Islamic State had repeatedly sought to capture the airport. Deir ez-Zor was Syria's oil centre. Syria's oil reserves are mostly in the surrounding region, though some smaller fields are in the centre and northeast of the country. Deir ez-Zor is also situated on a potential route for an Iranian or Qatari pipeline if either were ever built. The aerial attack and Islamic State's immediate follow-up were more than strange.

* * *

Another chemical attack took place in early 2017. The effort to influence hearts and minds gained momentum. On April 4, according to the UK-based Syrian Observatory, the Syrian air force bombed the Idlib provincial town of Khan Sheikhun with sarin gas, killing at least 59 civilians. The White Helmets, not seen since the siege of East Aleppo, reappeared with photos and videos. Without waiting to verify facts, President Trump ordered a punitive attack on a Syrian air force base. He allowed time for Syrians and Russians to vacate the base. On April 7, US destroyers fired 59 Tomahawk missiles. The attack came with a cost. With each Tomahawk costing roughly US$1.4 million, the replacement bill amounted to some US$83 million. Their manufacturer

Raytheon added about US$1 billion to market value overnight.[54] The base was reportedly operational again within 12 hours.[55]

The whole incident was reminiscent of the Ghouta chemical attack in 2013. But, this time, the US president took unilateral action based on information from the White Helmets. Official Washington was ecstatic, as was the US press corps. But the UN Security Council had passed no resolution authorizing the attack. The Syrian government had eliminated its sarin stockpile in 2014, and there were no obvious grounds to suppose it would cheat. The Organization for the Prohibition of Chemical Weapons (OPCW), an intergovernmental organization based in The Hague, never visited the town or air base to verify facts on the ground. The Syrian air force admitted to bombing a target at Khan Sheikhun but denied the use of sarin. The Russians corroborated the Syrians. As ever, the question was: *Cui bono* — who benefited?

After the incident, the White House distributed a four-page National Security Council document on the attack[56] and accused Russia of covering up the Syrian government's role in the attack.[57] Not everyone agreed. Theodore Postol, the MIT professor and rocket expert who had investigated the 2013 chemical attack, observed that the only source the document cited in evidence was a crater identified north of Khan Shaykhun.[58] From White House photos, he determined the munition was almost certainly placed on the ground, with a detonator that crushed the container and dispersed the alleged sarin. He concluded the attack was staged — executed by individuals on the ground — and he accused the National Security Council of producing a fraudulent report. Postol once served as scientific adviser to the Pentagon's chief of naval operations.

Journalist Seymour Hersh, too, challenged Washington's narrative. Drawing on inside sources, he noted Trump was briefed that no evidence existed against the Syrian government but ordered the military to retaliate anyway.[59] The Russians had already given the Americans advance details of the planned Syrian air strike, the target being a building in which senior leaders of al-Nusra were meeting. Recognizing the air strike's importance, the Russians had given the Syrian air force a GPS-guided bomb, but the explosives were conventional, not chemical. Hersh said the US military later determined the bomb triggered secondary explosions that could have

Map 9. Who Controlled Syria, 2016 and 2018

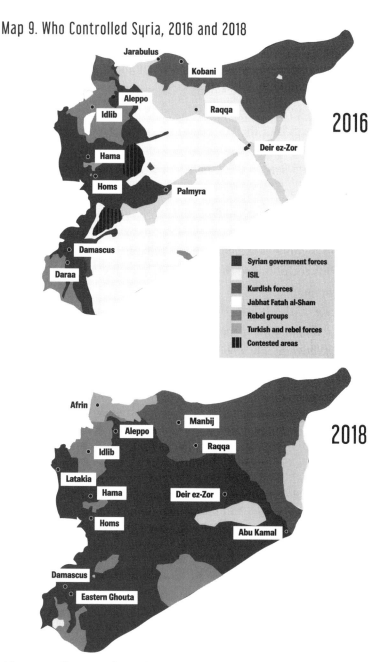

After controlling significant land mass in Syria, including much of its oil and gas, Islamic State was forced out by Syrian government forces west of the Euphrates River and by Kurdish forces east of the river.

generated a toxic cloud over the town, formed by release of fertilizers, disinfectants and other goods stored in the basement.[60]

The OPCW played its part. It launched a fact-finding inspection to determine whether chemical weapons had been used — not who might be responsible. Its preliminary report in May found people were exposed to a sarin-like substance.[61] The OPCW Board voted down a Russian-Iranian proposal that it despatch investigators to the air base and Khan Sheikhun.[62] The inspection team visited Turkey instead to meet with NGOs, including the White Helmets, who provided samples, interviewees, videos and images. Scott Ritter, the UN weapons inspector who stated before the invasion of Iraq that it possessed no weapons of mass destruction, excoriated the OPCW for its forensic testing of samples in Turkey.[63] The NGOs lacked the training for taking samples, failed to offer a seamless chain of custody and so were compromised.[64] Online journalists picked up on the theme.[65] Nevertheless, the OPCW's full findings, released on June 30, echoed its May report.[66]

As an exercise in managing public perception, Washington was successful. Western leaders pointed fingers at the Syrian government as the guilty party. Mainstream media blazoned the White House narrative and buried counterviews. Postol, Hersh and Ritter were heavyweight experts, yet received no mention. Mainstream media let the public down by avoiding discussion of contrary views.

* * *

The oil fields east of the Euphrates remained under rebel control. With Aleppo back in government hands and the northeast in Kurdish hands, the race was on between government troops and Kurdish forces to defeat Islamic State along the southern border and in the east.[67] Government troops were supported by Russian air cover and Kurdish forces by US-led special forces and air cover. The prize was twofold: Syria's land routes to Iraq, Iran and Jordan for transportation and potential pipelines, and Syria's vital oil and gas fields east of the Euphrates. Each protagonist wanted to establish facts on the ground ahead of any peace initiatives. Government forces planned a pincer movement from three directions: moving troops directly across the desert road from Palmyra, eastward along the southern border and down the west side of the Euphrates. Troops encountered stiff opposition along the direct central route.

Troops along the southern border were obstructed at Al-Tanf, a crucial crossing into Iraq. Al-Tanf had been controlled by rebels since 2015 and seized by US Special Forces in 2016. Its recapture by government forces would reopen the road between Damascus, Baghdad and Tehran, an unwelcome prospect to the United States and Israel.[68] During the first half of 2017, US aircraft targeted government forces approaching Al-Tanf several times, alleging it was a deconfliction zone which they were not obeying.[69] The statement was curious, as the US had declined to participate in the Astana, Kazakhstan, negotiations where Russia, Iran and Turkey created four such zones, and this was not one of them. In June 2017, government forces pulled a surprise move, outflanking the crossing and racing over the desert to the border 55 kilometres east of Al-Tanf. They were greeted by an Iraqi militia force which had raced north. It was a coordinated strategy to isolate Al-Tanf, reopen the road and facilitate recapture of the whole border to the east. US Special Forces remained at Al-Tanf in an isolated pocket.

Government troops moving from the northwest along the Euphrates encountered several US coalition attempts to block their progress, including air attacks and the destruction of bridges across the Euphrates. The incidents occurred near Raqqa, which Syrian Democratic Forces — a US-backed alliance of Kurdish and Arab forces — were battling to seize from Islamic State. They succeeded in October after a four-month battle, though the city was ruined.

Government troops eventually skirted Raqqa and, in September, managed to relieve Deir ez-Zor, which Islamic State had besieged for several years. That enabled them to regain territory west of the Euphrates down to the border crossing at Abu Kamal. Iraqi forces moved north and met them at the adjacent border town of Al-Qa'im. This restored to government hands the vital highway linking Damascus, Baghdad and Tehran. Kurdish forces, however, won the strategic race for control of Syria's oil and gas fields east of the Euphrates, giving them a powerful bargaining chip with Damascus.

* * *

Another region of unrest was the southwest, adjacent to Jordan and Israel. In July 2017 at the G20 Summit, Presidents Trump and Putin agreed on a de-escalation zone in the southern provinces of Daraa, Quneitra and Sweida. Trump also announced an end to the CIA covert program of arming and training Salafist/jihadist rebels along the Jordanian border — as well as in the northwest near Turkey.[70] (The Pentagon continued to support Kurdish forces in the east.)

Israel expressed concern. The region was close to the Golan Heights, which Israel had annexed in 1981. It had long supported rebels in Syria adjacent to the Golan Heights, with air support, cash, food, fuel and medical supplies. Its aim was to carve out a "buffer zone populated by friendly forces."[71] The Golan Heights were strategically important to Israel both militarily and as a source of water. A newer interest was petroleum.

In 2013, Israel awarded an exclusive licence for oil exploration there to Afek Oil and Gas Ltd., a subsidiary of the US company Genie Oil and Gas. Afek began drilling in 2014 and announced in 2016 it had struck oil. Its chief geologist told Israeli media "we're talking about significant amounts" of oil and gas.[72] The Israeli media evinced huge excitement. Genie Oil and Gas lined up a powerful array of Washington insiders to support its position geopolitically. Its Strategic Advisory Board included former US Vice-President Dick Cheney, media mogul Rupert Murdoch, former CIA director James Woolsey and other heavyweights. Though Syria maintains the Golan Heights are still Syrian, Israel clearly intends to stay there indefinitely.

* * *

Action moved to East Ghouta in early 2018. Despite Russian and Iranian support, government forces had been able to address only one part of Syria at a time. East Ghouta, just east of Damascus, had for several years been in the hands of rebels, who repeatedly fired rockets and mortar shells into the city. Who were the rebels? While most Western media obfuscated, respected journalists such as Robert Fisk and Patrick Cockburn reported they were groups allied to al-Nusra, also known as al-Qaeda in Syria, financed by Saudi Arabia and Kuwait.[73]

When the Syrian government launched a campaign to retake East Ghouta, Western governments alleged the Syrian regime was bombing, starving and making chemical attacks on civilians. The White Helmets reappeared, claiming the Syrian government was bombing hospitals and killing children. Washington turned on the heat. On March 12, the US ambassador to the United Nations, Nikki Haley, warned the US was prepared to act against any nation seeking "to impose its will through chemical attacks and inhuman suffering, most especially the outlaw Syrian regime."[74] The information blizzard was a reprise of East Aleppo two years earlier.

By late March 2018, Syrian government forces regained most of East Ghouta. In so doing, they located a well-equipped chemical laboratory hastily abandoned by rebels. Middle East scholar Sharmine Narwani visited it 24 hours later, reporting it in a *RT News* article replete with photos.[75] Russian Foreign Minister Lavrov warned rebels might stage chemical weapons provocations to invoke American assistance.[76] This came to pass in the rebels' last foothold, the town of Douma. The White Helmets alleged a chlorine attack with hundreds killed and posted horrific photos and videos. President Trump vowed a punitive strike against Syria. He tweeted Assad was a "gas killing animal" and called on the Russians to leave Syria. Moscow made clear that, if Russian military lives were endangered, it would take measures against both missiles and launch pads.[77]

With US ships and planes at risk, Washington chose its targets with care. On April 14, the United States, Britain and France launched 103 missiles. They did so without UN Security Council backing and one day before an OPCW site investigation. Moscow reported 71 were shot down. No one was killed, few injured, no Syrian aircraft destroyed, no airfield hit. The whole affair smacked of orchestrated theatrics to draw attention away from US and British political woes closer to home.

In the Kurdish northeast, the US strengthened its military foothold. Through its Kurdish partnership, it gained control over much of Syria's oil and gas production. In February 2018, Secretary of State Rex Tillerson said US and coalition forces controlled 30 per cent of Syrian territory, a large amount of the population and a large amount of Syria's oil fields. He said the idea "that the US has very little leverage or role to play is simply false."[78] With Western sanctions prohibiting oil imports into Syria, Damascus faced the prospect of buying its own oil from the Kurds.

* * *

Would Syria re-emerge as a unitary state or become balkanized? With ten US military bases ensconced in Syria's northeast, Turkey suspected Washington of supporting Kurdish aspirations for an independent state carved out of Syria, Iraq, Iran and Turkey itself. Turkey reached out to Iran and Russia. In a seismic shift, the three countries emerged as strategic Middle Eastern partners. Washington was caught between a rock and a hard place. In November, President Trump assured President Erdoğan by phone that the US was preparing to stop supplying weapons to ethnic Kurdish fighters in Syria.[79] However, US Defense Secretary Mattis told media the US military was not going to vacate Syria before a UN-brokered settlement at Geneva was achieved.

By 2018, the Kurds, supported by US air power and special forces, had seized most of the land east of the Euphrates, including key oil and gas fields. The US announced plans to train and equip a 30,000-strong border force in the Kurdish northeast of Syria. The force would be under control of the Syrian Democratic Forces — mostly Kurdish troops backed by US Special Forces. The action would create a *de facto* Kurdish state under US protection. For Turkey, the prospect of a Kurdish state on its border was a red line. Its troops crossed the border west of the Euphrates, evicting Kurdish forces from the Kurdish-majority province of Afrin.

Russia and Iran were in Syria because of an explicit request from the Syrian government in conformance with international law. Their support for the Syrian government remained legal. The US, Saudi Arabia, Qatar and Turkey were operating in Syria with neither an invitation from President Assad nor an enabling UN Security Council resolution. Countries participating militarily with the US included Australia, Britain, Denmark, France, Germany and the Netherlands, supporting so-called moderate rebels. Saudi Arabia, Qatar and Turkey were backing rebels of all sorts. In 2017, Qatar stopped supporting the rebellion and revealed its previous connivance. Turkey's overarching focus remained the Kurds, and Israel's concern was the Golan Heights. Canada participated in sanctions but avoided military involvement. The situation was a tinderbox, with potential conflict among many countries, including nuclear powers (the US and Russia) and NATO allies.

Who would be responsible for paying for Syria's reconstruction after the war? China would likely have a major role. It had been advocating a diplomatic rather than military solution since the war began, and provided humanitarian aid. China held fairs and expositions on Syrian reconstruction in 2017 and announced plans to invest US$2 billion in a Syrian industrial park for Chinese companies. The Syrian ambassador to China stated China, Russia and Iran would have priority over other countries for infrastructure investment and reconstruction when the war ended.[80]

Understanding all these complexities is a challenge. Finding a diplomatic solution had already proven difficult. Amid the ever-changing soundbites of numerous incidents, Western attention focused publicly on Syria's President Assad and on Russia's role in helping defeat rebels. Many realities of the conflict have been obscured, including financial and military support for rebels, accidental bombings, legitimate questions about chemical attacks and US support for Syrian Kurds. Through all this, the actions of major powers have been consistent *inter alia* with securing a pipeline route that supports their interests. The prospects for a pipeline from Iran or Qatar were still non-existent as of June 2018, but the long term is full of unknowns.

CHAPTER 4
IRAN — OUT OF THE COLD?

"Contrariwise," continued Tweedledee, "if it was so, it might be; and if it were so, it would be; but as it isn't, it ain't. That's logic."

—Lewis Carroll, *Through the Looking Glass* (1871)

In his State of the Union address in 2002, US President George W. Bush named Iran (along with Iraq and North Korea) to the "Axis of Evil," a term he used to describe countries he thought were involved with terrorism and weapons of mass destruction. He accused Iran of having a clandestine nuclear weapons program and "arming to threaten the peace of the world."[1]

Alarm bells went off around the world. The EU was about to negotiate a trade and cooperation agreement with Iran.[2] European Commissioner for External Relations Chris Patten said the phrase Axis of Evil was deeply "unhelpful"; the European policy of "constructive engagement" with Iran was much more likely to bring results.[3] French Foreign Affairs Minister Hubert Vedrine accused Washington of a "simplistic" approach that reduced "all the problems of the world to the struggle against terrorism."[4] Novelist John Le Carré commented, "What is at stake is not an Axis of Evil — but oil, money and people's lives."[5]

For its part, Iran maintained it had no intention of acquiring a nuclear weapon. Repeated investigations failed to find evidence of a nuclear weapons program. Yet the accusations continued. With the focus on the nuclear issue, other relevant topics received scant attention — topics such as Iran's massive oil and gas reserves and how wealth generated from petroleum might challenge the power of other countries in the region.

IRAN'S IMPORTANCE

Iran is a big country, larger than Québec and more than twice the size of Texas. It has 70 million people. Strategically situated between Europe and Asia, Iran stretches from the oil-rich Persian Gulf in the south to the oil-rich Caspian Sea in the north. It borders seven countries — Turkey, Iraq, Afghanistan, Pakistan, Armenia, Azerbaijan and Turkmenistan.

Iran is a proud and independent nation, a regional power and a pre-dominantly Shia country in the Middle East. Its outreach in recent years to like-minded countries (Iraq, Syria, Hezbollah in Lebanon) has nettled Arab States adjoining the Persian (Arabian) Gulf, which are predominantly Sunni. Since Iran's 1979 Revolution, the United States — a strong ally of Saudi Arabia and Israel — has sought to reduce Iranian power in the Middle East through political interference, sanctions and covert actions.

Iran has immense oil and gas resources. According to BP's 2018 *Statistical Review*, Iran's oil reserves are the world's fourth largest and its gas reserves are the world's second largest. Its oil exports are shipped through the Persian Gulf and the Strait of Hormuz to world markets, especially China, Japan, India, Turkey and, with the sanctions lifted in 2016, Europe again. Iran's gas exports are piped to Iraq and Turkey.

THE NUCLEAR ISSUE

Between 2002 and 2016, the nuclear issue dominated Western perspectives and relationships with Iran. Much public discussion focused on the nuclear issue as if that meant developing a nuclear weapon. Iran asserted time and again that it wanted only to generate electricity from nuclear power plants, saving oil and gas for other uses. Two supreme leaders of Iran — Grand Ayatollahs Khomeini and Khamenei — issued fatwas (rulings) prohibiting Iran's manufacture or use of nuclear weapons.[6] Even so, Western leaders continued to assert Iran was working toward nuclear weapons.

Nuclear energy is a UN right allowed to all countries. Iran's nuclear power aspirations date back to the 1950s, when they were supported by the United States under its Atoms for Peace program.[7] Iran is a signatory of the Nuclear Non-Proliferation Treaty, which explicitly allows the development of civilian nuclear power. Iran has a nuclear power station at Bushehr, built with Russian help. It has its own uranium mines, enrichment facilities and reactor for medical isotopes. It is self-reliant. The power station uses five per cent enriched uranium and the reactor, 20 per cent. That is quite normal.

The West said Iran might or could build a bomb. But that would require enrichment to 90 per cent — a very difficult process. Israel consistently refused to rule out a military option to prevent Iran from obtaining a nuclear bomb.[8] The US kept "all options" on the table. Between 2010 and 2012, four Iranian nuclear scientists were assassinated and a fifth wounded. Israel neither confirmed nor denied involvement, but Israeli Defence Minister Moshe Ya'alon hinted, "We will act in any way and are not willing to tolerate a nuclear-armed Iran ... Israel should be able to defend itself."[9] During 2007–2010, a sophisticated computer virus (Stuxnet) was unleashed mysteriously in computers at the Natanz uranium enrichment facility, destroying one-fifth of its centrifuges. *The New York Times* revealed Stuxnet was a joint US/Israeli effort, and President Obama personally authorized the cyber-attacks.[10]

The UN International Atomic Energy Agency (IAEA) investigated repeatedly and failed to confirm the assertions that Iran was attempting to build a nuclear weapon. In 2008, under Mohamad El Baradei's leadership, the IAEA was close to clearing its last remaining "issues of concern."[11] His successor since 2009, Yukiya Amano, kept closer to the Western narrative while producing no solid evidence in support. The US government's own National Intelligence Estimates found no evidence that a nuclear weapon was in process.[12]

Western political leaders ignored the lack of evidence and repeated their assertions. President Obama, in his 2012 State of the Union address, proclaimed, "Let there be no doubt: America is determined to prevent Iran from getting a nuclear weapon, and I will take no options off the table to achieve that goal."[13] Under US pressure, the UN Security Council passed a series of resolutions against Iran between 2006 and 2012. Western countries, including Canada, imposed additional unilateral sanctions, including restrictions on oil exports. In his 2014 book *Manufactured Crisis*, US journalist Gareth

Porter concluded the diplomacy surrounding Iran's nuclear program was a crisis manufactured by certain countries for their own reasons.

Israel was especially upset about Iran's nuclear capabilities. Israel, which, as of 2018 had not signed the Nuclear Non-Proliferation Treaty, had neither confirmed nor denied its own possession of nuclear weapons.[14] It accused former Iranian Premier Mahmoud Ahmadinejad of saying that Israel "must be wiped off the map." In fact, this was a mistranslation. In 2005, US professor Juan Cole and UK journalist Jonathan Steele clarified the translation as "the regime occupying Jerusalem must vanish from the page of time."[15] That indicated regime change, not war.[16] No matter, the mistranslation has been repeated time and again.

Big steps toward resolution took place in 2015. In July, the UN Security Council's five permanent members (Britain, China, France, Russia, the United States), plus Germany (the so-called P5+1), signed with Iran a Joint Comprehensive Plan of Action in Vienna, Austria.[17] The deal took effect January 16, 2016; and the United Nations, the US and other countries lifted their nuclear-related sanctions, including those on Iran's oil exports. However, under a "snap-back" plan, sanctions may be renewed if Iran violates the agreement; and some UN non-nuclear sanctions continue — on conventional weapon sales until 2021 and ballistic missile technologies until 2024. US sanctions related to human rights abuses, missiles and terrorism remain in place indefinitely.

For its part, Iran agreed to eliminate its stockpile of medium-enriched uranium, cut its stockpile of low-enriched uranium by 98 per cent, reduce the number of centrifuges for 15 years, and limit uranium enrichment to just 3.67 per cent. It will confine enrichment to its Natanz facility, converting the Fordo facility into a technical centre for isotopes and the Arak reactor into a peaceful nuclear research centre.

Western leaders praised the deal. US Secretary of State John Kerry declared the Middle East would be more manageable.[18] EU Foreign Affairs chief Frederica Mogherini saw the deal as opening up "unprecedented possibilities of peace for the region."[19] Some observers saw the deal somewhat differently. Professor William Beeman at the University of Minnesota commented dryly that Iran had won the diplomatic struggle over its nuclear program "by giving up activities in which it had never engaged and never intended to engage."[20]

BACKSTORY: IRAN BEFORE 1979

It is always interesting to look at history from the other person's point of view. What Americans remember is 1979 and their diplomats being taken hostage. What Iranians remember is foreign interference in the 1950s. From an Iranian perspective, Western countries have interfered and exploited repeatedly.

The first commercial discovery of oil in the Middle East dates back to 1908, when British explorers in southern Persia (now Iran) — after seven futile years — struck oil near the city of Masjid-i-Suleiman. In 1909, they formed the Anglo-Persian Oil Company to develop the oilfield. In 1913, the company built an oil refinery at Abadan in southern Persia, which for 50 years was the world's largest. The company was renamed the Anglo-Iranian Oil Company (AIOC) in 1935 when Persia became Iran, and then morphed into the British Petroleum Company (BP) in 1954.

BP has always had a close relationship with the British government. In the reign of Edward VII, before World War I, the British Empire ruled supreme and the Royal Navy ruled the waves. Like other navies of the time, it relied on coal-firing for its ships. At that time, Britain had a huge coal industry. But bunkering a battleship could take three days and required a coal dock, with all hands on deck to load the coal and wash off the dust. Winston Churchill, as First Lord of the Admiralty, and Lord Fisher as First Sea Lord, decided to switch the navy to oil. Bunkering with oil required just a few hours and a few sailors, and could even be done at sea. It also required less bunker space, as the calorific value of one ton of oil is roughly equivalent to one and one-half tons of coal.

However, the world's major source of oil then was the US Gulf of Mexico, and the United States was ambivalent about the British Empire. Britain preferred to remain independent from US oil. In 1914, the British government acquired a 51 per cent shareholding in the Anglo-Persian Oil Company and switched the Royal Navy to Persian oil.

Thereafter, Persia's oil became vital to the British economy. The company had a 60-year monopoly concession over southern Persia and produced oil on very advantageous terms. The concession — a gold mine to Britain — was renegotiated in 1933 to improve terms in Persia's favour. During World War II, Britain and the Soviet Union jointly occupied Iran to secure its oil for the Allies. After the war, the Iranian government sought once more to improve revenues from the concession. In 1951, negotiations having stalled, the elected government under Prime Minister Mossadegh nationalized AIOC's Iranian assets and assigned them to the newly created National Iranian Oil Company (NIOC). Foreign companies blackballed Iran, and no oil flowed for 18 months.

In 1953, the US and Britain engineered a coup, installed the Shah (a brutal regime) and inserted a foreign oil consortium, Iranian Oil Participants. Oil flowed again.[21] As a price for intervention, the US wanted its oil companies in on the deal. BP emerged as the largest consortium participant (40 per cent), but five American companies (Chevron, Esso, Mobil, Texaco, Gulf) together acquired 40 per cent, and two European companies (Shell and CFP), the other 20 per cent. The companies were the so-called Seven Sisters plus an eighth (CFP) that dominated the world oil business.

NIOC formally owned Iran's oil deposits and installations. The consortium controlled operations and produced oil on behalf of NIOC, which in turn sold the oil to the consortium's shareholders. The consortium shared profits with Iran on a 50:50 basis but had no Iranians on its board of directors. The Iranians had little choice in the matter. The consortium's head office was in London.

For its part, BP was well satisfied. It was already enjoying increased production from Kuwait. It was no longer conspicuously unique in Iran. It transformed its corporate culture in 1954 from a benevolent colonial company to a modern international company. It pensioned off expatriate staff based in southern Iran and recruited a new management cadre in London. I was one of the new recruits, joining the company three years later, in 1957.

The same year, NIOC started offshore exploration and development of fields in the Persian Gulf. It did so initially through joint ventures with foreign oil companies and later through long-term service contracts.[22] In 1973, Iran — like other OPEC countries — negotiated tougher terms with foreign oil companies. Participants in the onshore consortium remained privileged oil customers but gave up management and control of oil assets and instead carried out specific services for NIOC.

The Iranians, a proud people, were suspicious in those days — as now — of Western intentions. I experienced this when part of a World Bank economic

90

mission visiting Iran in 1973. Our mission leader briefed us our rooms were bugged. My role was to assess the contribution of petroleum to the Iranian economy — the balance of payments, government revenue, investment requirements. The government meetings were somewhat strained, but I was allowed to visit the oil province of Khuzestan in the southwest. This province has 90 per cent of Iran's oil reserves, the other ten per cent being in the Persian Gulf. I recall the super-giant Ahwaz oilfield with its huge pipelines going to the marine terminal, and the vast Abadan refinery with its soaring distillation columns. In those days, the refinery was a major source of refined products for BP's markets overseas in Asia, Africa and Europe.

CONFLICT AND PETROLEUM SINCE 1980

The 1979 Revolution overthrew the Shah of Iran and installed an Islamic Republic under the Grand Ayatollah Khomeini. The Revolution was massively popular in Iran, though many Iranians fled into exile. Even Iranians at the World Bank in Washington, DC, expressed excitement. Previously, they would not speak even privately about political issues lest the Shah's far-reaching Savak secret police overhear.

During the Revolution, Iranian students took over the US Embassy in Tehran. For 444 days (November 4, 1979, to January 20, 1981), 52 American diplomats and citizens were held hostage. The hostage crisis was the nadir in US-Iran relations. In Iran, many saw the hostage-taking as a slap at the United States for having supported the Shah and attempting to undermine the Revolution. But Americans were outraged. President Jimmy Carter called the hostages "victims of terrorism and anarchy" and said "the United States will not yield to blackmail."[23] Ten days after the hostage taking, he signed an Executive Order freezing Iranian government accounts in US banks, about US$8 billion. The hostages were finally released and bank accounts unfrozen on the last day of the Carter Administration.

Canada played a well-known role in the hostage crisis, with its ambassador Ken Taylor and diplomat John Sheardown sheltering and helping arrange the escape of six American diplomats. Canada closed its embassy for eight years. In 1988, Canada reopened the embassy and pursued a cautious policy of "controlled engagement" with restricted bilateral ties. Relations with Iran remained rocky.

Iran's 1979 Revolution had consequences for the oil sector. In 1980, NIOC terminated its offshore joint ventures and service contracts with foreign companies, and in 1981, Iran abrogated its agreement with the onshore oil consortium.

Then came the Iran-Iraq War (1980–1988). Two of Saddam Hussein's motives for attacking Iran were petroleum-related. First was the desire to take complete control of the Shatt al-Arab river (Arvand Rud in Persian) that forms the border between Iraq and Iran. Iraq's major rivers, the Tigris and Euphrates, flow into the Shatt al-Arab and thence the Persian Gulf. The port cities of Basra in Iraq and Abadan and Khorramshahr in Iran are situated along the Shatt al-Arab. The precise border line along the waterway has been a contentious issue for centuries. A second motive was the desire to annex the adjacent Iranian province of Khuzestan, which Saddam claimed was historically part of Mesopotamia. Khuzestan is Iran's key oil province.

In 1980, Saddam perceived the Iranian military to be severely weakened by the 1979 revolution, with many officers executed, exiled or retired. That was his opportunity; he initiated hostilities in September. Iraqi forces crossed the Shatt al-Arab, seized Khorramshahr, besieged Abadan and attacked other cities in Khuzestan, including its capital Ahwaz, the centre of Iran's oil production. They destroyed the Abadan refinery.

In many ways, the war was about oil. Oil provided the government revenues to buy weaponry. Each country sought to block the other's oil exports. Iraq repeatedly bombed Kharg Island, Iran's main crude oil terminal, located in the northeastern Persian Gulf, and destroyed most of the terminal facilities. It later bombed Iran's oil transfer terminals farther away in the southeastern Gulf at Sirri, Lavan and Larak islands. Iran's crude oil production fell dramatically, from 3.2 million b/d in 1979 to 1.3 million b/d in 1981.

For its part, Iran blockaded the Shatt al-Arab, preventing oil shipments from Iraq's southern fields. Iran's ally Syria closed the Kirkuk-Banias oil pipeline connecting Iraq's northern fields to the Mediterranean Sea. Iraq's remaining link to a marine terminal was the pipeline from Kirkuk to the Turkish port of Ceyhan. Iraq's oil production sank from 3.5 million b/d in 1979 to 900,000 b/d in 1981. By 1982, Iraqi revenues from oil were insufficient to finance the conflict. The war was going badly for

Iraq militarily. In June, Saddam sued for peace and withdrew his troops from Iranian territory. Khomeini refused peace — he wanted to eliminate Saddam's regime. He called on Iraq's Kurdish and Shia population to rise up. The Kurds obliged; the Shia did not.

Map 10. Iran: Locations of Petroleum Facilities

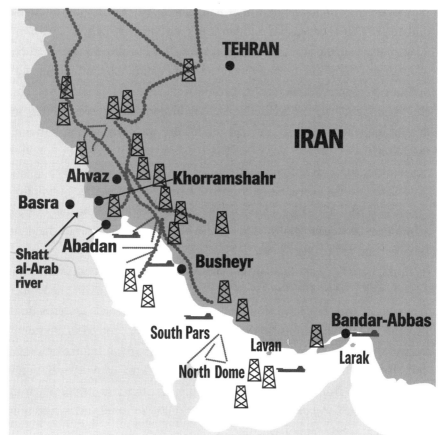

Iran's oil reserves are the world's fourth largest, and its gas reserves are the world's second largest. Its oil exports are shipped via the Persian Gulf to world markets. Its gas exports are piped to Iraq and Turkey.

Saudi Arabia, Kuwait and UAE stepped into the breach, making huge war loans to Iraq. Saudi Arabia later allowed Iraq to build an oil pipeline to the Saudi export terminal at Yanbu on the Red Sea, bypassing the hazardous Strait of Hormuz.

The Soviet Union and Western countries supported Iraq, regarding it as a counterweight to post-revolutionary Iran. The Soviet Union, France and China were the main suppliers of armaments to Iraq. US support began in mid-1982, after Iran rejected Saddam's overture to end the war. President Reagan decided "the United States could not afford to allow Iraq to lose the war to Iran."[24] The US provided loans, military equipment and intelligence on Iranian troop movements obtained from satellites and radar planes. The US, West Germany, the Netherlands, Britain and France assisted Iraq in developing chemical weapons. Iraq used those weapons against Iran and Iraqi Kurds.

Countries supporting Iran were fewer in number. Its main arms suppliers were China, North Korea, Libya, Syria and Japan. The US indirectly supplied weapons as part of the illegal program that became known as the Iran-Contra affair. The sales were designed to secure the release of hostages held in Lebanon and to launder money to Contra rebels in Nicaragua.

Throughout the war, Iraq targeted tankers carrying Iranian oil. Iran desisted until 1984, when it began targeting tankers carrying Iraqi oil. The Tanker War spread, with both countries attacking merchant vessels under neutral flag. In 1987, Kuwait appealed to the United States for protection. President Reagan signed an Executive Order banning US imports of Iranian crude oil and all other Iranian imports.[25] The US Navy started convoy operations, allowing ships from neutral countries to fly the stars-and-stripes when in the Persian Gulf and gain US protection. It did not extend such protection to tankers carrying Iranian oil.

During the Tanker War, the US Navy sank several Iranian warships. In 1988, the cruiser USS *Vincennes* shot down a commercial airliner, Iran Air 655, killing all 290 on board. The Tanker War was devastating. Lloyd's of London estimated the war damaged 546 commercial vessels and killed about 430 civilian sailors.[26]

Only toward the end did Iran become war-weary. The UN brokered a ceasefire. The war ended in stalemate, with immense casualties and financial cost on both sides. Iraq owed the Arab Gulf States US$37 billion, which it was unable to repay and they were unwilling to waive. This may have been one motive for Saddam's attempt to annex Kuwait two years later, in 1990.

After the crippling war, the National Iranian Oil Company had to rebuild its damaged oil infrastructure. Oil production rose gradually to 2.3 million b/d in 1990. Iran expressed interest in working with Western companies to develop new oil and gas projects, and the first deal was agreed in March 1995 with the US company Conoco. Ten days later, President Bill Clinton signed an Executive Order banning all US participation in Iranian petroleum development.[27] That squashed Conoco's US$1 billion deal. Iran subsequently awarded the contract to France's Total.

Two months later, Clinton signed a second Executive Order, imposing a total embargo on US trade and investment in Iran.[28] That ended purchases of Iranian crude by US companies for refining in non-US markets (the US market being closed since 1987). The two Executive Orders deemed Iran "an extraordinary threat to the national security, foreign policy and economy of the United States."

Nailing Iran further, Congress passed the US *Iran-Libya Sanctions Act* (ILSA) in 1996, renamed the *Iran Sanctions Act* in 2006 when Libyan sanctions were lifted. The *Act* imposed sanctions on both US *and* foreign businesses investing more than $20 million per year in Iran's petroleum sector. A spokesman for the Washington lobby group American Israel Public Affairs Committee (AIPAC) was quoted as saying, "These guys [Congress] wrote their thing with us sentence by sentence."[29]

Canada and the European Union opposed the US law's extraterritorial application to their firms and promptly adopted blocking legislation to prevent them from complying with it. European, Russian and Chinese companies went on to sign huge contracts with NIOC for oil and gas field development in Iran. These contracts were so-called *buyback* agreements, in which NIOC reimbursed expenses but owned the oil or gas field and marketed the production.[30]

Ten years later, in 2006, the international community fell into line with the United States. The UN Security Council imposed four rounds of sanctions on Iran in response to its nuclear program. The United States issued various Executive Orders freezing assets of firms and individuals, as did the EU and Canada. The EU, once Iran's largest oil market, prohibited the export of specific products to Iran and, in 2012, imposed an oil embargo. Canada broke diplomatic relations entirely and formally listed the Iranian regime as a state sponsor of terrorism. Prime Minister Stephen Harper claimed Iran was "a clear and present danger," and Foreign Minister John Baird called it "the most significant threat to global peace and security in the world."

Canada's stated reasons for the embassy closure were Iran's support to Syria during the civil war, non-compliance with UN resolutions regarding its nuclear program, threats to Israel and fears for safety of Canadian diplomats. Iran responded by closing its embassy in Ottawa. Israel's Prime Minister Benjamin Netanyahu praised Canada's decision as a moral, courageous step and a message to the international community that it could not allow "the dark regime in Iran to get nuclear weapons." When the Liberals came to power, Prime Minister Justin Trudeau expressed his intention to reopen Canada's embassy in Tehran, but as of April 2018 it remained closed.

ONGOING ISSUES AND PETROLEUM

With the lifting of sanctions in January 2016, Iran rapidly implemented its plan to raise oil exports to pre-sanction levels (2.5 million b/d).[31] Oil production rebounded to an average 5.0 million b/d in 2017 and exports to 3.0 million b/d. Exports to Iran's main markets — Asia and Europe — regained pre-sanction levels.

Iran began requiring payment for oil in euros and yuan, to the detriment of the petrodollar. As explained by Deputy Petroleum Minister Masoud Esfahani, Iran suffered much from US sanctions, including the freezing of significant assets acquired from oil sales. Iran's decision not to trade in dollars was "an attempt to protect Iranian assets from new unilateral US sanctions."[32]

European companies flocked to Tehran, looking to revive investment in the oil and gas sector. At an Iran-EU Investment Conference in 2015, Iran's deputy oil minister said Tehran identified nearly 50 oil and gas projects worth US$185 billion that it hoped to sign by 2020.[33] In August 2016, the government approved a new model contract for petroleum exploration and production.[34]

Distrustful of past Western policies, Iran looked increasingly toward Russia and China. Russia became a close partner. In 2014, Russia and Iran signed protocols for a strategic partnership that would vastly expand trade and investment, including petroleum investment and an oil-for-goods barter deal. Under the oil-for-goods deal, Iran agreed to supply 100,000 b/d of oil to Russia, which in return would export to Iran goods worth US$45 billion annually.[35] China had major investments in Iran's petroleum sector and accounted for one-third of Iran's foreign trade.[36] Iran was a crucial link in China's One Belt One Road initiative to strengthen transportation links to Europe, and was an early member of China's new Asian Infrastructure Investment Bank.

In 2016, China's President Xi Jinping made a state visit to Iran — the first foreign leader there since the nuclear deal was implemented — and announced massive trade and investment plans. The two countries agreed to upgrade their relations to a strategic partnership and unveiled a 25-year cooperation plan.[37] President Xi announced support for Iran becoming a full member of the Shanghai Cooperation Organization, a political, economic and military organization comprising China, Russia, Kazakhstan, Kyrgyzstan, Tajikistan, Uzbekistan and — since 2017 — India and Pakistan.

Iran remained wary of US investment. In January 2016, the day after the nuclear deal was implemented and sanctions lifted, the US Treasury imposed sanctions on 11 entities and individuals for their involvement in procurement for Iran's ballistic missile program.[38] Days after, Iran's Supreme Leader, Ayatollah Ali Khamenei, explained to President Xi that Iranians never trusted the West, and that was why Tehran sought cooperation with more independent countries like China.[39] President Hassan Rouhani said Iran would not pursue the development of economic links with the US beyond the purchase of specific goods such as airplanes, nuts or carpets. In that context, Iran Air signed agreements in December 2016 to buy 80 passenger aircraft from Boeing and 100 from Airbus. The Boeing deal was the largest between a US business and Iran since the 1979 Islamic Revolution.[40] The US House of Representatives passed a bill to block the deal but the Senate failed to follow through. Boeing signed another Iranian deal in 2017, with Aseman Airlines for 30 passenger airplanes and an option on 30 more.

International banking remained bedevilled by US non-nuclear sanctions. It was still illegal for US banks to lend to Iran. European banks were free to resume lending, but the larger banks were apprehensive lest the US re-impose its nuclear-related sanctions.[41] In previous years, they had paid enormous fines to the US Treasury for having financed trade with Iran. As a result, Iran turned to Asian and smaller European banks without US banking interests. As well, various European countries began offering euro-denominated credits and export guarantees to Iranian buyers, avoiding the need for US dollars.[42]

Washington continued its war of words against Iran. Before his election, Donald Trump told the American Israel Public Affairs Committee, "My number-one priority is to dismantle the disastrous deal with Iran ... This deal is catastrophic for America, for Israel and for the whole of the Middle East." In May 2017, he visited Riyadh and outlined to leaders of 55 Muslim countries his vision for US-Muslim relations. He urged them to "isolate Iran, deny it funding for terrorism, and pray for the day when the Iranian people have the just and righteous government they deserve." He said nothing about Saudi or Qatari support for terrorism. Instead, he signed a US-Saudi arms deal worth at least US$110 billion and called Qatar, which hosts US Central Command, a crucial strategic partner. Journalist Patrick Cockburn commented that Washington and London "will look in any direction except Saudi Arabia when seeking the causes of terrorism."[43]

* * *

Trump also met in Riyadh with leaders of the Gulf Cooperation Council, comprising Bahrain, Kuwait, Oman, Qatar, Saudi Arabia and UAE. Two weeks later, on June 5, the group erupted in dissension. Saudi Arabia — joined by Egypt, UAE and Bahrain — abruptly cut diplomatic ties with Qatar; suspended air, sea and land transport links; and expelled it from their coalition fighting in Yemen. They accused Qatar of supporting terrorism, the Muslim Brotherhood, Hamas and Iran. Their actions smacked of hypocrisy, given long-term Saudi support for Wahhabism, an extreme form of Sunni

Islam. Trump appeared supportive of Saudi Arabia, tweeting "there can no longer be funding of Radical Ideology. Leaders pointed to Qatar — look!"

A few days later, the Pentagon and State Department conducted damage control, selling 36 F-15 combat aircraft to Qatar and conducting joint naval exercises. The US Central Command's operational headquarters and its largest Middle Eastern airbase, both in Qatar, were at risk. Nor were all Gulf States supportive of Saudi Arabia. Iraq, Kuwait and Oman distanced themselves. Turkey overtly supported Qatar, rushing troops to its recently opened base there. Facing the suspension of food and water imports from Saudi Arabia, Qatar turned to Iran and Turkey for alternative supplies.

What caused the rift? Qatar had long challenged the Saudi claim to Arab hegemony. It maintained peaceful relations with Iran, despite supporting opposite factions in Syria. It shared with Iran the world's largest gas reservoir, offshore in the Persian Gulf. Without US protection, Qatar would be vulnerable to Saudi invasion. The prize would be the world's third largest gas reserves, a bonanza for the much depleted Saudi treasury. There were parallels with Iraq's invasion of Kuwait in 1990, when Iraq badly needed funds after its war against Iran and misguidedly believed the US had no objection.

On June 23, Saudi Arabia and its allies presented a list of demands, notably that Qatar scale down ties with Iran, close the Turkish military base, shut down the Al Jazeera news network and sever links with the Muslim Brotherhood, Hezbollah, al-Qaeda and Islamic State.[44] Qatar was given ten days to comply.[45] Qatar rejected the ultimatum, which would basically make it a vassal state. The boycott continued as of June 2018, and the Gulf Cooperation Council was riven. But the fear of invasion passed, and Qatar's LNG tankers traversed the Persian Gulf and Suez Canal unimpeded.

As of 2018, Qatar intended to remain the world's largest LNG exporter. It announced plans in July 2017 to raise LNG output by 30 per cent in the next few years, competing head-on with fast-expanding exports from Australia and the US. It ended a 12-year moratorium on developing the North Dome gas fields and initiated technical discussions with Iran on managing the shared reservoir.[46] Could it lead someday to a joint pipeline project to Europe via Iraq and Syria? Some analysts envisioned the possibility.[47] (The two proposed pipelines — from Iran and Qatar — are outlined in Chapter 3.)

The long-planned Iran-Pakistan Pipeline was linked symbolically in March 2013. With ongoing US opposition and sanctions threats, Pakistan's section still remained uncompleted as of 2018.

* * *

What about Iran's gas reserves? They are the world's second largest, scarcely tapped. In July 2017, the National Iranian Oil Company signed a contract with France's Total and the China National Petroleum Corporation to develop the second phase of South Pars. The gas would supply the Iranian domestic market. This was the first major Western energy investment in Iran since the lifting of sanctions in 2016. France's Total had worked on the project's first phase until sanctions forced it to stop work in 2009. The National Iranian Petrochemical Company also signed a preliminary agreement with Total to build three petrochemical plants in Iran.

The French led the European countries in trade and investment with Iran. Following Total's gas and petrochemical deals in July 2017, the French firm Renault signed a US$780 million deal in August to raise its production in Iran by about 150,000 cars a year. Total happens to be a major player in Qatar as well. In July 2017, Qatar Petroleum and Total implemented a 25-year 70:30 joint venture to develop the Al Shaheen oilfield, which produced about 200,000 b/d and lies above the North Dome gas field. Total is the field operator, taking over from the Danish company Maersk.

Europeans have expressed interest in importing Iranian gas, but Iranians doubt this is viable at low gas prices, such as those in early 2018. In July 2017, the deputy petroleum minister said, "export of gas to Europe is not among Iran's top priorities. The neighbouring countries and India are Iran's main options."[48] The war in Syria — plus US sanctions on Iran reimposed in 2018 — blocked the building of an Iranian pipeline to Europe. In contrast, the fast-expanding Chinese market for imported gas opened new opportunities unaffected by US sanctions.

* * *

Among options for exporting gas to Asia is a long-planned project to bring gas by pipeline to Pakistan. India was originally part of the project but withdrew from negotiations in 2009 after signing a nuclear deal with the United States. The pipeline would deliver gas from Iran's massive South Pars gas field in the Persian Gulf to the city of Nawabshah in Pakistan, where it would tie into the existing transmission system.

The Iranian section is virtually complete. The Pakistani section languished because of US opposition and frequent threats of sanctions.[49] For instance, in 2010, the US Special Envoy for Pakistan and Afghanistan, Richard Holbrooke, warned Pakistan against the pipeline deal because the US was preparing sanctions that could affect the project.[50] Despite numerous warnings and delays, the presidents of Pakistan and Iran met in March 2013 to inaugurate construction of the Pakistani section. Three months later, Pakistan's newly elected prime minister, Nawaz Sharif, confirmed his government's commitment to the project. Notwithstanding, Pakistan failed to go ahead. In October 2013, US Under Secretary of State for Political Affairs Wendy Sherman briefed the Senate Foreign Relations Committee that the pipeline was "not going anywhere anytime soon," and the Pakistanis "certainly understand where we are and what our sanctions require, should it proceed."[51]

With sanctions on Iran lifted, Pakistan at last appeared to be going ahead. In April 2015, China's President Xi made a red-carpet visit to Islamabad and met Prime Minister Sharif. The two leaders agreed on an economic corridor

Map 11. Iran-Pakistan Gas Pipeline Project

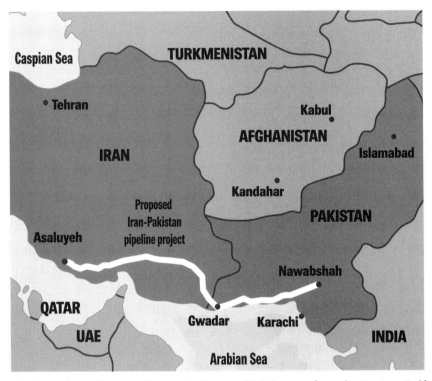

The long-planned Iran-Pakistan pipeline would bring gas from the Persian Gulf to central Pakistan. The Iranian section is virtually complete. The Pakistani section remained still unfinished in 2018 because of US opposition and threat of sanctions.

linking their countries. Investment agreements worth about US$45 billion will link China's western province of Xinjiang to Pakistan's Gwadar port on the Arabian Sea. Gwadar is strategic to China's One Belt One Road initiative. The economic corridor included the gas pipeline from Iran. Under an agreement initialled in May 2016, the China National Petroleum Corporation would finance and build the section in Pakistan from Gwadar to Nawabshah. Pakistan would finance and build the 80-km link from the Iranian border to Gwadar. There was even talk of a possible pipeline extension all the way to China.[52] Notwithstanding, the Pakistani government continued to drag its feet, expressing concern over possible US sanctions.

With the lack of progress on building the pipeline from Iran or its rival project from Turkmenistan through Afghanistan (discussed in Chapter 7), Pakistan faced an acute energy shortage and, in February 2016, signed a 15-year LNG import deal with Qatar Petroleum. Pakistan opened its first LNG import terminal in 2016, its second in mid-2017 and planned to open its third in 2018, all at Port Qasim, Karachi. It was also planning, with Russian support, a 1,200-km North-South gas pipeline from the port of Karachi to the eastern city of Lahore. The pipeline would transport natural gas (after regasification) from the Karachi LNG terminal, and a Russian company would build, own and operate the project.[53] At an Energy Cabinet Committee presided by Prime Minister Nawaz Sharif in June 2017, the Ministry of Petroleum and Natural Resources was directed to drop the Gwadar-Nawabshah pipeline project and start work on the third LNG terminal at Karachi.[54] The Iran-Pakistan pipeline was placed in limbo.

In 2018, Pakistan's relations with the United States took a turn for the worse. In January, President Trump suspended military aid and accused Pakistan of deceit and giving safe haven to Afghan terrorists.[55] US Ambassador to the United Nations Nikki Haley accused Pakistan of playing "a double game for years." Pakistan took measures to immunize itself. Its central bank announced steps to promote the use of Chinese yuan in trade and investment with China.[56] Pakistan became the fourth country to announce such plans, after Russia, Iran and Venezuela. As well, China announced plans to build a naval base in Pakistan at the port of Jiwani, near the Chinese-built commercial port of Gwadar and the Iranian border. Jiwani was to be China's second naval base overseas, following the one at Djibouti opened in 2016.[57]

* * *

President Trump continued Washington's vendetta against Iran. In August 2017, he signed a congressional bill codifying sanctions against Iran, North Korea and Russia. The new law — *Countering America's Adversaries Through Sanctions Act* — included sanctions on Iran's missile program. In January 2018, Trump threatened to withdraw from the nuclear deal unless

European countries joined in altering its terms. He had earlier called it "catastrophic for America, for Israel, and for the whole Middle East."[58]

In May 2018, Trump announced the US withdrawal from the nuclear deal. Israel and Saudi Arabia welcomed the withdrawal. Europe was shocked upon learning details of the sanctions to be reimposed. US licenses for Iran's airplane orders from Airbus (Boeing, too) were revoked. European companies and banks would face punitive fines if they continued business with Iran. Britain, France and Germany (the three European signatories to the nuclear deal) strongly deprecated the US action. Germany's Chancellor Merkel said Europe had to take its destiny into its own hands. Countries prepared a blocking mechanism to protect firms against extraterritorial US sanctions. Even so, France's Total, the largest foreign investor in Iran's oil sector, planned to halt work on the South Pars gas field without a specific waiver from Washington.

As a regional power in the Middle East with immense oil and gas resources, Iran is a proudly independent nation. After more than a century of sporadic Western interference and years of accusations, Iranians are wary of Western intentions. As of 2018, China and Russia remain steadfast in support of Iran while European countries are increasingly pursuing their own interests, despite American pressure, and although Canada has intentions to resume relations with Iran no steps have been taken to do so. Within this climate, Iran is moving closer to its supporters China and Russia.

CHAPTER 5
LIBYA — NATO CREATES A FAILED STATE

"I object to violence because when it appears to do good, the good is only temporary; the evil it does is permanent."

—Mahatma Gandhi

Muammar Gaddafi was a revolutionary hero when he came to power in a bloodless coup in 1969 at the age of 28. For more than four decades, he held Libya together. Early in 2011, a rebellion grew in the eastern part of the country. Protesters used violence and took over the oil capital, Benghazi. Western leaders accused Gaddafi of using excessive force and demonized him as a dangerous autocrat. NATO prepared to take action.

In the lead-up to NATO's air strikes on Libya in 2011, the focus was on protecting the people of Libya who had risen against Gaddafi. Western leaders argued that the principles of Responsibility to Protect (R2P) must be applied. R2P is a global commitment endorsed by UN members as a measure to protect people from genocide and war crimes. When a government fails to protect its own citizens, the international community has a responsibility to protect, using diplomatic, humanitarian and other means. In Libya, R2P became a precursor to outright war, even though it was always called a mission.

LIBYA'S IMPORTANCE
Libya is a big country with a small population — highly tribal with local loyalties. It is arguably an artificial country, soldered together by Italian

colonial conquest. Libya's capital is Tripoli, in the west; its oil capital is Benghazi, in the east.

Libya has large oil reserves, the world's ninth largest. Their production cost is low. The crude oil is top quality, light in gravity and low in sulphur content. Few oil-producing countries can match this quality. The oil is easy to refine in simple distillation refineries. Unlike heavier crude oils, it does not require costly secondary equipment to crack the fuel oil content into lighter, more valuable hydrocarbons before distillation. Libyan oil's low sulphur content means the refined gasoline and diesel can meet European regulations without being run through expensive desulphurization units. Libyan oil is prized and commands top dollar.

Map 12. Libya: Locations of Petroleum Facilities

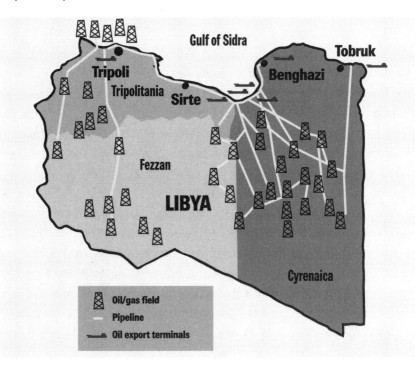

Libya has the world's ninth largest oil reserves. The crude oil is top quality, light in gravity and low in sulphur content.

Libya is close to southern Europe, notably Italy. For oil, the tanker voyage to refineries across the Mediterranean Sea is much shorter and cheaper than routes from the Middle East through the Suez Canal or around the Cape of Good Hope. Since 2004, Libya has also exported natural gas by a 516-km undersea pipeline to Sicily, where the gas enters the Italian gas system.

Gaddafi used the oil wealth to Libyan advantage. Among African countries, Libya was a jewel. Gaddafi made education and health care both free. Until the air strikes of 2011 and his death in October that same year, Libya had a 90 per cent literacy rate, the lowest infant mortality and the highest life expectancy of any country on the African continent.

NATO'S INTERVENTION, WESTERN INTERESTS AND PETROLEUM

Colonel Gaddafi had been both a friend and a foe of Western countries. Through the years, Western leaders made many accusations against him. Disputes swelled and receded. Clearly Gaddafi refused to be a puppet of the West. He had a vision for the African continent. He proposed a single African military force, a single currency and a single African passport. When chairman of the African Union, he pushed for a federation of some or all of the 54 African nations — a United States of Africa. He sought to expedite the creation of the African Union's three proposed financial institutions — the African Monetary Fund, African Investment Bank and African Central Bank — and envisaged them as purely African with no Western participation.

In Gaddafi's vision, the African Central Bank would be the sole issuer of a single gold-backed African currency, gold dinars, as an alternative to the main trading currencies in Africa — the US dollar, British pound and CFA franc. He called on African nations to export oil for gold dinars instead of US dollars. The response in Washington, London and Paris was predictable. French President Nicolas Sarkozy called Libya a threat to the financial security of the world.[1] A declassified email sent on April 2, 2011, to Secretary of State Hillary Clinton reveals the Libyan government held gold and silver valued at more than US$7 billion. The bullion was to be used to establish an alternative currency for African Francophone countries. It went missing during the invasion, and, as of 2018, no one knows what happened to it.

Gaddafi was an autocrat, and he had the finances and the vision to create a new African centre of power. He irritated the United States; he annoyed European countries that had ruled North Africa in the colonial era and now sought to maintain close ties with their former colonies.

The precipitating events of the 2011 Libyan conflict happened in quick succession. The uprising began in Benghazi on February 15, when police arrested lawyer Fethi Tarbel. He represented families of 1,200 or more prisoners allegedly massacred in 1996 at Abu Salim prison in Tripoli. That evening, several hundred people gathered in front of the police headquarters to protest his arrest. The protests escalated on February 17, designated a Day of Rage. Police tried to disperse crowds with water cannons, tear gas, rubber bullets and batons. Protesters broke into local barracks to seize weaponry. Soldiers fired on them. The situation spiralled out of control. By February 20, the city was in rebel hands.

The next day, according to the BBC, Libyan warplanes fired on protesters in the city.[2] The day after, according to Al Jazeera, Libyan fighter jets bombed portions of the city, focusing on ammunition depots and control centres around the capital.[3] Were these reports true? Western countries and NATO produced no supporting evidence. The Russian military, monitoring via satellite, said the air attacks never occurred.[4] Be that as it may, the rebellion was ignited.

Oil companies, concerned for employees' safety, began to shut down production, partly or completely.[5] The Chinese government evacuated 36,000 of its citizens within 48 hours — an extraordinary feat.[6] The Chinese had been highly involved in Libya, with 75 firms working on telecommunications, railways and petroleum exploration; and China had been Libya's third largest purchaser of crude oil.

The following week, February 26, the UN Security Council placed an arms embargo on Libya and froze the assets of Gaddafi's family and certain government officials.[7] This was the first time a Security Council resolution cited the Responsibility to Protect (R2P). R2P had been approved by the UN General Assembly in 2005 to prevent genocide, war crimes, ethnic cleansing and crimes against humanity.

The next day, February 27, rebel forces formed a National Transitional Council to act as the "political face of the revolution."[8] A day later, US Secretary of State Hillary Clinton said, "It is time for Gaddafi to go, now, without further violence or delay." The EU's foreign policy chief, Catherine Ashton, announced sanctions on Libya and declared: "What is going on — the massive violence against peaceful demonstrators — shocks our conscience."[9] UK Prime Minister David Cameron called for a no-fly zone, saying, "For the future of Libya and its people, Colonel Gaddafi's regime must end and he must leave."[10] President Sarkozy said the same in Paris.

Special Forces covertly entered Libya to protect the rebels. Canadian special forces were already on the ground by February 28, according to CTV News.[11] UK special forces were in Libya "since before the launch of air strikes to enforce the no-fly zone," per the *Daily Mail*;[12] French and Qatari special forces were there, too, according to *The Guardian*.[13] CIA operatives had been working in Libya "for several weeks," per the *New York Times* (March 30).[14]

On March 17, the UN Security Council authorized "all necessary measures" and a no-fly zone to "protect civilians." It froze the foreign assets of the National Oil Corporation and the Central Bank of Libya, both described as a potential source of funding for Gaddafi (Resolution 1973).[15] Brazil, China, Germany, India and Russia abstained from voting. The West used the UN Resolution as an authorization to bomb. In subsequent years, China and Russia became wary of how Western countries reinterpret UN Resolutions.

On March 19, Britain, France and the US began a "limited military action in Libya in support of an international effort to protect Libyan civilians." So said President Obama. He asserted: "This is not an outcome that the United States or any of our partners sought. Even yesterday, the international community offered Muammar Gaddafi the opportunity to pursue an immediate ceasefire ... He has ignored that opportunity."[16] Prime Minister David Cameron said: "Gaddafi has broken his word, broken the ceasefire and continues to slaughter his own civilians ... We have to make it stop."[17]

The rebel National Transitional Council wasted no time. That very day, it announced the creation of a new central bank, temporarily based in Benghazi. It would replace the existing Central Bank of Libya based in Tripoli, whose foreign assets the UN Security Council had just frozen. The announcement was puzzling. How was a new central bank promulgated so speedily? Who were the brains behind the scenes?[18]

The next day, March 20, Tomahawk cruise missiles launched from a British submarine hit a building in Gaddafi's compound, 50 metres from his residence.[19] They missed Gaddafi. A week later, March 28, President Obama told the US nation, "The task that I assigned our forces [is] to protect the Libyan people from immediate danger and to establish a no-fly zone. ... Broadening our military mission to include regime change would be a mistake."[20] Of course, without specific authorization, forcible regime change is illegal under the UN Charter.

The same day, the *Financial Times of London* reported, "Western oil companies operating in Libya have privately warned that their operations in the country may be nationalised if Colonel Muammar Gaddafi's regime prevails ... especially if their home countries are taking part in air-strikes."[21] Clearly, oil companies were alarmed and saw no future for operating in Libya if Gaddafi stayed in power.

The Western coalition was initially led by France, Britain and the United States. Other participants included Belgium, Canada, Denmark, Italy, Norway, Qatar and Spain. NATO took control of all operations on March 23. For its part, Canada assigned a naval frigate, six CF-18 fighter jets, four other aircraft and 200 personnel, plus special forces whose tasks went unreported.

NATO provided close-air support for rebel forces by attacking government troops retreating across Libya.[22] Under the command of Canadian Lieutenant General Charles Bouchard, NATO flew 9,700 strike sorties over seven months. Libya's infrastructure was devastated. The elegant port city of Sirte — Gaddafi's home town — was destroyed. The war was bloodless for the West, but many thousands of Libyans perished, and the country was fragmented. Many Libyans became refugees, fleeing to Europe. Hundreds of African migrant workers were imprisoned by rebels, accused of being mercenaries for Gaddafi.[23]

By September, rebel ground forces, with Western planes and special forces, prevailed. On September 15, Cameron and Sarkozy made a joint victory visit to Benghazi. Cameron declared: "The message to Gaddafi ... is: it is over. Give up."[24] Sarkozy promised: "France, Great Britain, Europe, will always stand by the side of the Libyan people."[25] The next day, the UN General Assembly, after much argument, recognized the National

Transitional Council as Libya's legal representative in lieu of the Gaddafi government.[26]

On October 20, NATO planes fired on Gaddafi's convoy as it fled his home city of Sirte. Rebel forces captured, sodomized and killed Gaddafi. US Secretary of State Hillary Clinton expressed jubilation on CBS television: "We came, we saw, he died."[27] Was the war really about saving civilians or was it about regime change?

The war ended officially on October 23, 2011. President Obama congratulated the people of Libya: "After four decades of brutal dictatorship and eight months of deadly conflict, the Libyan people can now celebrate their freedom and the beginning of a new era of promise."[28] Prime Minister Stephen Harper affirmed: "Canada has played a critical role both politically and militarily to protect innocent civilians against a cruel and oppressive regime." The government later held a ceremony on Parliament Hill for Canadian military who had served in Libya, with a flyby of ten airplanes. NATO's Secretary General Anders Fogh Rasmussen declared: "We have fully complied with the historic mandate of the United Nations to protect the people of Libya, to enforce the no-fly zone and the arms embargo."[29] UK Defence Secretary Philip Hammond claimed the Libyan people had "liberated their country from a ruthless tyrant," and NATO had "averted a humanitarian disaster."[30]

In 2016, the US State Department released a tranche of Hillary Clinton emails under the *Freedom of Information Act*. The emails provided new information regarding Western interests and the intervention in Libya. An email from Sidney Blumenthal, adviser to Secretary Clinton, confirmed that Western special forces were on the ground in Libya before the earliest protests. During the week NATO operations began, special forces transferred weapons and supplies to rebels, thereby assisting what was publicly assumed in the West to be a popular uprising.[31]

Further State Department emails revealed that all was not as it seemed. French President Nicholas Sarkozy was facing a difficult election and wanted to assert power to enhance his domestic reputation. He regarded Gaddafi's huge gold and silver reserves and plans for an African currency as a threat to the CFA French franc widely used in Francophone African countries.[32]

The State Department emails also proved that rumours alleging Gaddafi staged bodies at NATO bombing sites and dispensed Viagra to troops were fabricated, yet no efforts were made to prevent top-level officials from repeating them as if they were fact. Western leaders were well aware of Libya's high-quality oil. Behind the scenes, NATO governments were scheming to get rid of Gaddafi and share the spoils.

The Manchester bombing atrocity in May 2017 shed embarrassing light on the UK government's covert policy of early 2011. Some Libyan exiles and British-Libyan citizens had been subject to counter-terrorism control orders (i.e., house arrest).[33] They belonged to the extremist Libyan Islamic Fighting Group, proscribed in Britain as a terrorist organization opposing Gaddafi and seeking a hardline Islamic state in Libya.[34] In early 2011, when Prime Minister Theresa May was Home Secretary, the control orders were suddenly lifted, MI5 returned their passports and they were encouraged to travel and fight with anti-government forces, first in Libya and then in Syria.[35] The Manchester suicide bomber Salman Abedi was a member. He visited Libya several times after the overthrow of Gaddafi, just weeks before conducting the Manchester bombing.

These new revelations were widely reported just a few days before the 2017 general election in Britain. The Manchester bombing led people in Britain to realize the connection between Libya in 2011 and homegrown violence. The link was undeniable. The British government used Salafi jihadis from the UK to eliminate Gaddafi. Journalist Patrick Cockburn commented "the Manchester bombing is part of the legacy of failed British military interventions abroad."[36] Labour leader Jeremy Corbyn emphasized the same theme in his election campaign. It evidently struck a chord with the electorate. Corbyn nearly toppled Theresa May's Conservative government.

THE BACKSTORY — INTERVENTIONS AND OIL

Libya's history is a long and convoluted story of Western intervention, including manoeuvring for oil. In 1911, Italy seized the coastal regions — Cyrenaica and Tripolitania — from the Ottoman Empire, initiating almost two decades of fighting. The two provinces united in 1929 and became Italian Libya in 1934.

British and Italian/German armies fought over Libya during World War II.

They knew nothing of the oil beneath the desert. They perceived Libya as the gateway to Egypt, the Suez Canal, the Middle East oilfields. Finally, the British triumphed in 1943 and administered Tripolitania and Cyrenaica until 1951, while the French controlled Libya's other province, Fezzan, in the south. In 1951, Libya became a federal monarchy headed by King Idris. It was a puppet regime, with British and American military bases. The Wheelus Air Base was an important location for US Strategic Air Command.

The new Libyan government quickly enacted a legal framework for oil exploration (Mineral Law 1953 and Petroleum Law 1955). The fiscal terms were far more generous to companies than arrangements in the Middle East. That made for a Klondike-like stampede to Libya, with the government awarding concessions to a multitude of companies, mostly American. Companies were not permitted to sit on the land indefinitely — as they had in Iraq and Iran — but were required to relinquish one-quarter of their acreage after five years and more later. The terms of the concessions encouraged newcomers to explore where the original companies had failed.

In 1959, Esso made major oil discoveries, and soon thereafter so did Mobil and the Oasis consortium (comprising US independents Amerada Hess, Conoco and Marathon). Other companies, too, found oil during the 1960s, including BP (partnering with Texan billionaire Bunker Hunt), Occidental Petroleum (created by New York entrepreneur Armand Hammer) and AGIP (a subsidiary of Italy's ENI). Companies began exporting in the early 1960s.

In 1969, an army coup, led by Muammar Gaddafi, deposed the monarchy. The new government nationalized the banks, evicted the US military (the British having already left) and successfully negotiated higher oil export prices and oil tax revenues. Oil production rose rapidly and peaked in 1970 at an incredible 3.4 million b/d, most of it exported. The oil quickly entered the European market, underpricing Middle East oil supplied by the Seven Sisters — the seven Western companies dominating world oil from the mid-1940s to the 1970s.

In 1970, the new Gaddafi government expropriated BP's Libyan assets. In 1973, it created a national oil company and acquired a controlling interest in all other oil companies. Libya played an active role in the 1973 Arab oil embargo that was imposed on the US, the Netherlands, Portugal and

South Africa for supporting Israel in the Arab-Israeli War that year. Libyan oil production averaged about 2 million b/d during the 1970s.

Since the beginning, Italy has been Libya's largest oil customer, though the United States was a major customer prior to the Arab oil embargo. After that, US-Libyan relations plummeted. In 1973, President Gaddafi claimed much of the Gulf of Sidra (Gulf of Sirte) as territorial waters by drawing a straight east-west line across the north of the Gulf. He named it the Line of Death and threatened a military response if it were crossed without permission. The US insisted the waters were international up to 12 nautical miles from the shoreline.

During the 1980s, a series of tit-for-tat incidents dominated Libya's exchanges with the United States. In 1981, the US Navy asserted freedom of navigation and sailed into the Gulf of Sidra, crossing Gaddafi's Line of Death. The provocation led to active battle, with US naval aircraft shooting down two Libyan fighter jets. Washington turned up the diplomatic heat, invalidating US passports for travel to Libya, advising US citizens in Libya to leave, banning US imports of Libyan oil, restricting US exports and financing to Libya and imposing other economic sanctions. In March 1986, a US armada comprising three aircraft carrier task force groups with 225 aircraft and 30 warships entered the Gulf of Sidra, sinking a Libyan corvette — all onboard lost.

Two weeks later, in April 1986, a bomb exploded in a Berlin discotheque, killing two US soldiers and injuring 120 other people, including 79 US soldiers. Washington blamed the Libyan government and retaliated by bombing targets in Libya, including Gaddafi's compound near Tripoli. Gaddafi was tipped off by Italian Prime Minister Craxi and escaped with family, but an adopted daughter was killed and several family members injured. The raid was widely regarded as an attempt to assassinate Gaddafi. President Reagan dubbed him "the mad dog of the Middle East," adding "I find he's not only a barbarian but he's flaky."[37] In June 1986, Reagan ordered all American oil companies to leave Libya. European countries declined to follow suit.[38]

Then came the mid-air explosions onboard Pan American 103 in 1988 over Lockerbie, Scotland, and the French airliner UTA 772 in 1989 over the Sahara. Western leaders blamed Libyan intelligence agents for placing bombs on these flights. Though evidence was circumstantial, Gaddafi became an international pariah. In January 1989, the US retaliated with another show of naval force in the Gulf of Sidra, again shooting down two Libyan planes.

Later in 1989, a French court convicted six Libyan intelligence officials *in absentia* for the bombing of flight UTA 772. The UN Security Council followed up with three resolutions. The first required Libya to surrender the suspects for trial, to cooperate with investigations and to compensate victims' families. The second resolution imposed sanctions to induce compliance. The third resolution placed an embargo on specific oil equipment.

As regards Pan Am 103, Scottish authorities issued arrest warrants for two Libyan intelligence agents in 1991. Eight years passed before Libya surrendered them in 1999 to a Scottish court specially held in the Netherlands. In 2001, the court acquitted one agent and convicted the other, Abdelbaset al-Megrahi, of murder, sentencing him to life imprisonment. The West was satisfied. In 2003 the UN lifted sanctions on Libya. A few years later, following a protracted appeal, al-Megrahi fell ill, was allowed to return to Libya and died in 2012. Finding some measure of justice was a strange and murky business.

In March 2003, just before the invasion of Iraq, Libyan intelligence officials approached UK and US intelligence and offered to reveal the scope of Libya's programs of weapons of mass destruction (WMD). The ensuing covert negotiations resulted in Gaddafi's renouncing programs to develop WMD and welcoming international inspection to verify their termination.[39] Whether Libya, any more than Iraq, really had WMD capabilities is a moot point. Nonetheless, Gaddafi's renunciation had its desired effect. The United States ended economic sanctions, resumed diplomatic relations and rescinded Libya's designation as a state sponsor of terrorism. To clinch matters, in 2008 Libya paid US\$1.5 billion into a US compensation fund for relatives of American victims of the Lockerbie bombing, Berlin discotheque bombing and UTA Flight 772 bombing, as well as Libyan victims of the 1986 US bombing of Tripoli and Benghazi.

What about the oil? Production recovered from about 1.4 million b/d in the 1990s to about 1.8 million b/d in the five years from 2005 to 2010. In 2007, BP returned to Libya after a three-decade absence. In a £450 million deal, it was granted the right to explore for gas in the offshore Gulf of Sidra basin and the onshore Ghadames basin.[40] The deal coincided with a meeting in the Libyan desert between President Gaddafi and Prime Minister Tony Blair, attended by BP's chairman Peter Sutherland.[41] Blair called the meeting positive and constructive, saying, "the relationship between Britain and Libya has been completely transformed in these last few years."[42]

ONGOING CONFLICT AND PETROLEUM

Although the NATO air strikes on Libya ended in October 2011, rival militias continued fighting for control of Libya — and its petroleum. After national elections held in June 2014, two rival governments emerged, each vying for political power and for control of Libya's petroleum facilities.[43] The General National Congress was based in the capital Tripoli, and the House of Representatives (Council of Deputies) was based in the eastern city of Tobruk. The General National Congress was backed by Libya Dawn and other militias, and the House of Representatives by the Libyan Army under General Haftar. Reflecting the fight for control of the oil revenues, each government claimed authority over the National Oil Corporation and Central Bank of Libya, which were de facto split in two.[44] The National Oil Corporation was reunified in 2016 but the Central Bank remained divided as of April 2018.

Attempting to restore political unity, the UN brokered an agreement in December 2015 between the two governments, under which an interim Government of National Accord (GNA) would be formed as the sole legitimate government, the House of Representatives would continue as the legislative assembly and elections would be held within two years. The interim GNA arrived in Tripoli in March 2016, but governance remained unstable, with the House of Representatives voting in August 2016 not to approve the GNA.[45]

Amid the political and military chaos, Islamic State set up a Libyan branch in November 2014. In addition to local recruits, it attracted Libyan jihadists returning from Syria. In the next few months, it captured the city of Sirte and neighbouring towns along the coast, and attacked various oilfields and export terminals.[46] The success of Islamic State drew Western attention. In

May 2016, US aircraft bombed targets in Libya. In June, armed forces allied to the new Government of National Accord and militia allied to the House of Representatives advanced independently from west and east toward Sirte, each vying to liberate the city from Islamic State.[47] Special forces from the US,[48] UK,[49] France[50] and Italy[51] provided support. After months of fighting, the GNA proclaimed in December it had recaptured the city. ISIS still remained in control of other coastal communities.

The strife since 2011 took its toll on the Libyan oil scene. Several companies, such as BP and Shell, reduced or stopped exploration and production. Some others, such as Italy's ENI, continued despite the risk. Oil production fluctuated like a yo-yo. Having averaged 1.65 million b/d in 2010, it collapsed to just 480,000 b/d in 2011. It rebounded in 2012 to 1.5 million b/d. It sank again in 2013, beset by militia harassment, to 1.0 million b/d. Production plummeted again in the next three years, averaging 500,000 b/d or less.[52] It recovered in 2017, averaging 865,000 b/d. Five of Libya's six export terminals are in the east, frequently shut by militias seeking higher oil revenue for the east.[53]

Libyan sales of natural gas also suffered. The GreenStream underwater pipeline from Libya to Sicily operated at close to capacity prior to the 2011 war. Since then, it has operated at less than two-thirds of capacity. The pipeline is owned by Agip Gas BV, a joint venture of Italy's ENI and the National Oil Corporation of Libya.[54] The company operates in a high-risk environment. In 2015, militants kidnapped four employees of the Italian contractor Bonatti, subsequently killing two and releasing the others.

Long-term recovery of petroleum exploration and production will require an end to the stand-off between rival governments, a central bank capable of handling oil revenues and defeat of Islamic State in Libya.[55]

In a 2016 BBC interview, US President Obama was asked what was the greatest mistake of his presidency. His response: failing to plan for a post-Gaddafi Libya.[56] He also blamed France and the UK for the mess. A few months later, the Foreign Affairs Committee of the UK Parliament concurred. They issued a damning report based on interviews with people who were senior ministers at the time of the war. The report slammed Prime Minister David Cameron for failing to do an intelligence assessment, failing to consider opportunities for negotiation before moving

Libya: refugees fled to Europe after 2011 NATO intervention.

toward military action and failing to secure the weapons of the Gaddafi regime.[57]

The 2011 Libyan war can be seen as a repeat performance of earlier Western interventions. Through NATO, powerful Western nations usurped the concept of R2P for their own purposes. While they claimed humanitarian motives, underlying reasons included regime change, petrodollar concerns, showing what NATO was capable of and a quest for control of vast petroleum opportunities in Libya. As in Iraq, they failed to plan for a Libya without an autocratic leader.

Whatever the motivations, the intervention failed. Many thousands died or were injured; many others fled. Homes and infrastructure were destroyed. Libya's strongman leader was brutally assassinated. The country descended into anarchy.

Years later, Libya remained fragmented, bankrupt, chaotic. Governance was unclear. Health care was in crisis. Libya's proud standards of living were in tatters. Oil facilities were damaged or destroyed, and oil and gas flows much reduced. Libyans and other nationals who had worked in Libya fled as refugees to Europe, many drowning en route. Weapons and militants flowed from Libya to Syria and back again. Western special forces were still there, supporting militias against Islamic State. Libya is a failed state. Even with the best of intentions, what was torn asunder is very hard to put back together. The NATO intervention left a sordid legacy. Conflict was still ongoing in 2018.

CHAPTER 6
MARITIME TRADE ROUTES AND CONFLICT

"We will bankrupt ourselves in the vain search for absolute security."

—Dwight D. Eisenhower, US President, 1953–1961

On the morning of October 12, 2000, the US Navy guided-missile destroyer USS *Cole* moored in the Yemeni port of Aden to refuel. It was a routine stop en route to a carrier battle group in the Persian Gulf. A small fibreglass boat with two men on board approached the destroyer. Alongside, it exploded, creating a huge gash in the ship's port side. Seventeen American sailors were killed, and 39 were injured. The terrorist organization al-Qaeda claimed responsibility for the attack, in which two suicide bombers also died. After the attack, the US and NATO emphasized the importance of boosting security along sea lanes and in adjacent countries.

MARITIME TRADE ROUTES – IMPORTANCE

The security of port infrastructure and tanker routes from the Middle East is crucial to Western and Asian countries alike. Maritime powers such as the United States have long sought to secure the safe passage of shipping along the world's trade routes. NATO cites freedom of navigation and the flow of energy as critical to the security of NATO members.[1] In its heyday, the British Empire held a series of naval bases along the trading routes to India, Australia and China. Aden was one of them.

Almost 30 per cent of the world's shipping is dedicated to moving petroleum.[2] Of the world's oil production, 64 per cent moves to market by sea in immense tanker fleets.[3] Of the world's gas production, ten per cent moves by sea as LNG.[4] Any interruption in this massive flow of seaborne petroleum could have devastating effects on modern economies.

Narrow marine waterways are of particular concern to governments and companies. A strait, where ships pass closely between two shorelines, could be blocked by pirates or enemy ships and become a dangerous choke-point. In open water, ships have scope to manoeuvre away from danger; in chokepoints, vessels are particularly vulnerable. The US Energy Information Administration describes world oil chokepoints as "a critical part of global energy security."[5] Gibraltar, which the British captured in 1704 during the War of the Spanish Succession, is a chokepoint at the western end of the Mediterranean and remains under British sovereignty.

Map 13. World Oil Chokepoints

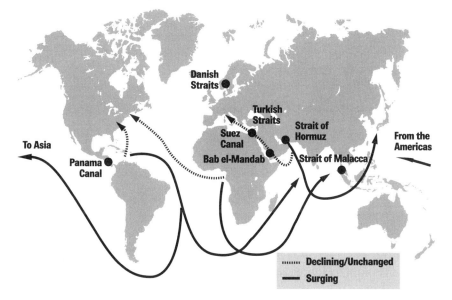

Narrow seaways can be dangerous chokepoints for shipping. Navies patrol Straits of Hormuz, Mandab, Malacca, South China Sea and beyond.

After the attack on the USS *Cole*, the United States gave increased atten-tion to guarding sea lanes and adjacent countries in the Middle East.

To that end, it organized in 2002 a naval coalition of 31 nations, the Combined Maritime Forces, as part of its War on Terror. Their formation was five months after the Twin Towers attack on September 11, 2001, and a year before the invasion of Iraq. Member countries comprise a dozen NATO countries (including Canada), several Arab Gulf States and Asia-Pacific countries.[6] Excluded are China, Iran and Russia. Canada assigned a Halifax-class frigate once every two years and a CP-140 Aurora Maritime Patrol Aircraft once per year.

HMCS Regina *patrolling off East Africa, 2014, as Canadian contribution to Combined Maritime Forces.*

The Combined Maritime Forces are located in Bahrain and under US command. The US Fifth Fleet, too, is based in Bahrain and patrols the Persian Gulf, Red Sea, Arabian Sea and Indian Ocean. As well, NATO operates Operation Ocean Shield, a counter-piracy mission in the Gulf of Aden and off the Horn of Africa. Maritime Forces enforce the Carter Doctrine (1980); an attempt by any outside force to gain control of the Persian Gulf region will be regarded as an assault on US vital interests and be repelled by any means necessary, including military force.

THE STRAIT OF HORMUZ

The Strait of Hormuz is the narrow waterway connecting the Persian Gulf and the Indian Ocean. It is 180 kilometres long. On its northern shore is Iran. On its southern shore lie Oman and UAE, with Qatar, Saudi Arabia and Iraq on the Gulf farther north. At the strait's narrowest point, the width of the shipping lane in either direction is only three kilometres. About 30 per cent (18.5 million b/d in 2016) of the world's seaborne oil goes through this strait every day, originating from the Gulf States, Iraq and Iran.[7] Its closure would be an economic calamity for both exporting and importing countries.

Map 14. Persian Gulf and Strait of Hormuz

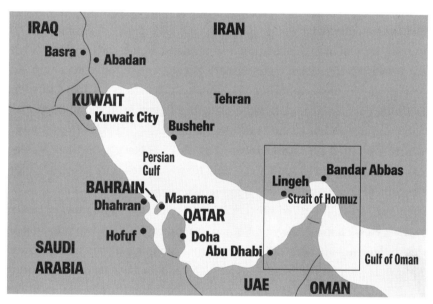

Thirty per cent of the world's seaborne oil passes from the Persian Gulf through the Strait of Hormuz to reach the Indian Ocean. The area bristles with warships.

Given the risk of closure of the Strait of Hormuz and attacks on oil tankers in the Persian Gulf, as happened in the 1980–1988 Iran-Iraq War, several pipelines have been built or planned from Arab Gulf State fields to ports on the Red Sea, Arabian Gulf and Mediterranean. These pipeline routes avoid the Strait of Hormuz.

As well, the Combined Maritime Forces have been patrolling the international waters of the Persian Gulf and the Strait of Hormuz since 2004. For its part, Iran's navy keeps close watch over its territorial waters. The Persian Gulf is almost 1,000 kilometres long and varies in width from a maximum of about 340 to a minimum of 55 kilometres. It is quite shallow, with the deeper water closer to the Iranian side. Suffice to say, the Persian Gulf is bristling with warships. It would be easy for a war to start accidentally.

During the Iran-Iraq War of the 1980s, the Persian Gulf *was* the scene of a tanker war. Commercial passage along the Gulf and through the Strait of Hormuz was a hazardous business. From the very beginning, Iraq attacked tankers carrying Iranian oil. Iran did not retaliate until 1984. Starting in 1987, the US Navy protected ships heading to and from Arab Gulf ports, but not Iranian ones.

A key Iranian naval installation is Farsi Island, in the middle of the northern Persian Gulf. It is a base for fast attack craft, which Iran's Revolutionary Guards use in unconventional warfare and the defence of Iran's offshore facilities, coastlines and islands. During the Tanker War, naval speedboats operating from Farsi Island laid mines and attacked tankers from Kuwait, which supported Iraq. In October 1987, the US Navy sank three Iranian patrol boats near Farsi Island, claiming they had fired on a US observation helicopter.

In April 1988, the US frigate *Samuel B. Roberts*, escorting a Kuwaiti tanker, was severely damaged by an Iranian sea mine. The US Navy retaliated, destroying two offshore drilling platforms, sinking an Iranian frigate and hitting another in the Strait of Hormuz. Accidents happened, too, during the Iran-Iraq War. In May 1987, an Iraqi jet aircraft fired missiles at the American frigate USS *Stark*, killing 37 crew members and wounding 21.

Around the Persian Gulf, the territorial waters of littoral countries stretch 12 nautical miles (22 km) offshore and overlap between Iran and Qatar in the Strait of Hormuz. Both countries allow freedom of passage to all shipping, including foreign naval vessels. In July 1988, the US Navy cruiser USS *Vincennes* entered Iranian waters in the strait in pursuit of Iranian speedboats, which had fired warning shots at one of its helicopters flying in Iranian airspace. Coincidentally, an airliner, Iran Air 655, was on its way from the Iranian airport of Bandar Abbas on a regular flight across the strait to Dubai. The ship fired two missiles at the airliner, having mistakenly identified it — according to the Pentagon — for a warplane. All 290 onboard perished. Eight years later, in 1996, the United States and Iran reached a settlement at the International Court of Justice, including an *ex gratia* payment of US$61.8 million to next-of-kin.

Tensions flared up again following the 2003 Anglo-American invasion of Iraq. The British occupied the south around Basra, including the Shatt al-Arab waterway between Iraq and Iran. In June 2004, eight British sailors and marines conducting a river patrol were seized by Revolutionary Guards in Iranian waters and detained three days. In March 2007, 15 sailors and marines from the British frigate HMS *Cornwall* searching a merchant vessel in disputed waters were surrounded by Revolutionary Guards and detained 13 days.

Farsi Island also hit the headlines in January 2016, when the Revolutionary Guards seized two US Navy riverine command boats in Iranian waters offshore the island. The US Navy claimed mechanical failure and navigational errors. The incident took place four days before the implementation date set for the nuclear deal. The timing was curious. The US and Iranian foreign ministers spoke by telephone, crew members were promptly released and the boats sped away with no apparent mechanical or navigational difficulties.

The US Fifth Fleet has been in the Persian Gulf since 1995. The Combined Maritime Forces have been there since 2002 as part of the US War on Terror. Who is the enemy? Al-Qaeda has no navy nor does Islamic State. Piracy suppression in the Gulf hardly requires a naval coalition of such dimension. Is the purpose to enforce the Carter Doctrine, keeping the Persian Gulf under US hegemony? Or is the purpose the continued containment of Iran? For sure, the naval coalition is less an impartial policeman than a demonstration of hegemonic power in the regional geopolitics. But at what cost and risk?

THE STRAIT OF BAB EL-MANDAB AND RELATED COASTLINES

Another key chokepoint is the Strait of Bab el-Mandab or Mandab Strait, a vital sea link between Europe and Asia. Its name is Arabic for "gate of tears." Just 20 kilometres wide, it connects the Indian Ocean to the Red Sea — thence to the Suez Canal. Eight per cent (4.8 million b/d) of the world's seaborne oil passes through the strait every day. In addition, a constant procession of container ships and warships use the strait. Their safety of passage is of paramount importance.

Map 15. Mandab Strait

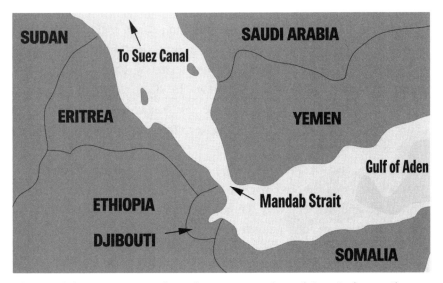

The Mandab Strait connects the Indian Ocean to the Red Sea. Seaborne oil passes both ways — to and from the Suez Canal.

Piracy in the region's waters has been a scourge for centuries. The British colony of Aden (Yemen) was established in 1839 as a naval base against piracy, and the British stayed 130 years, until 1967. Piracy resurrected in Somalia as a major problem after the 1989 collapse of Siad Barre's government led to anarchy. Pirates started attacking vessels in Somali waters and the Gulf of Aden, robbing cargo or hijacking ships and crew for ransom. As shipping companies took steps to protect and reroute their vessels and naval forces began patrolling the Gulf of Aden, pirates extended operations as much as 2,000 kilometres from the Somali coast.

Oil tankers have not been immune. In the years 2008–2010, three Very Large Crude Carriers (VLCCs) were hijacked in the Indian Ocean, taken to Somalia and released for ransom.[8] In 2011, the *Irene SL* was hijacked in the Arabian Sea and ransomed for a record US$13.5 million. The ransoms were large but even so represented a small fraction of the cargo value. The VLCCs have a cargo capacity exceeding 300,000 tons deadweight (DWT), or 2.2 million barrels. The cargo was worth more than US$150 million at then prevailing prices.

To counter the surge in piracy, naval vessels patrol the western Indian Ocean. They are the Combined Maritime Forces; NATO's Operation Ocean Shield; an EU naval force; and ships from China, India and Russia. In 2015, an average of 19 warships were on station and engaged in counter-piracy operations. The worst seemed to be over. Pirate attacks declined from over 170 in 2010 to just a handful in 2013, and the last major vessel hijacked by Somali pirates was in 2012.[9] The non-profit organization Oceans Beyond Piracy recorded in 2015 five dhow hijackings, a failed attack on a Thai fishing vessel, nine incidents suspected of being piracy-related and one armed robbery.[10]

The Western media has limelighted the Somali piracy issue, while shedding little light on parallel problems of the intrusion of foreign fishing vessels and the dumping of toxic waste.[11] With the anarchy that followed the 1991 breakdown of central government came the collapse of Somalia's fishery protection service. Foreign trawlers moved in from southern Europe, Arabia and East Asia, ruining the fishing for Somalis. Local Somali fishermen created a self-help protection force trying to expel or capture foreign fishing vessels in Somali waters.

A report published by the UN Food and Agriculture Organization in 2005 estimated 700 foreign vessels were engaged in unlicensed fishing in Somali waters, and there was "strong suspicion of illegal dumping of industrial and nuclear wastes along the Somali coast."[12] The Italian mafia and others dumped toxic and radioactive waste in international waters offshore Somalia. After the tsunami in 2004, drums washed ashore causing strange illnesses.[13] In 2005, the UN Environmental Program told Al Jazeera that toxic waste washed on to Somalia's coastline by a tsunami had spawned diseases bearing symptoms of radioactive exposure in villagers along the shore.[14] It appears Somali fishermen became pirates in desperation. Yet the focus was on protecting shipping, not addressing root causes.

Maritime security stretches along the coastlines of Djibouti, Eritrea and Somalia beside the Red Sea, the Mandab Strait, the Gulf of Aden and the

Indian Ocean. It extends along Yemen's coastline beside the Mandab Strait and Gulf of Aden. Each country has a unique situation but all share a strategic location and military or petroleum significance.

Djibouti has become an important transshipment hub for regional container freight. A new Chinese-built railway links Djibouti to Addis Ababa in landlocked Ethiopia. Djibouti has petroleum significance, too. It provides oil refuelling for merchant vessels and warships traversing the Red Sea and Indian Ocean. It is planning a pipeline to bring petroleum products from the port of Djibouti to Ethiopia. Djibouti has five ports serving different purposes.

As well, Djibouti is host to four foreign military bases. US Africa Command has maintained a large base at Camp Lemonnier since 2003. The US operates a major drone base at Chabelley airfield, from which drones cruise over Somalia and Yemen ready to dispatch troublemakers.[15] The US Navy has secure refuelling facilities in Djibouti, a major consideration after the 2000 attack on the USS *Cole* at Aden. France has maintained a military base in Djibouti since its colonial days. Japan opened a naval base at Djibouti in 2011, to help combat offshore piracy.[16] China opened a naval base there in 2017 for its anti-piracy warships in the region, its first overseas military facility.[17] All these countries are interested in who owns which port. It affects their global strategies.

The Tadjourah terminal was operated by Allana Potash Corporation, a Canadian/Israeli company. The Doraleh Multipurpose Port was operated by China Merchants Holdings, a Hong Kong company. The Port of Djibouti and the Doraleh Container terminal were operated by DP World, a Dubai company, until February 2018, when the Djibouti government took over operation of the two ports. Visiting in March 2018, US Secretary of State Rex Tillerson stressed Djibouti's geopolitical importance.[18]

Eritrea's mainland stretches 1,150 kilometres beside the Red Sea. Formerly an Italian colony, Eritrea was occupied by British forces in World War II and ceded to Ethiopia in 1950. After a protracted struggle, it gained independence in 1993. Eritrea is one of the world's poorest countries and highly dependent on external aid, particularly from Italy and the European Union. Nonetheless, it is subject to UN sanctions since 2009 for having supported the Islamist insurgent group al-Shabaab in Somalia.[19] The Eritrean navy was placed under US sanctions in April 2017 for receiving communications equipment from North Korea.[20] However, Eritrea is important to the Gulf States. In 2015, it signed a security and military partnership agreement with UAE and Saudi Arabia, including use of the port and airfield at Assab for their ongoing war in Yemen.

Eritrea's offshore territory, according to an article in *The Guardian*, has "massive oil and gas reserves," but incessant conflict with Ethiopia has left Eritrea's natural resources little explored.[21] A few foreign companies explored offshore in the past but to no avail. The government is now pursuing new investors. The Ministry of Energy and Mines, assisted by UK consultants, has compiled technical information of Red Sea prospective areas to help investors determine hydrocarbon potential.[22]

Somalia has the longest coastline (3,000 km) in Africa, along the Gulf of Aden and Indian Ocean. It has been plagued with civil war since 1991, when armed opposition groups overthrew President Siad Barre's 22-year regime. Thousands of Somalis have died in the war; many thousands more fled for safety abroad. The war is a complex conflict of rival tribal loyalties, with a succession of administrations struggling to exercise governance over Somalia. The northern regions — Puntland and Somaliland — broke away in the 1990s to become semi-autonomous. In the south, an austere militia known as the Union of Islamic Courts seized power in 2006. In a six-month period, the Islamic Courts restored a modicum of law and order to Somalia before being driven out of power by a Western-backed transitional government reinforced by Ethiopian troops.

The Union of Islamic Courts broke up, but a splinter Islamic militant group, al-Shabaab, has fought a guerrilla war ever since. The government has been supported militarily by the African Union (with troops from Burundi, Djibouti, Ethiopia and Uganda) and the United States (with special forces and drones). In 2018, al-Shabaab held no major towns but remained strong in the southern countryside. The whole situation was eerily reminiscent of the war in Afghanistan. Somalia is the world's poorest nation. It ranked bottom in per capita income, per UN data for 2014.[23] To alleviate its poverty, Somalia receives huge amounts of external assistance.

Does Somalia have petroleum potential? In the 1980s, major US companies (Amoco, Chevron, Conoco, Phillips) signed exploration agreements but most abandoned work when the government collapsed. Conoco kept its office open, providing space for a temporary US embassy in 1992. This reinforced the view of some Somalis that foreign assistance was all about oil, an allegation US officials staunchly denied.[24] With the recent decline in violence and piracy, foreign companies are returning. In 2013, the Somali Ministry of Petroleum engaged a start-up UK company, Soma Oil and Gas Exploration, to process and evaluate all existing seismic data; and in 2014, BP signed an agreement to resume exploration. Ignoring federal government objection, the two northern semi-autonomous regions of Somaliland and Puntland have also issued exploration licences to oil companies.

Yemen has a strategic location, with Saudi Arabia on its northern border and the Gulf of Aden to the south. The port of Aden was an important base for the Royal Navy during 130 years of British rule (1839–1967). BP built a refinery there in 1952. Nationalized in 1977, the refinery continues to operate. Aden remains a major bunkering port. It is where the USS *Cole* was sabotaged while refuelling in 2000.

In addition, Yemen has oil and gas. There are two onshore fields with proven reserves, Marib in the west and Masila in the southeast. They are small by Middle East standards but important for the Yemeni economy. Yemen has yet to be fully explored, and some analysts speculate the possibility of considerable offshore resources in the Red Sea and the Sea of Aden.

Oil pipelines link the Marib field to a Red Sea oil terminal, and Masila to the Gulf of Aden. A gas pipeline also links Marib to an LNG terminal on the Gulf of Aden. Yemen's oil production began in the mid-1980s and reached about 440,000 b/d in 2011. With the outbreak of civil war, production fell precipitously and in 2015 stopped altogether, as did gas production. Masila resumed oil production in August 2016 but Marib remained shut. As well, Saudi Arabia planned to build a pipeline from its main producing fields to Yemen on the Gulf of Aden, bypassing the Strait of Hormuz.

Yemen is a highly tribal, fractious country. It is the uneasy union of two countries, North and South Yemen, that existed from the end of British rule until 1990. The civil war began in September 2014, when Houthi tribesmen loyal to ex-President Saleh captured the capital city of Sana'a and overthrew President Hadi's Western-supported government. Hadi fled to the port of Aden, where he remained recognized by numerous countries as president of

Yemen. The Houthis are a Zaidi Shia movement allegedly backed by Iran.

In March 2015, a coalition of Sunni Arab states, led by Saudi Arabia, joined the fray, aiming to evict the Houthi from power. The coalition conducted heavy aerial bombing and imposed an air and sea blockade, resulting in dire shortages of food, water and fuel. Military staff from the US and Britain helped identify targets. Much of the fighting occurred in the oil province of Marib, sandwiched between the Houthi-held provinces of Saada and Sana'a.[25] In early 2018, Yemen was a humanitarian disaster. Many thousands of civilians had died from injuries, starvation and cholera. Many more had fled. Ceasefire initiatives had led nowhere.

The United States has used armed drones in Yemen since 2002 and in Somalia since 2007. Compared with conventional military aircraft and troops on the ground, Washington sees drones as less costly to operate than manned planes and as surgically precise. They also attract relatively little publicity. Drones are used to eliminate so-called enemies. President Obama signed off on a weekly kill-list.

The Bureau of Investigative Journalism, an independent, not-for-profit organization in the UK, tracks US drone strikes in Pakistan, Somalia and Yemen. According to its records, during the first seven years (2009–2015) of the Obama Administration, drones killed a range of 2,753 to 4,333 people, of whom 380 to 801 were civilians.[26] In July 2016, the White House released a lower estimate of 2,372 to 2,581 total deaths during those years, of which a mere 64 to 116 were defined as non-combatants.[27] Researchers from Stanford and New York University law schools have questioned this assessment. Interviews of victims and witnesses of drone strikes in Pakistan revealed death, injury and harm to the daily lives of ordinary civilians, who heard drones hover 24 hours a day and lived in fear a strike could occur at any moment of day or night.[28]

In his 2013 prize-winning documentary and book *Dirty Wars*, Jeremy Scahill, a US investigative journalist, described drone wars as "conducted in the shadows, outside the range of the press, without effective congressional oversight or public debate."[29] All this effort to secure the Strait of Bab el-Mandab and related coastlines receives little public attention in the West. Meanwhile, the people in Somalia and Yemen live in misery.

THE SUEZ CANAL

The Suez Canal is a vital sea link across Egypt, connecting Europe and Asia. Port Said is at the northern end, on the Mediterranean, and Port Suez is at the southern end, on the Red Sea. The canal is owned and maintained by the Suez Canal Authority of Egypt. Tankers move in both directions, north and south. Most bring Persian Gulf oil to European and North American markets, but some bring North African oil south to Asian markets.

Some oil tankers are too large to transit the canal. Since 1977, the Suez-Mediterranean Pipeline (Sumed) has provided an alternative route across Egypt.[30] Tankers from the Persian Gulf offload their cargo at the pipeline's Red Sea terminal and other tankers reload at the Mediterranean. The pipeline transports about 1.5 million b/d of crude oil northward. The very large crude carriers avoid Suez completely and pass round the Cape of Good Hope at the southern tip of Africa. While that adds some 15 days of transit to Europe and 8 to 10 days to the US, the economies of scale make the voyage worthwhile.[31] In 2016, total shipments through the Suez Canal and Sumed pipeline averaged 5.5 million b/d, about nine per cent of the world's seaborne traded oil.

In 2018, the canal — an international waterway — was firmly guarded by Egypt, a country financially reliant on the West, reconciled with its neighbour Israel and on good terms with Russia and China. Egypt's strategic position on trading routes between East and West makes its stability an international concern to all. Western countries maintain a low-key watch, insisting that Egypt respect their interests.

The canal's history includes several interventions. It was completed in 1869 as a French-Egyptian joint venture but soon ran into financial difficulties. The British moved in, buying Egypt's share, imposing resident advisers on the Egyptian government, and making the canal a neutral zone under British military protection. Egypt remained under British indirect rule until 1952, when a military coup ousted King Farouk and shortly brought Colonel Nasser to power in 1954. It was Britain's lifeline to its empire in the east.

In 1956, when President Nasser nationalized the Suez Canal Company, Prime Minister Anthony Eden believed he needed to make a stand. Two-thirds of Europe's oil passed through the canal. The British and French had no faith in Egyptian ability to run the canal. They sought to remove Nasser from power and brought Israel into the plot. The British and French sent a vast armada to Port Said, and the Israelis swept through the Sinai Desert toward the canal.

I experienced this intervention first-hand, as a sub-lieutenant in the Royal navy. Our tank landing craft was the first to enter Port Said. When the armada arrived offshore Port Said, the Egyptians had sunk ships to block the harbour. Our landing craft was ordered to thread through the block-ships. We did so and tied up at a jetty, in time to witness a real-life shoot-out.

The scene was surreal that beautiful sunny morning. On the jetty, a Royal Marine commando was firing at an upper window of the hotel opposite. We were gawking on the foredeck. A bellow came from the bridge: "Get down — it's for real." Later, we watched naval aircraft strafe the historic Admiralty Building. We opened the bow doors, lowered the ramp and unloaded communication vehicles and port experts primed to control Port Said. We unloaded a generator, too, which vanished overnight despite the swarm of troops on the jetty. A few days later, I went ashore to collect the ship's payroll. I passed a bloated Egyptian corpse in the ditch and thought: "He's dead because we're here."

Although we were told we had invaded Egypt for important reasons, the Suez landings incurred the wrath of the United States. Canada's Secretary of State for External Affairs Lester B. Pearson proposed a way out — the creation of the first United Nations peacekeeping force that would ensure unfettered access to the canal for all and an Israeli withdrawal from the Sinai. British opinion was divided and angry. There were many who said, "Finish the job, advance to Port Suez, take the whole canal." Did they wish to take Egypt, too? It wasn't clear. Anthony Eden resigned in March 1957, the canal reopened in April 1957 with UN assistance and Egypt has ably run the canal ever since.

After the 1967 and 1973 Arab-Israeli Wars, Israel and Egypt settled their differences at the 1978 Camp David Accords. The United States began its huge annual program of economic and military support to both countries, and Cairo has remained faithful to Washington since then. Egypt is firmly aligned with the United States and Israel. For the past 60 years, the Suez Canal has remained secure, with tankers and other ships moving freely.

STRAIT OF MALACCA

The Strait of Malacca is a strategic waterway traversed by all but the largest oil tankers voyaging from the Persian Gulf to East Asia. This waterway, 850 kilometres long, links the Indian Ocean to the South China Sea — thence China, Japan, Taiwan and South Korea. On its western shore lies the Indonesian island of Sumatra, and on its eastern shore are West Malaysia and Singapore. It is one of the world's most crowded waterways. Approximately 100,000 vessels pass through the strait each year, carrying about one-quarter of the world's maritime trade. Twenty-six per cent of the world's seaborne oil (16.0 million b/d in 2016) passes through it.

From the Strait of Malacca, tankers enter the Strait of Singapore before sailing into the South China Sea. The Strait of Malacca is only 18 kilometres wide at its southern end, and the Strait of Singapore is only 2.8 kilometres at its narrowest point. The navigable waters are shallow and have a 25-metre draught limit. Large vessels specifically designed for the waterway are called Malaccamax ships, and a typical Malaccamax tanker has a draught of 20.5 metres and tonnage of 300,000 DWT. Larger tankers have to detour through the Lombok Strait between the Indonesian islands of Bali and Lombok.

Piracy has long been a threat to ships passing the Strait of Malacca. Unlike Somalia, pirates have not taken hostages or hijacked vessels for ransom, preferring to rob cargos instead. Navies of Indonesia, Malaysia, Singapore and Thailand have maintained a coordinated patrol of the strait since 2006 and met with some success in reducing piracy and robbery at sea.[32]

SOUTH CHINA SEA

From the Strait of Singapore, tankers sail east into the South China Sea. This sea is important both as a strategic trade route to East Asia and for the unproven petroleum resources that may lie beneath. Its shoreline stretches south from China and includes Brunei, the Republic of China (Taiwan), Indonesia, Malaysia, the Philippines, Singapore and Vietnam. The South China Sea matters to all these countries. It is also a major tanker route to northern China, South Korea and Japan.

The US government insists on freedom of navigation in the South China Sea to ensure access to vital shipping and air routes.[33] Secretary of Defense

Map 16. Strait of Malacca and South China Sea

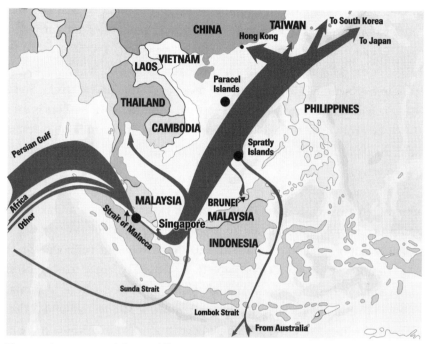

Twenty-six per cent of the world's seaborne oil passes through the Strait of Malacca from the Indian Ocean to the South China Sea — a strategic trade route to East Asia.

Ash Carter asserted in 2015 that the United States "will fly, sail and operate wherever international law allows, as we do around the world, and the South China Sea ... will not be an exception." He said the US would continue its "role as a pivotal security partner in this region," increasing maritime cooperation "from Vietnam to India, to the Philippines, to Japan."[34] Putting words into action, the US Navy conducted naval exercises and surveillance flights in the South and East China Seas by itself and with these countries.

Is the objective really freedom of navigation? Or is it the naval containment of China, a cordon round the South China Sea? In March 2016, China's Foreign Minister Wang Yi said China upholds the freedom of navigation but this does not equal the "freedom to run amok."[35] As of 2018, the South China Sea remained one of the safest shipping lanes in the world. China conducts exercises in the South China Sea by itself and jointly with Russia.

China, Japan and South Korea are all highly dependent on the Middle East. A major disruption of shipping through the Strait of Malacca and South China Sea would be catastrophic for their economies and for world trade. China is the world's eighth largest oil producer, 3.8 million b/d in 2017. In the 1970s it was self-sufficient but, reflecting its phenomenal economic growth, has been importing more and more oil each year. Since 2013, it has become the world's largest net importer (9.1 million b/d in 2017), exceeding the United States. For their part, Japan and South Korea have no oil production and are the world's third and fifth largest oil importers respectively.

To alleviate its vulnerability to sea routes, China was strenuously developing alternative trade routes overland. Its massive One Belt One Road infrastructure program delivers goods by rail to Europe. Recently built pipelines import oil and gas from Russia, Kazakhstan and Turkmenistan.

In addition, China built two pipelines across Myanmar to southwest China, one in 2013 to import natural gas from fields offshore Myanmar and the other in 2014 to import crude oil from the Middle East and Africa. The two pipelines avoid the Strait of Malacca and provide a shorter route to southwest China. The pipelines run in parallel and start at Myanmar's port of Kyaukphyu. The pipelines and port are strategically important to both China and Myanmar. The port happens to be located in Rakhine State, the centre of the Rohingya crisis and refugee flight to Bangladesh.[36] Western countries castigated Myanmar's handling of the unrest. In October 2017, Ottawa appointed a special envoy, Bob Rae, who made a fact-finding visit to the region. In December, Washington imposed sanctions on a Burmese general for repressing the Rohingya. In 2018, Ottawa acted similarly, and the European Union prepared to do the same.

Chinese companies are vigorously exploring for petroleum outside the Middle East. An exploration area of much interest is the South China Sea. Malaysia and Vietnam already produce oil and gas offshore the Gulf of Thailand — an inlet of the South China Sea — and they allow joint development in areas claimed by both countries.

The offshore boundaries between countries around the South China Sea are highly contentious. Their determination is complicated by the hundreds of uninhabited islands, shoals, reefs and sandbars, on which the countries

Map 17. Myanmar-China Oil and Gas Pipelines

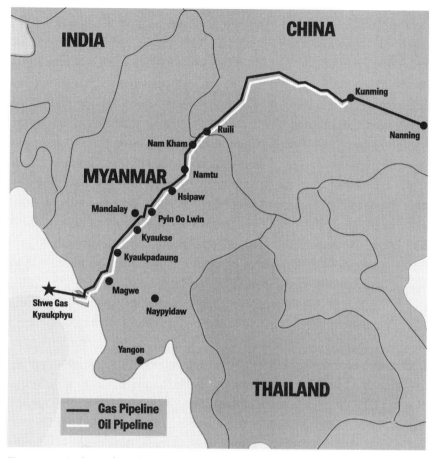

Two new pipelines for oil and gas across Myanmar from the Bay of Bengal to southwest China avoid the Strait of Malacca.

have competing territorial claims. Two major archipelagos are the Paracel and Spratly Islands. For several decades, Malaysia, the Philippines, Taiwan and Vietnam have all occupied islands in the Spratlys, built outposts and airstrips and reclaimed land, with a view to influencing boundaries. China started doing so in the 1980s. In 2014, it began constructing artificial islands, with military airstrips on seven reefs. China and Taiwan both claim much of the South China Sea as theirs.

In 2013, the Philippines filed a case with the Permanent Court of

Arbitration in The Hague, seeking a ruling on its right to exploit the South China Sea waters within its exclusive economic zone. China boycotted the proceedings, claiming the court had no jurisdiction in the matter. In July 2016, the court ruled in favour of the Philippines, giving it an exclusive economic zone of 200 nautical miles from its archipelagic baseline into the South China Sea.[37] Western leaders and press praised the ruling, but it is unenforceable. China rejected the decision. China and the Philippines are amicably examining possibilities for offshore economic cooperation, including joint petroleum exploration in disputed areas.[38]

The Philippines and other southeast Asian countries are looking increasingly to Beijing. They are interested in being part of China's One Belt One Road initiative. As members of the Association of Southeast Asian Nations (ASEAN), they were negotiating a free trade agreement with China and other countries with which ASEAN had partner agreements.[39] This is the Regional Comprehensive Economic Partnership, an alternative to Washington's moribund Trans-Pacific Partnership.

For the Trump Administration, a big concern has been to stop North Korea's missile and nuclear weapons program. The US and South Korea held massive military exercises close to the thirty-eighth parallel each year. Each time, North Korea responded to these provocations with missile launches and nuclear tests. Neither side backed down from such confrontation. In 2017, North Korea tested an intercontinental ballistic missile on July 4 (US Independence Day), conducted an underground nuclear test in September and sent a missile over the Japanese island of Hokkaido the same month. The US trumpeted all options were on the table, including military action.

In September 2017, the UN Security Council imposed sanctions on North Korea's exports of coal, iron, lead and seafood. In December, it imposed stronger sanctions, capping annual exports of crude oil and refined products to North Korea. Washington imposed unilateral sanctions on companies and banks of countries trading with North Korea.

In January 2018, Canada and the United States co-hosted an international meeting in Vancouver, B.C., to discuss the security threat posed by North Korea. Foreign ministers were invited from the 16 countries that participated in the UN-led coalition during the 1950–1953 Korean War, as well as South Korea, India, Sweden and Japan. The meeting included Colombia and Greece but excluded China and Russia, two countries bordering on North Korea. The US called for naval interdiction of North Korean shipping. Canada sent a submarine, HMCS *Chicoutimi*, to keep watch in the region's waters.

From the perspective of China and Russia, the US/South Korean military exercises were a provocation. Both China and Russia had long-standing policies of engagement with North Korea rather than confrontation. They ruled out regime change, seeking instead a "double-freeze" — a cessation of North Korea's nuclear weapons program and an end to US military exercises in South Korea.[40] They frowned on a naval blockade and a total ban of oil imports into North Korea. In 2017, President Putin said pursuing further sanctions was useless, as the North Koreans would "rather eat grass" than give up their nuclear program. North Koreans remember what happened to Saddam and Gaddafi after abandoning weapons of mass destruction.[41] Putin proposed a trilateral economic cooperation program to include construction of a gas pipeline, electricity grid and rail link from Russia through North Korea to South Korea. At separate meetings in Russia, both Koreas showed guarded interest in the proposal. It was reminiscent of Germany and the Soviet Union reaching out during the Cold War through trade and investment in petroleum and pipelines.

The ice dividing North and South Korea showed signs of melting in 2018. At the Winter Olympics hosted by South Korea, the South and North Korean teams marched into the opening ceremony under the Korean unification flag. In women's ice hockey, there was a single united Korean team. Kim Yo Jong, sister of President Kim Jong Un, represented North Korea. Washington rained on their parade, imposing more unilateral sanctions.[42] Meetings between North and South Korean officials took place in February, followed by the visit of a South Korean delegation in March to Washington. The delegation presented an invitation to President Trump to meet with North Korean leader Kim Jong Un for a summit. President Trump accepted. Whether they could bridge the chasm separating their countries remained to be seen.[43] The stakes were high, and any missteps could devastate North and South Korea alike.

* * *

Each of the five strategic waterways — the Strait of Hormuz, Mandab Strait, Suez Canal, Strait of Malacca and South China Sea — is important in petroleum trade. Each has its own history, and each could be the site of future conflict. Since 2001, enormous security efforts have aimed to protect maritime routes and port infrastructure and to ensure freedom of navigation. Under US command, a dozen NATO countries and various Asia-Pacific countries participate in these activities. China, Russia and Iran are excluded.

What is the payoff of the efforts to secure chokepoints? The benefits and costs are hard to quantify. Are the benefits justified by the cost? How much security is enough? The cost is a real subsidy to petroleum borne by taxpayers and not included in the price. As always, there are winners and losers. The winners include armaments suppliers, security system people, mercenaries and the military. The losers are taxpayers and people who are inevitably collateral damage in countries being patrolled. An uneasy question remains. How far has the super-abundance of Western navies, special forces and drones engendered peace and stability rather than hostility and conflict along the region's waters and shorelines? It merits reflection.

CHAPTER 7
AFGHANISTAN — THE TAPI PIPELINE

"America did not want peace for Afghanistan because it had its own agendas and goals."

—Afghan President Hamid Karzai, 2014[1]

Petroleum is seldom associated with Afghanistan, a very poor country in which roughly 70 per cent of the population is illiterate. Afghanistan has been the epicentre of geopolitical struggles for centuries. The US motive for invading Afghanistan was ostensibly to capture Osama bin Laden, assumed to be the brains behind the 9/11 attack. Yet the motives kept evolving. The United States still has troops in Afghanistan. NATO countries continue to provide financial resources. Why? One important reason is rarely discussed in the West — Afghanistan's strategic location as a transit country for energy exports. Linked to petroleum are power and politics in the region.

AFGHANISTAN'S IMPORTANCE

Afghanistan has been a frequent battleground between nations and empires vying for dominance of the region. In efforts to conquer Afghanistan, foreign powers have expended great sums in blood and treasure. Today, the rivalry in Asia is in part a quest for control of energy export routes. The rivalry is sometimes called the New Great Game, an update of the nineteenth century Great Game in Central Asia between the Russian and British Empires. Afghanistan is at the fulcrum of this rivalry.

Afghanistan is also rich in mineral resources. Russian geologists in the

1980s drew attention to its mineral potential. The Pentagon did so in 2010, trumpeting the existence of minerals worth nearly $1 trillion — copper, iron, gold, cobalt and lithium.[2] President Karzai claimed his country's minerals could be worth much more. Lithium, for example, is highly valued for its uses in modern electronics, ceramics and numerous other industries. Some minerals are already being developed. A Chinese consortium is developing huge copper deposits at Aynak, and an Indian consortium, the iron ore at Hajigak. According to the *New York Times*, President Trump views mining as one justification to stay engaged in Afghanistan, giving the US "a valuable new beachhead in the market for rare-earth minerals, which has been all but monopolized by China."[3]

Afghanistan has geopolitical importance because of its location. To the west is Iran, with its enormous reserves of oil and gas. To the north are Central Asian countries that became independent when the Soviet Union collapsed. Along Afghanistan's northern border are Turkmenistan, Uzbekistan and Tajikistan. Further north are Kazakstan and Kyrgyzstan, also Central Asian republics. They all have resources to be developed. To Afghanistan's east are Pakistan and, via a narrow corridor of land, China. Strategically, Afghanistan is a bridgehead into Central Asia. US General David Petraeus briefed the Senate Armed Services Committee in 2011: "It's very important to stay engaged in a region in which we have such vital interests."[4] Phrases such as "vital interests" are clues to Washington's attention to the region's resources. In effect, the US presence in Afghanistan brings its military bases closer to Russia, China and Central Asia.

Afghanistan's petroleum reserves, primarily in the north, are modest. But its location between Central and South Asia makes it a critical link in long-standing plans to build a gas pipeline from energy-rich Turkmenistan, through Afghanistan, to Pakistan and India. Turkmenistan has vast reserves of natural gas. It exports much of its gas east to China and smaller amounts southwest to Iran. It used to export gas north to Russia and then on to Europe but stopped in 2016. Afghanistan offers a route to the south — to Pakistan and India. As of 2018, the US has been working toward the creation of this pipeline for more than 20 years.

THE PROPOSED TAPI PIPELINE

The TAPI pipeline is named after the initials of the four countries who would benefit from its creation — Turkmenistan, Afghanistan, Pakistan and India. Turkmenistan would earn revenue from sales of natural gas. Pakistan and India would benefit because they are currently energy deficient. Afghanistan plans industrial centres along the pipeline route. With few interruptions, the TAPI pipeline has been actively planned since the mid-1990s — and even earlier. A long gestation period is often the case with pipelines. Agreement among countries can be difficult. Pricing is complicated; politics are involved; and in the case of Afghanistan, security is of paramount concern.

Map 18. TAPI Gas Pipeline Project

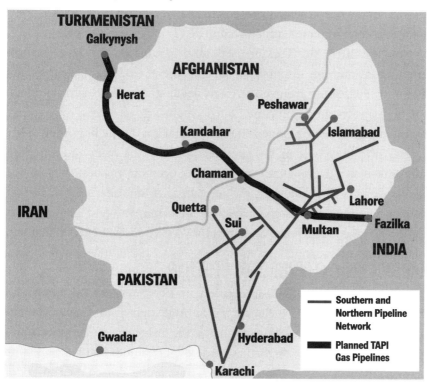

The TAPI pipeline project is planned to bring gas from Turkmenistan through Afghanistan to Pakistan and India.

The proposed TAPI pipeline would be 56 inches in diameter and have an annual capacity of about 30 billion cubic metres (BCM). It would extend 1,700 kilometres from the giant Galkynysh gas field (earlier known as South Yoloten-Osman) in Turkmenistan, through Afghanistan alongside the Herat-Kandahar highway, past Quetta and Multan in Pakistan, to the Indian border town of Fazilka.

Turkmenistan, a country with the world's fourth largest reserves of natural gas, sits on Afghanistan's northern border. In 2007, US Assistant Secretary of State for the region Richard Boucher stated, "One of our goals is to stabilize Afghanistan," to link South and Central Asia "so that energy can flow to the south."[5] This policy priority carried forward to the Obama Administration. In 2009, George Krol, a senior US diplomat, told Congress that a US priority in Central Asia was "to increase development and diversification of the region's energy resources and supply routes."[6] Washington's New Silk Road initiative, announced in 2011, had the same goal.

Note the absence of "Turkmenistan" and "natural gas" in the quotations from senior officials. In public statements, these two terms have generally been avoided. Some groups offered misleading statements such as "there are no plans for an oil pipeline." Such statements were technically correct — the pipeline being planned was for natural gas. Or perhaps they didn't know. In reality, planning has continued through the years, and American efforts to ensure the pipeline's creation have been stupendous. The pipeline is part of a US global strategy, put in place after the collapse of the Soviet Union, when numerous countries that were formerly part of the Soviet Union became independent and open for Western investment and markets.

THE BACKSTORY: GEOPOLITICS OF A PIPELINE

After the Soviet Union's disintegration in 1991, Western oil companies flocked to Central Asia. Included was an Argentinean firm named Bridas. Its chief executive, Carlos Bulgheroni, was the first to call on Turkmenistan's president. Turkmenistan signed agreements with Bridas in 1992 and 1993 to develop two gas fields, Yashlar and Keimir, and endorsed the concept of building a pipeline south through Afghanistan to Pakistan. In June 1994, Turkmenistan's President Niyazov sent Mr. Bulgheroni to Pakistan as special emissary, with power of attorney to negotiate on the government's behalf. In March 1995, Turkmenistan and Pakistan agreed to do a feasibility study on the pipeline.

In May 1995, executives from Unocal (Union Oil of California), a US firm, arrived in Turkmenistan interested in a similar pipeline. The two companies held friendly discussions, and Bulgheroni offered Unocal participation in his consortium. However, Unocal proceeded separately and signed a pipeline deal with Turkmenistan in October. In November, Turkmenistan declared Bridas' agreements unacceptable and seized its field installations. Bridas promptly filed a US$15 billion suit against Unocal in a Texas court, alleging it had illegally interfered in Bridas' talks with Turkmenistan. After much litigation, the case was dismissed for lack of jurisdiction.

Meanwhile, Bridas was negotiating a pipeline agreement with the Afghan government and met with tribal leaders along the pipeline route in Afghanistan. In February 1996, it signed an agreement with the government. Seven months later, the Taliban seized power.[7] Wasting no time, Bridas renegotiated and reached agreement in November with the Taliban as well as the northern warlord General Dostum, through whose fiefdom the pipeline would pass.

In April 1997, the Taliban backtracked and announced it would award the contract to whoever were to start first (whatever that meant). A Taliban delegation visited Argentina in September for meetings with Bridas and visited the United States in November for meetings with State Department and Unocal. The Taliban team also visited Unocal's regional headquarters in Sugar Land, Texas, a modern metropolis close to Houston. In their traditional Afghan dress and loose black turbans, the men stayed in a five-star hotel and were shepherded around in a company minivan. Unocal wanted to win.

Just before the meeting, Unocal, Turkmenistan and five minority partners had formed a joint venture for the project, Central Asia Gas Pipeline Ltd. (CentGas).[8] The Unocal proposal was a key component of Washington's geostrategy for Eurasia.[9] Pakistani journalist Ahmed Rashid detailed the Bridas/Unocal rivalry in his book *Taliban: Militant Islam, Oil and Fundamentalism in Central Asia*.[10] He wrote, "Unocal's real influence with the Taliban was that their project carried the possibility of US recognition, which the Taliban were desperately anxious to secure." Bridas was out of the running.

The Taliban movement had emerged in 1994 from the Mujahedin, a coalition of Muslim guerrillas heavily financed by the CIA. The Mujahedin had been receiving covert US aid since July 1979 because they opposed the pro-Soviet government in Kabul and later the Soviet occupation. Zbigniew Brzezinski, national security adviser to President Carter, later explained the secret aid "had the effect of drawing Moscow into the Afghan trap" and a "conflict that brought about the demoralization and finally the breakup of the Soviet empire."[11] He expressed no regret about supporting the Mujahedin: "What is most important to the history of the world? The Taliban or the collapse of the Soviet empire? Some stirred-up Moslems or the liberation of Central Europe and the end of the cold war?"

When the Soviets withdrew from Afghanistan in 1989, the Afghan government collapsed and various Mujahedin groups fought for power. The Taliban were victorious and took power in 1996, ruling until the US invasion of 2001. In power, they used a strict code of Sharia (Islamic) law to achieve law and order — public executions for murder, amputations for theft. Men were required to grow beards; women were required to wear burkas; girls over ten were forbidden from going to school. Music, cinema and television were banned.[12]

Negotiations for the pipeline continued, with the US government supporting Unocal. Shortly after the Taliban visit to Unocal, the company made a donation to the University of Nebraska's Center for Afghanistan Studies and opened a training centre to train Afghans in pipeline construction technology. Later, Unocal's CEO John Imle estimated the company spent US$15–20 million on feasibility studies and various efforts to encourage Taliban support for the proposed pipeline.[13]

American and international women's groups were upset by the Taliban's misogyny. In 1997, five female Afghan employees working for the international humanitarian organization CARE were forced from their minibus, humiliated and publicly beaten with metal and leather whips for "associating with foreigners." Though the Taliban apologized (an apology later rescinded on Radio Shariat), restrictions for women — dress code, prohibitions on education and employment — continued. This was only one of many incidents of Taliban misogyny.[14]

In February 1998, John J. Maresca, Unocal's Vice-President for

International Relations, testified before the US Congressional Committee on Asia and the Pacific. He indicated that Unocal had held meetings with all factions of the Afghanistan government and found all in favour of the pipeline. But the pipeline would not be built, he said, until there was a single Afghan government. Further, he said, "we have to look 10, 20 years out into the future because the projects are vast."[15] Unocal wanted a unitary government so they could negotiate once for the whole country. A unitary government would also facilitate loans from international financial institutions.

Pipeline planning continued until August 1998 when the US Embassy in Nairobi, Kenya, was bombed by al-Qaeda. Since the Taliban leadership had approved the presence of Osama bin Laden in Afghanistan, Unocal broke off negotiations in December 1998 and withdrew from the CentGas Consortium. A Saudi company, Delta, took over leadership, but to little effect. In July 1999, President Bill Clinton signed an Executive Order prohibiting commercial transactions with the Taliban.[16] His Administration's focus was no longer on the pipeline but on the extradition of Osama bin Laden. Even so, the US maintained informal contact with the Taliban.[17]

When George W. Bush became president in 2001, his Administration continued contact with the Taliban."[18] A Taliban envoy, Rahmatullah Hashimi, visited the United States for six weeks in March–April 2001 for discussions with government officials and meetings with think-tank analysts.

In July, the United Nations hosted a meeting in Berlin to brainstorm Afghanistan, attended by senior retired diplomats from the US, Russia, Iran and Pakistan. A representative of the anti-Taliban Northern Alliance attended, but the Taliban declined. According to *The Guardian*, the meetings were designed to offer a free and open-ended forum for governments to pass messages and sound out each other's thinking. A former Pakistani foreign minister who attended, Niaz Naik, said the Americans indicated that, if the Taliban did not cooperate, the US would have no option "but to take an overt action against Afghanistan.[19] Naik told French television that discussions addressed "the formation of a government of national unity. If the Taliban had accepted this coalition, they would have immediately received international economic aid ... And the pipeline ... would have come."[20] That was two months before the 9/11 attacks in New York and Washington, DC.

THE 9/11 ATTACKS, US INVASION AND PIPELINE PLANNING

After the 9/11 attacks, the stars-and-stripes fluttered outside homes all over the United States. Draped from overpasses, flapping from cars and displayed in shop windows, they represented an overwhelming wave of patriotism. On September 20, 2001, President George W. Bush told the American people, "Either you are with us, or you are with the terrorists. From this day forward, any nation that continues to harbour or support terrorism will be regarded by the United States as a hostile regime."[21] He launched the War on Terror and posed the question: "Why do they hate us?" He answered himself: "They hate our freedoms; our freedom of religion, our freedom of speech, our freedom to vote and assemble and disagree with each other." Of course, the War on Terror was about control — it had nothing to do with democratization.

It's difficult to explain to non-Americans what Washington, DC, was like just after 9/11. The freedom to criticize the government seemed to die overnight. My own impression, as an expatriate resident of the area, was that there was a seismic shift. I asked American friends their thoughts. In my office, a staunch Democrat didn't see anything to discuss. "We must follow the Commander-in-Chief," he said. Only in whispered conversations would anyone dare register concern for the direction the government was taking. Friends of mine were only willing to share their concerns about looming war during a walk in the woods, but by tacit agreement, there was no further discussion during dinner later at a restaurant where someone might overhear. I visited Canada the week after the attack and found people willing to entertain different points of view. In terms of freedom of discussion, Washington, DC, and Toronto, Canada, were like night and day.

In subsequent weeks, a church in Virginia held informative talks on current events. Hundreds showed up on a weekday evening to hear a local imam explain the Islamic faith and express words of sorrow. At another session, two speakers — a journalist who covered the Pentagon and a senior State Department diplomat — indicated the US government was planning retribution in Afghanistan. In response to my question about the illegality of regime change under the UN Charter, the speakers replied that Cheney and Rumsfeld were tough men and were bent on it. In the audience, I sensed a general mood for revenge.

Although 15 of the 19 hijackers were citizens of Saudi Arabia, the US planned retribution in Afghanistan. They demanded the extradition of Osama bin Laden, who had been living in Afghanistan for six years. The Taliban requested evidence of wrongdoing upon which they could act. Though the US had been tracking bin Laden, they offered none. Instead, they worked with the Northern tribes to attack the Taliban in October 2001 and bombed it out of power. The stated reason was to capture Osama bin Laden.

After the US invasion of Afghanistan, a conference of 25 Afghan leaders was held in December 2001 at Bonn, Germany. The Bonn Conference agreed on the framework for a new constitution and chose Hamid Karzai as interim leader. The conference envisaged a strong, centralized government. It ignored Afghanistan's tradition of informal, regional power-broking. In 2004, the new constitution was enacted, national elections were held and Karzai was elected president.

After the invasion, pipeline planning continued. The US government moved to the shadows. Leaders of Turkmenistan, Afghanistan and Pakistan agreed in 2002 to form a steering committee of energy ministers to oversee the project. They were joined by India in 2008. In subsequent years, the steering committee met regularly.

The Asian Development Bank (ADB) — the regional development bank for Asia — became the secretariat for the project in 2003. It began sponsoring and financing feasibility studies, consultants, legal services, meetings and negotiations.[22] The ADB is a regional cousin of the World Bank and is headquartered in Manila. Its members include the United States, Canada and other NATO countries who sent troops to Afghanistan — Britain, France, Germany, Italy, Norway. The ADB shielded the involvement of NATO countries from public scrutiny. The United States uses international lending agencies regularly to promote its world vision. A project as sensitive as TAPI must have the early blessing of the United States, which has 15.5 per cent of the ADB's shareholding (as does Japan). In effect, the same countries were deciding where to focus militarily and how to support the pipeline project. It was a bit like the Wizard of Oz, Professor Marvel — the hidden power behind the curtain.

At a Heads of State Summit in 2010, the four countries — Turkmenistan, Afghanistan, Pakistan and India — signed an Inter-Governmental Agreement committing them to cooperate and realize the project. Subsequently, Afghanistan, Pakistan and India signed individual Gas Sales and Purchase Agreements with Turkmenistan, specifying gas supply and off-take obligations. All of this was normal for a pipeline agreement.

The new plan was for TAPI to be built, owned and operated by a consortium comprising state-owned companies from the four countries and an international company as lead partner who would drive the project.[23] The countries appointed the ADB to identify the lead partner. In 2012, road shows were held in Singapore, New York and London to seek out private investors.[24] In 2014, the four countries approved bidding documents for companies taking part in the tender.[25] Several companies were later reported to be interested — Chevron and ExxonMobil (US), Petronas (Malaysian), Total (French) and RT Global Resources (Russian) — but a signed deal remained elusive.[26]

A key issue was the terms for developing and operating the gas field. Turkmenistan proffered a service contract, not the more lucrative production-sharing arrangement which foreign firms demanded. In 2015, when both Turkmenistan and foreign firms were unwilling to budge from their respective positions, the steering committee endorsed Turkmenistan's state-owned Turkmengaz as the consortium leader.[27] Turkmengaz declared the project remained open to foreign companies, but none had indicated interest by early 2018. Sometimes pipelines take years of talking before they happen.

Along the way, Western countries were privately supportive of the TAPI project. In 2006, donors at a New Delhi conference vowed to accelerate work on the pipeline and help Afghanistan become a regional "energy bridge."[28] The Canadian delegation was led by Parliamentary Secretary for Foreign Affairs Deepak Obhrai.[29] In 2008, donors at a Paris conference endorsed Afghanistan's National Development Strategy (2009–2013).[30] The strategy affirmed Afghanistan's central role as a land bridge connecting energy-rich Central Asia to energy-deficient South Asia.[31] The Canadian delegation was led by Minister of Foreign Affairs David Emerson.

In 2010, the G8 endorsed the project at Huntsville, Ontario, though they avoided mentioning it directly. What they endorsed was a new initiative to facilitate joint infrastructure projects identified in a Joint Declaration by Afghanistan and Pakistan.[32] The declaration included the TAPI pipeline.[33] It was a fascinating exercise in obfuscation. The pipeline was buried in layers of documents like a matryoshka doll.

None of the public pronouncements relating to the G8 meeting mentioned the pipeline. I had been curious about the project since 2006. I read about it in the South Asian press. The ADB listed the project in its website. Rarely was there mention of TAPI in the US or other NATO countries. The US Energy Information Administration's website, full of country energy backgrounders, stopped updating on Afghanistan after 2001.

The one exception came in 2008 when Shawn McCarthy, energy journalist at the *Globe and Mail*, wrote a front-page article on June 19, 2008, headlined *Pipeline Opens New Front in Afghan War*.[34] The article featured a paper I wrote at the request of the Canadian Centre for Policy Alternatives (CCPA), entitled *A Pipeline through a Troubled Land*.[35] The flurry in the Canadian media was not picked up in the US or European press. But the CCPA paper was downloaded more than 200,000 times; many people must have read it. The paper documented in detail what was going on and concluded that physical security of the pipeline was a paramount concern.

Canadian media asked federal officials if Canadian troops were in Afghanistan to defend a pipeline route. On a Halifax, Nova Scotia, talk show, Minister of National Defence Peter MacKay replied that Canadian troops were "not there specifically to protect a pipeline across Afghanistan," but "if the Taliban were attacking certain places in the country or certain projects, then yes we will play a role."[36] Unwittingly, I had been on the show the day before to explain the TAPI pipeline.

I've encountered people who said the pipeline would never happen — it was a pipe-dream. But governments had gone to great efforts to make it happen, and the ADB had spent several million dollars on feasibility studies. Just before I gave a talk in January 2010 at UBC's Liu Institute, the Canada-Afghanistan Solidarity Committee posted an online announcement for the talk but cautioned the pipeline was a myth.[37] I wondered why they'd discourage people from attending with an open mind. The next day, I was invited to appear on a Vancouver television program.[38] Its host, Peter Klein, used to be a producer for the US television program *60 Minutes*. He said that, in 2002,

60 Minutes heard pipeline rumours and sent him to Turkmenistan to learn more. He ran into a brick wall; nobody had anything to tell him.

Then in February 2010, perhaps because I was one of the few to write publicly, the *Journal of Energy Security* invited me to write a piece on Afghanistan and the TAPI pipeline. Its editor said the pipeline would shortly be a breaking story, and he wanted the *Journal* to be the first to run it. The *Journal* is published by the Institute for Analysis of Global Security, in Washington, DC. At the time, its advisers included a former CIA director, a national security adviser and two generals, all retired. I wondered whether the *Journal* would publish what I wrote, but they did so in March 2010 — without changes.[39]

Two months later, in May 2010, a joint think-tank report on *The Key to Success in Afghanistan: A Modern Silk Road Strategy* referenced my *Journal* article. The think-tanks were the Center for Strategic and International Studies, the School of Advanced International Studies and the Swedish Institute for Security and Development Policy.[40]

In 2011, officials in Washington began showcasing the pipeline. They launched a New Silk Road to link Central and South Asia. The TAPI pipeline was the centrepiece — the flagship project. Assistant Secretary of State for South and Central Asia Robert Blake enthused to a Houston audience, "TAPI's route may serve as a peace corridor."[41]

In July 2011, US Secretary of State Hillary Clinton visited India and referred openly to the TAPI pipeline: "Let's work together to create a New Silk Road ... more ... energy infrastructure, like the proposed pipeline to run from Turkmenistan, through Afghanistan, through Pakistan into India."[42] In September 2011, she announced the New Silk Road initiative at an intergovernmental meeting in New York, saying, "Turkmen gas fields could help meet both Pakistan's and India's growing energy needs and provide significant transit revenues for both Afghanistan and Pakistan."[43] Canada's Minister of Foreign Affairs John Baird was present.[44]

Hillary Clinton's successor, John Kerry, endorsed the New Silk Road initiative on a visit to India in June 2013.[45] Meanwhile, Washington kept strong pressure on Pakistan to abandon the rival pipeline project to import gas from Iran, described in Chapter 4.

Turkmenistan hustled to get the pipeline built. In 2016, it contracted a

Japanese consortium to develop the Galkynysh gas field for a service fee, and a Chinese company to build the first 300 kilometres of pipeline to the Afghan border. In 2017, the TAPI Pipeline Company engaged consultants, with ADB financing, to undertake engineering and project management of the entire pipeline. The firm selected was ILF Consulting Engineers, based in Austria and Germany with offices worldwide, including Calgary.

ONGOING CONFLICT AND THE TAPI PIPELINE

Security has long been a major concern for the project. The route passes through Pashtun tribal areas in Afghanistan (Helmand and Kandahar) and Pakistan — the scene of so much US/NATO military activity. The Afghan government promised to protect the TAPI pipeline. In December 2015, the Minister of Mines and Petroleum, Daud Shah Saba, told Parliament that Afghanistan would raise a 7,000-member security force to guard the project.[46]

Can Afghan security forces really protect the pipeline? They are mostly Tajiks and other tribes from the north — foreigners in the Pashtun south. Afghanistan is highly tribal. The Taliban are mostly Pashtun people from the conservative rural south. There are well over 30 million Pashtuns, living on both sides of the Afghan-Pakistan border. It's an artificial border — the Durand Line imposed by British India in 1893. It was drawn intentionally to break up the Pashtun tribes; in fact, local tribespeople move back and forth.

The Taliban are still viewed by the US and NATO as the enemy. They are Islamic fundamentalists who are primarily concerned with local matters. Initially, many were students at Saudi-financed madrassas (religious schools) in Pakistan. They see the Kabul government as a puppet regime, beholden to foreigners. They object strongly to foreign occupation. The Taliban remain excluded from the Kabul government, even though they have strong support in the Pashtun south and east of Afghanistan, and the Pashtun represent well over 40 per cent of the nation's population.[47]

When the Taliban ruled Afghanistan, non-Pashtun ethnic groups (Tajik, Uzbek, Hazara) in the north continued to resist them. During the 2001 invasion of Afghanistan, the United States relied on these northern tribes. Western support has been mostly to northern tribes. As of 2018, the war was continuing.[48]

In this context, the United States made huge efforts to build up the Afghan National Army. Up until mid-2017, the US spent more than US$60 billion to develop, train and equip Afghan National Security Forces.[49] NATO countries also supported the Afghan National Army through a trust fund that exceeded US$1 billion.[50] The government of Afghanistan spends about 15 per cent of its GDP on security.[51] Most countries spend less than two per cent. Yet the security situation is not improving. General John Nicholson, commander of US forces in Afghanistan, told Congress in 2017 it was a stalemate.[52]

Under a Bilateral Security Agreement signed in 2014, the US committed to keep a residual force in Afghanistan for ten years. With the withdrawal of combat troops, the US relied heavily on special forces, drones, private military contractors and night raids — the "dark side" as former Vice-President Cheney once termed it.[53] NATO, too, was committed to continued support for Afghanistan which, in 2010, it declared to be an "enduring partner." For its part, Canada ended its military mission in 2014 but undertook to continue funding for the Afghan national security forces until 2017.[54] In 2016, Canada announced a new three-year package of CAD$465 million for the Afghan security forces, women's and girls' rights and empowerment, and the basic needs of Afghans.

NATO countries had individual soldiers who behaved gallantly and did good things like digging wells or escorting girls to school. Yet US/NATO practices such as extra-judicial killing, torture and drone attacks have generated unending bitterness — likewise the erroneous targeting of wedding parties and hospitals.

The war has taken its toll on soldiers too — mostly American but other nationals also. Since 2002, more than 2,400 US military were killed and more than 20,000 wounded as of April 30, 2017. In Canada's case, a total of 159 soldiers were killed, and at least 62 committed suicide upon return or retirement.[55] Post-traumatic stress disorder (PTSD) has also taken its toll. According to the *Globe and Mail*, nearly one in ten Canadian troops who went to Afghanistan are collecting disability benefits for PTSD, much higher than the rate in the general public. The prevalence of PTSD is likely much higher among combat troops.[56]

The war's cost to Afghan civilians has been very high. While there are no

Afghan children greeted Canadian Forces patrolling village near Kandahar, 2010.

official statistics, various independent organizations have published estimates. For instance, Brown University's Watson Institute tallied more than 104,000 Afghans killed in the war (to August 2016), of whom 31,000 were civilians (howsoever defined).[57]

As of 2018, security in Afghanistan remained precarious. The Taliban remain strong. Rumours of peace negotiations come and go, but peace itself is elusive. Meanwhile, out of 168 countries in the world, Afghanistan ranked 166 for graft and corruption.[58] How much of the billions spent has actually been used effectively and how much has been siphoned off by officials?

Can enough security be achieved to build and maintain the TAPI pipeline? As of June 2018, that question remains unanswered. In 2009, NATO's Secretary General, Jaap de Hoop Scheffer said: "NATO is not in the business of protecting pipelines. But when there's a crisis, or if a certain nation asks for assistance, NATO could, I think, be instrumental in protecting pipelines on land."[59] Are US/NATO troops staying on in part to protect the pipeline route?

Meanwhile, the unrest provided a convenient reason for US and NATO troops to remain. In early 2017, the US had roughly 15,000 troops there. NATO and other coalition allies had roughly 5,000. The US had at least nine major military bases in Afghanistan and an agreement to stay until

2024.[60] It has a long record of retaining bases and remaining in countries for many years beyond initial conflicts. It still had 113 bases in Japan 60 years after the end of World War II.[61]

In 2017, President Trump gave a green light to the US military to intensify efforts in Afghanistan. His emphasis was on killing "the bad guys." In April, with much fanfare, the US military dropped the largest conventional bomb ever designed, the Massive Ordnance Air Blast (MOAB) bomb (18,000 lbs. of explosive) on a cave-bunker complex near Tora Bora, in eastern Afghanistan. The complex was said to be occupied by Islamic State militants. It was originally constructed with CIA finance for the Mujahedin and subsequently used by Osama bin Laden prior to 9/11. Speaking shortly after, Trump said he was "very, very proud" of the US military for dropping the "mother of all bombs" on Afghanistan.[62] This contrasts with comments he made before taking office. In 2013, he tweeted: "Let's get out of Afghanistan. Our troops are being killed by the Afghanis we train and we waste billions there. Nonsense! Rebuild the USA."

In August 2017, President Trump announced he intended to win the war with "strategically applied force" aimed at creating "the conditions for a political process to achieve a lasting peace." He hoped "someday, after an effective military effort, perhaps it will be possible to have a political settlement that includes elements of the Taliban in Afghanistan, but nobody knows if or when that will ever happen." To achieve that aspiration, he authorized sending additional troops to Afghanistan for an unspecified period of time, with Defense Secretary Mattis having the authority to set troop levels. After 16 years, the strategy sounded like more of the same, a recipe for continued misadventure.

In February 2018, the US Lead Inspector General for Afghanistan issued a bleak report. US and Afghan government forces had made no progress in 2017 in expanding control of the country or forcing the Taliban to the peace table.[63] The Taliban controlled nearly half of the country. They successfully attacked targets in Kabul and other cities.

The Office of the Special Inspector General for Afghanistan Reconstruction (SIGAR) is the US government's oversight authority on Afghanistan reconstruction. Its quarterly reports to Congress are, in some ways, disarmingly frank. For a couple of years, they published detailed information on areas under government and insurgent control. In 2017, areas under Afghan government control were at their lowest level in two years.[64] The Pentagon found this an inconvenient truth and stopped releasing the data. SIGAR called this decision deeply troubling, as the data were some of the few indicators on how the 16-year war was faring.[65] Other key data on the Afghan National Defence and Security Forces had already been banned, such as casualties, personnel strength, attrition, capability assessments and operational readiness of equipment.

* * *

Despite massive amounts of assistance over 17 years, Afghanistan was still a dangerous place with frequent attacks and much unrest. The Pashtun, a major ethnic group, were underrepresented in government and in security forces. The Taliban, drawn largely from the Pashtun, remained strong in 2018. In February, President Ashraf Ghani offered talks with the Taliban without preconditions.[66] He avoided the contentious issue of US military bases staying in Afghanistan. He made the offer at an international conference attended by officials from more than 20 countries participating in a new peace initiative, the Kabul Process for Peace and Security Cooperation.[67] Participants included China, Russia and US (the Big Three); regional powers, most notably Iran and Pakistan; and NATO countries including Britain and Canada. The Taliban were conspicuously absent.[68]

Five days earlier, President Ghani officially inaugurated construction of the TAPI pipeline in Afghanistan. The Taliban made a crucial announcement. They stated the pipeline was an important economic project in the region,[69] and they would cooperate in providing security for the project in areas under their control.[70] They noted that talks on the pipeline dated back to the 1990s when they governed Afghanistan.

Why is Afghanistan so important? It is a pipeline transit country, but it is also part of a geopolitical strategy that asserts US power in Asia. Power, politics and petroleum go together. Perhaps these are the agenda Hamid Karzai alluded to in his farewell speech when he suggested, "the Americans did not want peace because they had their own agenda and objectives."[71]

CHAPTER 8
UKRAINE AND PIPELINE RIVALRY — TWO NARRATIVES

"We recognize the deep and complex history between Russia and Ukraine. But we cannot stand by when the sovereignty and territorial integrity of a nation is flagrantly violated."

—President Obama at the UN General Assembly[1]

"In Ukraine ... the military coup was orchestrated from outside — that triggered a civil war as a result."

—President Putin at the UN General Assembly[2]

During three fateful days — February 18–20, 2014 — shots rang out in the Maidan, Kiev's Independence Square. When the carnage was over, about 130 people were dead — including numerous civilian protestors and 18 policemen. In previous weeks, demonstrations had been a daily occurrence, mostly peaceful and focused on widespread government corruption. Ukraine was a country in financial crisis, torn between stop-gap solutions offered by the East (Russia) and the West (Europe). The three days of violence changed the course of Ukraine's history.

The next evening (February 21), Viktor Yanukovych, the democratically elected president, fled and a new interim government was installed immediately. Even so, the crisis continued. Sporadic clashes among Ukrainians and in eastern parts of the country became outright battles. As of 2018, Ukraine remained a divided country with a deep-seated economic crisis and ongoing battles causing death and destruction. Why?

Two narratives exist for what's going on — one espoused by governments in the United States and NATO countries, the other by the government of Russia. The different narratives are rooted in geopolitics and history and show up within Ukraine itself.

UKRAINE'S IMPORTANCE

Ukraine is a big country, almost as big as France or the US state of Texas. Located in east central Europe, Ukraine borders Belarus, Hungary, Moldova, Poland, Romania, Slovakia and Russia, as well as the Bay of Azer and the Black Sea. Its land border with Russia is more than 1,900 kilometres in length. From Uzhorod in the west (near Slovakia) to Donetsk in the east (near Russia) is 1,534 kilometres, farther than the distance between London, UK, and Budapest, Hungary. This enormous distance illustrates the difference between the east and west of the country. Donetsk looks to Moscow, about 1,000 kilometres away. Uzhorod looks to Frankfurt, just 1,300 kilometres to the west. Differences in history, geography, ecology and economy abound.

Ukraine is rich in natural resources — coal, iron ore, manganese, nickel, uranium, sulphur, mercury and much more. The eastern part of Ukraine is its industrial heartland, with several large cities, mining centres and heavy industrial production. Ukraine has reserves of building materials such as marble and graphite. Its abundant arable land produces wheat, barley, corn, sugar beet and sunflower. Ukraine has Europe's third largest reserves of shale gas (after Poland and France), according to the US Energy Information Administration. Shale reserves are in Ukraine's west and east, untapped as yet.

With the breakup of the Soviet Union in 1991, Ukraine achieved independence, but linguistic and trade links remained in place. Russia was its largest trading partner. Pipelines continued to supply Ukraine with Russian natural gas and to move it across Ukraine to the European grid. Ukraine's rich agricultural lands continued to provide food to Russia. The population in the eastern part of the country was content with the close economic ties to Russia. The population in the western part of Ukraine dreamed of closer association with Europe. These differences were reflected in election results for many years before the unrest began in 2013.

Russia and Ukraine have an ancient interlinked history. People from both nations regard ancient Rus as their cultural ancestor. President Putin has frequently said the Russians and Ukrainians are practically one people. Many Ukrainians, however, remember how Stalin forced collectivization on Ukrainian farmers in the 1930s, causing immense famine and death from starvation.

Russia saw its existing trade links with Ukraine as mutually beneficial. After 1991, the United States and European Union looked for *new* opportunities for investment and trade in the former Soviet republics. They put in place numerous initiatives to build new relationships. Ukraine is important to the US and European Union for one set of reasons, and important to Russia for other reasons. Within Ukraine, some people look west while others look east. Therein lie the two narratives. Understanding requires thinking about Ukraine from both perspectives.

UKRAINE'S TWO NARRATIVES — GEOPOLITICS AND PETROLEUM

This section examines Ukraine's two narratives with respect to geopolitics, internal politics and petroleum. The three dimensions explain recent conflicts that led Ukraine to be front page news for many weeks in 2014 and 2015. They also underlie major pipeline rivalry involving Russia, the United States and Europe.

The geopolitical dimension of the two narratives is long-standing. Since the breakup of the Soviet Union in December 1991, Washington has been seeking to dislodge Ukraine from its close association with Russia. Within seven months (July 1992), the United States Agency for International Development (USAID) launched a major aid program that continues to this day. Its stated goal is to create a market-based economy, help build a participatory democratic political system and assist social reforms to ease the transition.[3] By the mid-1990s, Ukraine was the fourth largest recipient of American assistance after Israel, Egypt and Russia.

In September 1992, Ukraine joined the International Money Fund (IMF) and World Bank and, with their financial support, initiated economic structural reforms including the privatization of state enterprises. In October 1992, Ukraine joined the European Bank for Reconstruction and

Development (EBRD), which had just been created to finance private sector projects in Eastern Europe and the former Soviet Union. The following year, it joined the International Finance Corporation (the World Bank's private sector arm).[4] Notwithstanding all these initiatives, Ukraine experienced economic disaster in the 1990s. By the end of the decade, gross domestic product (GDP) in real terms had dropped to 40 per cent of its 1990 level. The World Bank attributed the fall to the lack of incentives for private enterprise to flourish.[5]

On December 13, 2013, US Assistant Secretary of State for European and Eurasian Affairs Victoria Nuland told a US-Ukraine Foundation Conference in Washington, DC, that the United States had been helping Ukrainians advance democracy since 1991.[6] "We've invested over $5 billion to assist Ukraine in these and other goals that will ensure a secure and prosperous and democratic Ukraine," she said.

Democracy promotion has been a key component of US foreign policy for many years and has been applied in many countries with varying results. The more than US$5 billion allocated to Ukraine came from USAID and the Departments of Defense, Energy and Agriculture. In 2015, USAID spent US$21 million on democracy, human rights and governance in Ukraine. Its programs stretched deeply. They included civic activism, non-governmental organizations and independent media. They helped political parties develop platforms and policy agendas, and supported political training for many individuals.[7]

An active promoter of democracy in the Ukraine is the National Endowment for Democracy. This is a US non-profit, grant-making foundation funded through an annual appropriation from the US Congress through the Department of State. In recent years, it has spent millions of dollars in Ukraine supporting NGO initiatives that profess democracy promotion.[8] Its president, Carl Gershman, said in 2013: "Ukraine is the biggest prize ... Ukraine's choice to join Europe will accelerate the demise of the ideology of Russian imperialism that Putin represents."[9]

In 2013, the government of Ukraine was in dire financial straits and sought assistance from both Europe and Russia. The European Union offered a trade agreement and political association, together with loans tied to specific economic and social reforms and the release of a former prime minister, Yulia Tymoshenko, from prison. She had co-led the 2004 Orange Revolution and was prime minister of Ukraine in 2005 and 2007–2010. A summit meeting was set for November 28–29 in Vilnius, Lithuania, where Ukraine, Georgia and Moldova were to sign association and trade agreements with the European Union. At the last minute, November 21, President Yanukovych balked and declined to sign. He argued Ukraine could not afford to sacrifice trade with Russia, which opposed the deal. He also described the EU offer to lend Ukraine €610 million (US$828 million) as inadequate and said Ukraine would need at least €20 billion a year to upgrade its economy to European standards.[10]

Moscow offered a huge financial bail-out. On December 17, Presidents Yanukovych and Putin signed an action plan, under which Russia would buy US$15 billion of Ukrainian Eurobonds. In addition, the cost of Russian gas to Ukraine would be substantially discounted. According to Russian presidential press secretary Dmitry Peskov, this deal was "not tied to any conditions."[11] Seven days later, Russia's National Wealth Fund bought a US$3 billion Ukrainian Eurobond.[12]

Yanukovych's rejection of the European deal sparked anger among those in Ukraine who leaned toward Europe. The Maidan demonstrations began the same day. They grew larger and larger, with various demands — an end to government corruption, respect for human rights, closer integration with the European Union, the resignation of President Yanukovych. They were peaceful at first but became increasingly violent and confrontational. Several actions during the next three months suggest outside interference leading to the change of government in February 2014.

Washington openly supported the Maidan protesters. On December 10, 2013, the US Assistant Secretary of State Victoria Nuland, accompanied by the US Ambassador to Ukraine Geoffrey Pyatt, was at Independence Square, offering cookies to the Maidan protesters. Five days later, on December 15, Senator McCain arrived. He told protesters: "We are here to support your just cause, the sovereign right of Ukraine to determine its own destiny freely and independently. And the destiny you seek lies in Europe." He told CNN: "What we're trying to do is try to bring about a peaceful transition here."[13]

Assistant Secretary Nuland was caught in an open phone call on January 28, 2014, with Ambassador Pyatt. They were discussing which opposition leaders to support after Viktor Yanukovych's ouster, and how to "midwife this thing."[14] They favoured Arseniy Yatsenyuk, who indeed became prime minister in the new government. They didn't want Vitali Klitschko, a former heavyweight boxing champion and the EU's preference, Nuland saying "F*** the EU." The call, made three weeks before the change of government, was posted on YouTube and went viral.[15]

Ukrainian politics are highly polarized and regional. President Yanukovich came from the eastern city of Donetsk, and his Party of Regions (dissolved in 2014) derived support from the Russophile in the east and southeast. The opposition parties, in power as of June 2018, derived their main support from western Ukraine. In 2013, the two largest were the Fatherland Party, led by Yatsenyuk; and the Ukrainian Democratic Alliance for Reform (later merged into President Poroshenko's bloc), led by Klitschko.

Two smaller ultra-nationalist parties that played key roles in the Maidan demonstrations were the Svoboda (Freedom) Party, led by Olev Tyahnybok; and the Right Sector Party, then led by Dmytro Yarosh. According to the BBC, the Right Sector was the most radical group among the Maidan protesters. In early February 2014, Yarosh boasted the Right Sector had 500 fighters on Independence Square. He was an acolyte of Stepan Bandera, a nationalist leader who fought Polish and Soviet rule in the 1930s and 1940s. Bandera is viewed in Russia and eastern Ukraine as a Nazi collaborator.[16] Demonstration organizers created a group called Self-Defence of the Maidan to provide security and protect protesters from police. In charge was Andriy Parubiy, who once headed Svoboda's paramilitary wing, Patriots of Ukraine. Their symbol was the Wolf's Angel, closely associated with Nazism.

The Maidan demonstrations exploded on February 18, 2014. The night before, the Right Sector called on all its members to be ready for a "peace offensive." That morning, some 20,000 demonstrators marched on the Verkhovna Rada (Parliament building), broke through the police barricade and fought with police. During the next four days, the clashes went from bad to worse. Some 130 people were killed, including 18 police; and more than 1,100 people were injured. The worst day was February 20, with demonstrators and police exchanging gunfire, and snipers on the rooftops picking off both protestors and police.

Hoping to end the crisis, the foreign ministers of France, Germany and Poland visited Kiev on February 21 to broker a compromise with President Yanukovych and three opposition leaders — Klitschko, Yatsenyuk and Tyahnybok. They agreed to hold early presidential elections, form a national unity government and revert to the 2004 constitution, removing some presidential powers.[17] Putin made a revelation later. The very moment the compromise was reached, "our American partners called and asked us to do everything to ensure that Yanukovich didn't use the army, so the opposition could clear the squares and governmental buildings and go on towards implementing the agreement." Moscow agreed, only to see the situation escalate the next day into a full-fledged armed coup.[18]

When the three opposition leaders who had signed the agreement presented it to the Maidan demonstrators, two groups, Right Sector and Self-Defence of the Maidan, expressed dissatisfaction and demanded Yanukovych's immediate resignation. Maidan activists seized government buildings, and Yanukovych fled the capital in fear of his life.

Yanukovych's party, the Party of Regions, disintegrated, and the opposition parties took control. Parliament stripped Yanukovych of his presidential powers, withdrew troops and police to barracks, released Yulia Tymoshenko from prison and set elections for May 25. An interim government took over pending the elections. The US, Canada and European countries recognized the interim government immediately, even though Yanukovych had been elected democratically. President Putin called the events an anti-constitutional coup and an armed seizure of power.[19] Russia did not recognize the new government.

Who was responsible for the snipers? Each side blamed the other. Estonia's foreign minister, Urmas Paet, visited Kiev on February 25 to assess the situation. Back home the following day, he phoned the EU High Representative for Foreign Affairs, Catherine Ashton, to brief her on his findings. The conversation was leaked and appeared on the Internet.[20] He said Olga Bogomolets, a doctor treating casualties at the fighting, told him all the evidence showed the snipers were killing people from both sides, police and protesters alike. He surmised: "Behind [the] snipers, ... it was not Yanukovych, but it was somebody from the new coalition." Ashton commented: "I think we do want to investigate. I mean, I didn't pick that up. It's interesting. Gosh." Both were shocked by the violence.

In April 2014, the Polish left-wing weekly *Nie* published an eye-witness account of training in Poland given to the Right Sector two months before the Maidan protests started. According to this source, the training was at the invitation of Polish Foreign Minister Radoslaw Sikorski. In September 2013, 86 party members attended a Polish police centre for four weeks of intensive training in "crowd management, person recognition, combat tactics, command skills, behaviour in crisis situations, protection against gases used by police, erecting barricades, and especially shooting, including the handling of sniper rifles."[21] Why would members of a political party require such training? Who funded it?

In October 2014, a detailed study of the snipers' massacre was published by Ivan Katchanovski, a professor at the University of Ottawa. He analyzed a large amount of evidence from publicly available sources and concluded that the massacre was a false-flag operation, planned and carried out with a view to overthrowing the government and seizing power. He fingered an alliance of far-right organizations, specifically Right Sector and Svoboda, and oligarchic parties such as Fatherland. His study uncovered videos and photos of armed Maidan snipers and spotters in at least 20 Maidan-controlled buildings. Evidence also included many testimonies of Maidan protesters; comparisons of entry wounds and the locations of protesters killed; and bullet impact signs.[22]

BBC journalist Gabriel Gatehouse corroborated the study's conclusions a year later. He interviewed a protester named Sergei, who described how he was given a hunting rifle and escorted on February 20 to the Kiev Conservatory, a music academy on the square. There, Sergei spent some 20 minutes firing on police, alongside a second gunman. The riot police chief at the square phoned Andriy Shevchenko — a protester and opposition MP — and said, "Andriy, somebody is shooting at my guys ... from the Conservatory." Shevchenko contacted Andriy Parubiy, commandant of the Maidan, who promised to send men to the building and find if there were "any firing positions." Meanwhile the police chief kept phoning Shevchenko, "I have three people wounded, I have five people wounded, I have one person dead." Parubiy, who became chairman of the Ukrainian parliament in 2016, said his men found no gunmen in the Conservatory. Nonetheless, a photographer managed to enter and took pictures of gunmen. Sergei said he was reloading his rifle when men ran to him, told him to stop and bundled him out of town by car. He believed they were from Parubiy's security unit.[23]

In December 2017, new evidence on the shooting surfaced during the trial in Kiev of Berkut special police officers accused of killing civilians in February 2014 in the Maidan. The defence presented evidence from Georgian army snipers Alexander Revazishvili and Koba Nergadze, who confirmed the presence of at least 50 foreign snipers operating in teams.[24] Italian journalist Gian Micalessin had brought this evidence to light in November in the Italian journal *Il Giornale*[25] [26] and television Canale 5.[27] He reported the two Georgians and a third were sent from Tbilisi to Kiev and briefed by a uniformed former soldier of the US Army's 101st Airborne Division, Brian Christopher Boyenger. They were given weapons, placed in buildings overlooking the Maidan and joined by snipers from other countries, including Lithuania. On February 20, they were ordered to shoot indiscriminately at both police and demonstrators.

* * *

The political dimension of the two narratives relates to a tug-of-war for Ukraine's soul. The country is divided linguistically between Ukrainian speakers who tend to look west, and Russian speakers in the east who lean toward Russia. Ukrainians in the west have the support of the current government. Ukrainians in the east have close economic and cultural ties to Russia. Roughly speaking, the dividing line is the River Dnieper, which flows from north to south through the middle of Ukraine.

Ever since taking power in February 2014, the Kiev government failed to reach out to Russian speakers. The previous government, led by President

Yanukovych, was elected democratically with strong support from the eastern part of the country. The new government showed indifference and even hatred for people in the east.

The tinderbox was recognition of Russian as an official language. During the Soviet era, both Russian and Ukrainian were official languages. Ukraine's new constitution in 1996 made Ukrainian the sole official language, though other languages spoken in Ukraine were guaranteed constitutional protection. Russian speakers were unhappy. In 2012, when Yanukovych was president, new legislation granted Russian and other minority languages the status of a regional language that could be officially used in areas where the percentage of minorities exceeded ten per cent of the population. On February 23, 2014, just one day after the interim government assumed power, Parliament passed a bill to repeal the 2012 law and make Ukrainian the sole official language at all levels.

The damage was done. The bill caused immediate uproar in the east, southeast and Crimea, where much of the population spoke Russian as their native language. Eastern Ukrainians felt disenfranchised and threatened. Ten days later, on March 3, acting President Turchynov declared he would not sign the bill until a replacement law was adopted. He was too late.

Clashes erupted immediately after the bill was passed. Within a week, protesters against the new government held large rallies in the east (Kharkiv, Donetsk, Luhansk), southeast (Mariupol, Melitopol), south (Odessa) and Crimea (Kerch, Simferopol, Yevpatoria). A poll carried out by the International Foundation for Electoral Systems, in Washington, DC, and funded by USAID, found that 56 per cent of respondents in eastern Ukraine (80 per cent in Donetsk) considered the new government to be illegitimate, much higher than the national average of 33 per cent.[28] The unrest escalated, first in Crimea, then spreading through eastern Ukraine. The Kiev government lost control over much of the region. The elements of a civil war were in place. The United States was invested in the new government. Russia was concerned for its fellow Russian-speakers and its interests in Ukraine, including extensive trade and a long border.

Crimea deserves special attention because of its unique status. Crimea was an autonomous republic within Ukraine from 1954 to 2014, and within Russia before that. The allocation of Crimea to Ukraine was made by Soviet President Khrushchev. In 2001, 77 per cent of the Crimean population spoke Russian as their native language, 11 per cent Tatar and only ten per cent Ukrainian.[29] The Crimean port city of Sevastopol has been home to the Russian Black Sea fleet since 1784. Sevastopol is a crucial Russian naval base on the Black Sea. At the time of Ukraine's change of government, Russia was leasing Sevastopol under an agreement that extended to 2042.

Westerners may have forgotten the Crimean War (1853–1856), but Russians and residents of Crimea have not. The loss of life was immense; 25,000 British, 100,000 French and up to 1 million Russians died, almost all of disease and starvation.[30] Russians also remember the Siege of Sevastopol (1941–1942) when the Soviets held back the German army for eight months. Control of Crimea gives control of the Black Sea, a vital link between Russia and the Mediterranean.

In 2014, after the new government was installed in Kiev, Crimea quickly held a referendum. On March 16, the residents voted overwhelmingly to rejoin Russia. The official result was a 96.77 per cent vote for integration into Russia with an 83.1 per cent voter turnout. Given the high proportion of Russian speakers and the importance of Sevastopol, this was not surprising.

Russia responded by granting Crimea full integration as the Crimean Federal District. On March 18, two days after the referendum, President Putin said: "Those who opposed the [February 22] coup were immediately threatened with repression ... The residents of Crimea and Sevastopol turned to Russia for help in defending their rights and lives, in preventing the events that were unfolding and are still underway in Kiev, Donetsk, Kharkov and other Ukrainian cities." He pointed out that Russia's armed forces never entered Crimea; they were there already in line with an international agreement.[31] They came out of barracks to keep law and order because gangs from Kiev threatened security in Crimea.

Ukraine regarded the referendum and Crimea's return to Russia as a violation of international law. The anger in western Ukraine was huge. A typical attitude was that expressed by Yulia Tymoshenko in a leaked phone call on March 18: "This is really beyond all boundaries. It's about time we grab our guns and go kill those damn Russians together with their leader." If she were in charge, "there would be no f***ing way they would get Crimea then."[32]

When Crimea rejoined Russia in 2014, the US, Canada and UK accused Russia of being in breach of its obligations under the Budapest Memorandum signed in 1994. Under the Budapest Memorandum, the US, UK and Russia agreed to respect Ukraine's independence, sovereignty and existing borders.[33] Russia responded that the Memorandum did not apply. The Russian ambassador to the UK explained that Russia "did not make any commitment to force any region of Ukraine to remain a part of the country against the will of its people. Ukraine's loss of its territorial integrity was a result of complicated internal processes ..."[34]

The West referred to what happened as annexation. Russia pointed to historical precedent indicating the Crimean people were entitled to self-determination. Two days before the referendum, Foreign Minister Lavrov compared it to independence referenda taken earlier with Western support in Kosovo, the Falklands (Malvinas) and Comoros. He emphasized: "For Russia, Crimea means immeasurably more than the Falklands mean for Britain or the Comoros for France."[35] Within Russia, a 2016 poll showed 88 per cent support for Crimea's "accession" to Russia. Only 5 per cent opposed it.[36] In January 2015, Germany's biggest market research organization, GfK, conducted a poll in Crimea and found 82 per cent of those polled said they fully supported Crimea's inclusion in Russia, 11 per cent expressed partial support and only two per cent said no.[37]

Russia would never give up its access routes to the Mediterranean by allowing Crimea to become home to NATO. Russia had already been evicted from Georgia — another former Soviet state and home to Russian troops for two centuries. Georgia terminated Russia's last base in 2007 and became an aspirant NATO country in 2011.[38] By comparison, Britain has held Gibraltar since 1704, and the United States has retained Guantánamo since 1898. Would either of those Western countries give them back? Referendum and annexation have become two more words representing the difference in view between Russia and the West. Russia's reaction with respect to Crimea would have been easy to anticipate in the West. Was Crimea a convenient excuse for sanctions against Russia?

On March 6, President Obama ordered sanctions, including travel bans and the freezing of US assets, against individuals (unnamed at the time) who had "asserted governmental authority in the Crimean region without the authorization of the Government of Ukraine." Two weeks later, the US, together with European Union, Canada and Japan, identified specific individuals for sanctioning. That was one day after the Crimean referendum and a few hours before President Putin signed a decree recognizing Crimea as an independent state.

The next month, CIA Director John Brennan visited Kiev for undisclosed discussions. Citing unnamed German security sources, the German newspaper *Bild am Sonntag* reported on May 5 that dozens of specialists from the US Central Intelligence Agency and Federal Bureau of Investigation were helping the Kiev government end the rebellion and set up a functioning security structure.[39]

In eastern and southern Ukraine, protests escalated upon Crimea's rejoining Russia. Police and military overwhelmed protesters in cities closer to Kiev; but protests in the Donetsk and Luhansk oblasts (administrative districts) escalated into an armed insurgency. These two oblasts adjoin Russia at Ukraine's eastern border and cover an area known as the Donbass (Donets coal Basin), an important industrial and coal-mining area. Historically, culturally and linguistically, the Donbass is highly Russian. The former President Yanukovych and his Party of Regions had their political base in the Donbass.

Insurgency leaders declared the creation of the Donetsk People's Republic on April 7, and the Luhansk People's Republic on April 27. The next day, the US banned various Russian officials and companies from business within American territory. The list included Igor Sechin, executive chairman of the state oil company Rosneft, though not the company itself. That was despite BP holding shares of almost 20 per cent in Rosneft, and despite ExxonMobil (US), Statoil (Norway) and ENI (Italy) partnering with Rosneft in exploration offshore the Russian Arctic.[40] The same day, April 28, the European Union and Canada followed suit. Western countries accused Russia of supporting the activists in eastern Ukraine — a claim denied by Moscow.[41]

Despite Western actions against Russia, Donetsk and Luhansk held referenda on May 11, and voters chose autonomy from Ukraine. On May 24, the republics merged into a confederation known as Novorossiya (New Russia). The new Ukrainian government regarded the confederation to be a terrorist organization. Western countries called the referenda illegal. The Russian government expressed respect for the results and urged a civilized implementation.

The Ukraine government made no attempt to reach out to its eastern citizens. Instead, it deployed the military to subjugate the Donbass, using airplanes, heavy artillery and tanks. It was supported by far-right volunteer militia such as the Azov Battalion and the Right Sector. The people of Donbass suffered repeated bombardment, with heavy destruction of housing, industry and airports. According to UN statistics, the conflict resulted in more than 6,000 dead, 17,000 injured and 2.3 million people displaced. More than 1.1 million people from the Donbass fled to Russia.[42] During this period, Russia provided numerous shipments of food and humanitarian aid. The shipments were announced publicly in advance and long convoys of trucks painted white brought food and medical supplies into the Donbass.

The growing hatred and mistrust were not confined to the Donbass. The southern port city of Odessa experienced continuous unrest, culminating in a horrific incident on May 2, when six pro-government protesters and at least 42 anti-government protesters were killed and over 200 people injured in violent clashes. The pro-government protesters were augmented by thousands of right-wing soccer fans visiting Odessa for a soccer match. Activists opposed to the new government had set up a tent city in Kulikovo Pole square. They wanted Ukraine to adopt a federal, instead of unitary, constitution. The two groups clashed. Pro-government gangs set fire to the tent city and drove hundreds of pro-federation protesters into the Trade Unions Building bordering the square. Subsequently, the building was set on fire, each side accusing the other of throwing petrol bombs.

Whatever the truth, many died inside or were beaten trying to escape. The police were inactive and the fire service slow to arrive. The shockwaves

On May 2, 2014, major clashes in Odessa, Ukraine, resulted in death of at least 42 people and over 200 injured.

reverberated throughout southern and eastern Ukraine. The Council of Europe delivered a report, criticizing Ukrainian authorities for their poor investigation[43] and faulting the police for complicity in mass disorder.[44] But none of those involved in the massacre was prosecuted.

People in the Donbass region of eastern Ukraine boycotted the presidential election on May 25, 2014, when President Poroshenko took office. Thus, they remained unrepresented in the new Kiev parliament. Poroshenko continued the interim government's hard line, making ill-founded accusations and outright war on the Donbass region.

Again, there were two narratives. The Kiev government and the West emphasized Russian meddling without providing evidence. They called the people in the Donbass Russian-supported rebels or terrorists. Russia said the Russian speakers in Ukraine had legitimate grievances and had been treated badly by the new Kiev government. Russia pointed to a previous pattern of easy migration back and forth for years and intermarriage between Ukrainians and Russians. It said some volunteer soldiers from Russia had chosen to support their kin in the Donbass.[45]

Then came the downing of Malaysian airliner MH-17 on July 17, 2014, in eastern Ukraine. It was another case of two narratives. Washington immediately accused Russia, without revealing any evidence from radar, satellite or air traffic control. The Russians immediately released radar data that was essentially ignored by the West. The same day, July 17, Washington expanded its sanctions to include two Russian petroleum companies (Rosneft and Novatek) and two banks. European governments lined up with Washington, as did Australia, Canada and Japan. Sanctions excluded Russia's Gazprom, a vital supplier of gas to Europe. On September 12, the US and EU imposed additional sanctions on Russia's financial, petroleum and defence sectors.

Europe imposed sanctions on Russia with evident reluctance. It was a reversal of 50 years of defusing European-Russian relations through trade and investment, notably in oil and gas. In a speech at Harvard University on October 3, 2014, US Vice-President Joe Biden revealed America's leadership had "to embarrass Europe to stand up and take economic hits to impose costs" on Russia; "it is true they did not want to do that." He said Putin had a simple choice: "respect Ukraine's sovereignty or face increasing consequences."[46]

Russia countered with a total ban on food imports from the United States, Canada, EU, Norway and Australia. Russia also imposed retaliatory sanctions on specific officials of those countries, banning them from entering Russia. The list of Canadians comprised parliamentarians from the three main federal parties, including Chrystia Freeland (foreign minister since January 2017) and Andrew Scheer (Conservative party leader since May 2017).

Sanctions have weakened the economies of both Russia and Europe. The French, for instance, had to cancel a contract in 2014 to deliver two Mistral aircraft-carriers to Russia. Polish apple growers, previously the world's largest apple exporters, struggled to find customers to replace the Russian market. Russian manufacturers and farmers, too, suffered initially but later appeared to be benefiting from import substitution and new overseas trading partners. As of 2018, the sanctions remained in place, though numerous politicians and business leaders in Europe have expressed the wish to end them and President Trump has doubted their worth.

As the situation escalated during 2014, President Obama made clear that NATO actions should avoid starting a war with Russia.[47] Nonetheless, US

General Breedlove, then supreme commander of NATO in Europe, sought insider assistance in Washington to build up military support for Ukraine. He claimed the Russians were planning a large-scale invasion of Ukraine. For its part, the Kiev government hired Washington lobbyists to persuade Congress to authorize the sale of sophisticated weapons for use against the Donbass.

The picture for Ukrainians opposing the Kiev government was grim. A series of assassinations and so-called suicides of opposition politicians and journalists occurred in the first four months of 2015.[48] Ukrainian leaders blamed the Russian secret service.[49] Russian media intimated Ukrainian special services were behind the assassinations, with NATO technical support.[50]

What was going on was essentially a civil war. Pressured by France, Germany and Russia, representatives of Ukraine, Russia, Donetsk People's Republic and Lugansk People's Republic met in Minsk, Belarus, in September 2014 and again in February 2015, signing agreements intended to stop the fighting. The agreements called for an immediate and full bilateral ceasefire, the withdrawal of all heavy weapons by both sides, and constitutional reform in Ukraine with decentralized special status for Donetsk and Luhansk.[51] The new constitution was intended to clear the way for local elections in Donetsk and Luhansk, and full Ukrainian government control over the border with Russia. A group of four countries (France, Germany, Russia and Ukraine), known as the Normandy contact group, has been meeting periodically to review progress since 2014.

During the next three years, the Ukrainian parliament failed to enact a new constitution, and left most of the agreement's other provisions unfulfilled. For this, Western leaders blamed Russia, though how Russia could influence the Ukrainian government was hard to imagine. European leaders were silent about the provocative actions of the US, UK and Canada, who were providing military training and equipment to the Kiev government. As well, NATO was building missile bases in Romania and Poland and conducting military exercises in the Black Sea and in Baltic countries, actions that Russia viewed as provocative.

At Washington's insistence, the sanctions against Russia remained in place, but Europeans showed increasing signs of discontent with their repeated renewal. The economic impact on the United States is minimal, but their impact on economies in Europe is substantial. The very real divisions within Ukraine are rarely discussed by politicians or media in the West, who prefer to denigrate Putin.

* * *

The petroleum dimension of the two narratives evolved because all countries want reliable trading partners and secure trade routes. At the heart of the Western narrative is a concern for buying natural gas from diverse sources, to limit the dependence of EU countries on Russia. Diversity of sources helps assure both reliability and security. If one source is blocked, another can be used.

At the heart of the Russian narrative is a concern for diverse routes for the sale of natural gas to EU economies. Diversity of routes helps assure both reliability and security. Without reliability, there can be no security of income from sales of oil and gas, Russia's major source of foreign exchange. Ukraine has become an insecure route, plagued by corruption and payment disputes. Russia wants to limit or discontinue dependence on Ukraine by building pipelines to bypass the country.

Both the Western and the Russian narratives have long-standing back-stories relating to market share and geopolitical struggles between East and West. In the 1960s, the pipelines traversing Ukraine were expanded to supply natural gas to Western Europe. Ukraine became the major pipeline route for Russian gas. At the time, Ukraine and Russia were both within the Soviet Union, so it was, in effect, Soviet natural gas coming from various parts of the Soviet Union. The arrangement was beneficial to all. European countries had abundant coal, but moved to oil and increasingly to natural gas for industrial purposes, electric power generation and residential use. Soviet supplies met the increased demand.

Germany and Italy were the first countries in Western Europe to step out front and import Soviet oil and gas. Their view was that energy security derived from a diversity of energy sources. Soon, more countries imported Soviet oil and gas — and nothing dire happened. Eastern European countries were already receiving Soviet oil and gas. The Soviet Union, with its immense petroleum reserves, was glad to supply Western Europe's growing market.

Map 19. Transit Pipelines Through Ukraine

Beginning in the 1960s, Ukraine provided the main pipeline transit routes for Russian gas to reach Europe.

American and European oil companies, including BP where I was working, watched the market changes closely. How would new Soviet imports of oil and gas affect their business? Western companies were major marketers of oil products in Europe refined from Middle Eastern crude. As it turned out, the binding of East and West by pipeline helped build trust. It was a precursor to the Soviet policy of Glasnost (openness) under President Gorbachev (1988–1991).

From the outset, Washington opposed this East-West energy trade on grounds of energy security. It saw Moscow as the enemy and argued that dependence on Soviet oil and gas was risky. This view was latent for many years but surfaced again under the George W. Bush and Obama Administrations, where high-level officials were hyping a New Cold War.

As of 2018, the pipelines traversing Ukraine continued to provide revenue from transit fees — more than US$2 billion per year.[52] This revenue was significant income for the economy, but the country had not managed the revenue prudently. Ukraine's national oil and gas company, Naftogaz, had long been regarded as one of the nation's biggest sources of corruption.

176

Various oligarchs have made their fortune by exploiting the differences between prices of gas imports, gas exports and energy subsidies to households and industry.[53]

Since 2005, several serious disputes have erupted between Ukraine's Naftogaz and Russia's Gazprom. A major issue was the failure of Naftogaz to pay for supplies to the local market and the diversion of transit gas that Gazprom intended for EU customers. For a few days in January of 2006 and 2009, Gazprom cut off all gas supplies passing through Ukraine until reaching agreement with Naftogaz. European nations were understandably unhappy with these disruptions.

Ukraine has several big problems that have contributed to its unreliability as a transit route. First, it has a long history of corruption. Transparency International ranks Ukraine 142 out of 174 countries.[54] Second, it is virtually bankrupt. Third, it has had long disputes with Russia over gas price and payments issues. When both countries were part of the Soviet Union, Ukraine received preferential treatment and reduced prices. After Ukraine became an independent country, Russia wanted it to pay full market price like any other European country. Ukraine balked, wanting the benefits of independence *and* special treatment from Russia. From 2010 onward, Russia began charging full market price.

After the change of government in 2014, Ukraine's financial crisis deepened. By non-payment and late payment for gas supplies, Ukraine built up an enormous debt. According to Gazprom, it reached US$4.5 billion by June 2014, after which Russia required prepayment for all new supplies. Ukraine used European Union and International Money Fund (IMF) loans to meet outstanding debts. The EU and IMF hoped the proposed privatization of Ukraine's gas sector might cure its problems.

In 2015, Ukraine stopped buying Russian gas directly for its internal market and began purchasing "reverse" supplies of Russian gas from Slovakia, Hungary and Poland. Deliveries from these countries were the same fuel that Ukraine could have obtained directly from Russia at lower prices. Russian gas exports to other European countries continued to transit Ukraine.

Within Ukraine itself, the development of shale reserves has been of interest to international companies. Ukraine signed production-sharing agreements in 2013 with Chevron (US), ENI (Italy) and Shell (Anglo-Dutch).

After the change of government and the ensuing unrest, Chevron and Shell pulled out in 2015, leaving behind ENI and a Ukrainian company, Burisma. The latter is Ukraine's largest private gas distribution company. One of its board directors, appointed in 2014, was Hunter Biden, son of former US Vice-President Joe Biden — the Obama Administration's point man on Ukraine.

Before the change of government, Ukraine had signed agreements for offshore exploration in the Black Sea — with ExxonMobil in 2012 and Italy's ENI in 2013. Crimea's assimilation into Russia implies that extensive offshore resources in the Black Sea may now belong to Russia but, with sovereignty over Crimea still disputed, ExxonMobil and ENI have yet to initiate further exploration there. ENI does have plans to drill elsewhere in the Black Sea jointly with Russia's Rosneft.

The petroleum dimension of the two narratives for the Ukraine crisis arose because Russia began to see Ukraine as an unreliable transit route for Russian gas. Some European countries agreed with Russia. Others, supported by the European Commission, sought alternate sources to reduce dependence on Russian supplies.

Overall, the two narratives are reflected in the words used by leaders and media in the West and in Russia. Washington says Ukraine is about democracy, that a new government was needed and Putin is meddling. Russia points to Washington's involvement in a coup in February 2014 and the presence of neo-Nazis in the Kiev government. NATO said it must expand to protect countries such as Estonia, Latvia and Lithuania from Russian threats. Russia asked what threats? Putin asserted repeatedly that he had no plans to invade other countries.

Canada's Conservative and Liberal governments had both been outspoken in support of Ukraine. The Liberal Foreign Minister Chrystia Freeland told Parliament in 2017: "The illegal seizure of Ukrainian territory by Russia is the first time since the end of the Second World War that a European power has annexed by force the territory of another European country. This is not something we can accept or ignore ... Russian military adventurism and expansionism pose clear strategic threats to the liberal democratic world, including Canada."[55]

Since 2015, Canada had deployed some 200 soldiers in Ukraine to provide training for the Ukrainian military. The mission fell under a Multinational Joint Commission comprising Canada, Ukraine, Britain and the United States. Other European countries eschewed military involvement. As of December 2017, the Joint Commission had trained more than 5,100 Ukrainian soldiers. Since 2017, Canadian forces were no longer restricted to western Ukraine, as long as they stayed away from the Russian border and the fighting in eastern Ukraine. Their focus was on tactical training, including marksmanship, weapons training, survival in combat and military police training. The stated intent was to help Ukraine remain sovereign, secure and stable.

Since 2017, the US and Canada have also been supplying lethal weapons to Kiev. They had previously supplied nonlethal military aid such as radar equipment and night-vision goggles. In 2017, the Trump Administration approved delivery of sniper systems and expressed willingness to supply "enhanced defensive capabilities" including anti-tank missiles. A State Department spokeswoman averred such assistance was "entirely defensive in nature."[56]

Ottawa followed in Washington's footsteps. The Canada-Ukraine Defence Cooperation Arrangement, signed in 2017, allowed Ukraine access to Canadian technology in precision-guided munitions and target identification systems, as well as communications and night-vision equipment. Foreign Minister Freeland avowed Canada "will continue to stand with the people of Ukraine and support Ukraine's territorial integrity and sovereignty."[57] The Ukrainian Canadian Congress welcomed the decision, asserting the weapons would contribute to Ukraine's ability to defend itself against Russia's ongoing invasion.[58] Ukraine matters politically to Canada. Canada is home to 1.3 million people of full or partial Ukrainian origin (the majority being Canadian-born citizens). They are Canada's ninth largest ethnic group. Canada has the world's third largest Ukrainian population, after Ukraine itself and Russia.

Russian diplomats protested that pumping Ukraine full of American and Canadian weapons would push Kiev toward "reckless new military decisions."[59] The deadlock between Washington and Moscow continued into 2018, with peace remaining elusive. The Western idea that military conquest could win hearts and minds in the Donbass is preposterous. More likely the idea was to entrap Russia in an intolerable quagmire.

PIPELINE RIVALRY AND GEOPOLITICS

The two narratives regarding Ukraine are embodied in wide-ranging geopolitical rivalry involving Russia, the United States and Europe. The key questions relate to sources of natural gas and pipeline routes: Who will supply gas to European markets? In what quantities? By what routes? The answers will be found in myriad diplomatic and military efforts to influence the course of history.

Pipelines are important today in the same way that railway building was important in the nineteenth century. They connect trading partners and they influence the regional balance of power. That's why they are so vital in understanding the geopolitics. When a pipeline crosses more than one country, each country becomes a stakeholder. The countries are bonded together physically, economically and diplomatically.

Europe offers a giant market. As the world's largest importing region for natural gas, its consumption has grown by leaps and bounds in the past five decades. Gas quickly replaced coal and oil in central heating, petrochemical manufacture and other uses. Europe's appetite for gas was met by the North Sea, North Africa and Russia. The European gas market is mature and supported by an extensive pipeline network. Since gas output from the North Sea began to decline, the largest source of gas to Europe is Russian. Just three countries — Russia, Iran and Qatar — have almost half the world's gas reserves. All have abundant natural gas for Europe. Russia has been planning new pipelines to bring its gas to Europe, bypassing Ukraine. Iran and Qatar were in the early stages of planning pipelines through Syria when they were stymied by the Syrian conflict.

Since the early 1990s, the United States has vigorously promoted new pipelines from the Caspian Sea to Europe. The new pipelines avoid passing through Russian territory, even though their route is therefore longer and more costly. The routing appears to be politically driven. Two are now open, bringing oil and gas from the Caspian offshore Azerbaijan through Georgia to Turkey. Oil and gas pipelines often run along parallel routes. The Baku-Tbilisi-Ceyhan oil pipeline, completed in 2005, terminates at Turkey's Mediterranean port of Ceyhan. The line is owned by an international consortium, of which BP is the largest shareholder. The South

Caucasus gas pipeline, completed in 2006, runs parallel as far as central Turkey. There it joins the Turkish gas grid.

The European Commission and US Administration backed an ambitious project from Turkey to Italy, the so-called Southern Gas Corridor. This comprised three interconnecting pipelines: the South Caucasus Pipeline, just described; the Trans-Anatolian Pipeline under construction across Turkey; and the Trans-Adriatic Pipeline under construction across Greece, Albania and the Adriatic Sea to Italy. The three pipeline companies have diverse shareholders, but BP and Azerbaijan's SOCAR have shareholding in all three pipelines. BP is also the operator for the consortium developing the offshore field. Not surprisingly, the British government is a big endorser of the Southern Gas Corridor and supports BP's effort strongly, as the UK ambassador to Azerbaijan told media in 2016.[60]

The European Commission eyed other sources of gas that an expanded Southern Gas Corridor could transport to Europe. One possibility was the Levantine (Cyprus and Israel) gas basin recently discovered in the East Mediterranean Sea. The US has been supportive. Visiting Cyprus in May 2014, Vice-President Joe Biden said: "Cyprus is poised to become a key

Map 20. Southern Gas Corridor

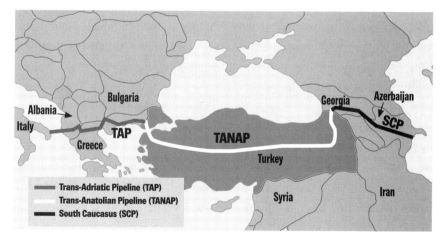

The Southern Gas Corridor (three inter-connecting pipelines built or under construction as of 2018) is designed to bring gas from Azerbaijan to Turkey, the Balkans and Italy, bypassing Russia.

player ... transforming the eastern Mediterranean into a new global hub for natural gas."[61]

In April 2017, the EU Energy Commissioner Miguel Arias Cañete met in Tel Aviv with energy ministers from Israel, Greece, Cyprus and Italy to discuss the East Mediterranean's gas potential for Europe. He believed it would offer a vital role in the EU's energy security in the next decades, and stated the European Commission strongly supported construction of the necessary energy infrastructure and developing a competitive market in the region.

The East Mediterranean could become an area of conflict. Israel and Lebanon dispute the offshore border between the two countries. In February 2018, Lebanon granted exploration rights in the contested waters to a consortium comprising France's Total, Italy's ENI and Russia's Novatek. The same month, Turkish warships stopped an Italian drill-ship on its way to a gas field offshore Cyprus. In March, the US Navy increased its Mediterranean fleet just before ExxonMobil sent two surveying vessels to explore offshore southern Cyprus.

The European market is big — but not big enough to accept every project. There will be winners and losers — and since the payoff in wealth is huge, there are intense rivalries.

In its search for reliable trading routes, Russia has made numerous efforts to diversify its pipelines to Europe so as to bypass Ukraine. These efforts are described in turn — Nord Stream, Nord Stream 2, South Stream and Turkish Stream. Only the first of these has so far led to construction of a pipeline. The unfolding of events illustrates how geopolitics is involved with pipelines and petroleum.

Nord Stream is a pipeline system built under the Baltic Sea directly to northern Germany. It is owned and operated by Nord Stream AG, a joint venture of Russia's Gazprom with German, Dutch and French companies. At 1,200 kilometres in length, it was the world's longest marine pipeline system as of 2018. It has throughput capacity of 55 BCM per year and comprises two parallel lines, the first commissioned in 2011 and the second in 2012. The gas, upon arrival at the import terminal, is delivered to two transmissions systems. One runs westward across northern Germany toward the Netherlands. The other runs south through Germany and connects with lines to Poland and the Czech Republic.

Map 21. Nord Stream Pipeline

The Nord Stream pipeline brings gas from Russia under the Baltic Sea to Germany. The disputed Nord Stream 2 is planned along a parallel route.

Nord Stream 2 is a new project parallelling Nord Stream, to bring a similar amount of gas under the Baltic Sea to Germany. In 2015, Gazprom signed a memorandum of intent with Shell, French, German and Austrian companies to form a new joint venture to implement the project.[62] Strategically, the project is significant. It would make Germany the main gateway for Russian gas to Europe and reduce Ukraine's importance as a transit country.

German politicians and German businesses are happy with Nord Stream 2. Eastern European countries are not, some because they derive transit fees from gas received from pipelines through Ukraine and others because they were hoping for transit fees from alternative new routes.

The US wants to kill the project. At a joint US-EU energy meeting in Washington, DC, on May 4, 2016, Secretary of State John Kerry said the Nord Stream 2 pipeline was a specific issue of deep concern for the US and EU. He was convinced it would "have an adverse impact on Ukraine, on Slovakia, and Eastern Europe."[63] Earlier, at a conference in Slovakia on November 5, 2015, the US Deputy Assistant Secretary for Energy Diplomacy Robin Dunnigan said Nord Stream 2 "threatens not only Ukraine's viability and their resources but is a risk to real diversification in Europe, especially in central and southeastern Europe."[64] She said cutting off all gas transit through Ukraine would deprive it of US$2 billion in annual revenue. "Why would you support Ukraine with one hand and strangle it with the other?"[65]

Later, on November 26, 2015, seven Eastern European countries, led by Poland, wrote to the European Commission, claiming Nord Stream 2 could have serious consequences for Ukraine and EU nations, and saying the route through Ukraine was in the strategic interest of the EU as a whole.[66] The signatories were Estonia, Latvia, Lithuania, Poland, Slovakia, Hungary and Romania. Slovakia's minister of economy said his country would lose up to US$400 million annually in transit fees if Nord Stream 2 went ahead. However, three other countries — Bulgaria, Czech Republic and Greece — declined to sign.

Poland already has one transit pipeline, named Yamal, bringing 33 BCM yearly from Russia through Belarus and Poland to Germany. At one time, Russia was considering a parallel pipeline, Yamal-2, but decided instead to build Nord Stream. On January 4, 2016, Poland's Foreign Minister Witold Waszczykowski declared: "We would like future gas pipelines from Russia to Western Europe to run through Polish territory."[67] Poland also seeks to diversify its sources of gas. It opened an LNG terminal in 2016 to receive monthly shipments of gas from Qatar, and it was contemplating an underwater pipeline to import Norwegian gas via Denmark. The two projects look politically driven, and whether they are cost competitive with Russian gas is open to question.

Poland adamantly opposed Nord Stream 2. With some consortium partners also marketing gas locally in Poland, the Polish competition agency ruled in 2016 the project could restrict competition and strengthen Gazprom's dominance in the local market.[68] Following the ruling, Gazprom's five European partners withdrew from the joint venture and researched alternative ways to contribute to the project.[69] In April 2017, they announced they would secure financing for 50 per cent of the project cost, with Gazprom becoming the sole shareholder of the project company.

The rift between European countries on Nord Stream 2 is reflected within the EU's secretariat. The European Commission has been seeking to insert itself into the pipeline negotiations. It has admitted it does not like the project politically but has no legal grounds to oppose it. In 2017, it failed to obtain a mandate from member countries to negotiate a special legal framework with Russia. Nord Stream 2 was an offshore project to which the Third Energy Package did not apply. In November, it proposed amended legislation to apply internal market rules (its Third Energy Package) to gas pipelines entering EU territory.[70] It would allow member countries to make exceptions for existing pipelines such as Nord Stream 1 and the Southern Gas Corridor. Whether the European Council would approve the amendment (clearly aimed at Nord Stream 2) remained an open question. With Austria, France, Germany and the Netherlands backing the pipeline, it seemed doubtful.

The next hurdle was US legislation passed in August 2017, codifying into law sanctions on Iran, North Korea and Russia previously imposed by presidential executive order. The codification made the sanctions far harder to lift. The law empowered the US to impose sanctions on European firms if they financed or participated in Russian energy export pipelines, and to fine European companies if they breached US law.[71] With this threat to Nord Stream 2's financing, one of the project participants, OMV of Austria, stated the project's management may look to Asian and Russian banks rather than European or American.

Before Trump signed, Germany and Austria protested vigorously. On June 15, 2017, the German foreign minister and Austrian chancellor wrote jointly: "To threaten to punish companies in Germany, Austria and other European nations if they participate in or finance natural gas projects such as Nord Stream 2 with Russia introduces a completely new and very negative quality into European-American relations ... Europe's energy supply is a matter for Europe, not for the United States of America!" They asserted the bill was an illegal attempt to boost US LNG exports to Europe by displacing Russian gas, and political sanctions should not be linked to economic interests.[72]

The European Commission followed up. Its President Jean-Claude Juncker warned on July 26 the new measures could harm European energy security, and the EU was ready to retaliate within days if European companies were punished for working with Russia on energy projects.[73] The Commission was reportedly considering statutes to make US extraterritorial decisions unenforceable within the European Union.

The Europeans had a legitimate fear. US fracking was causing a tidal wave of gas production, and LNG export terminals were being built apace on the US Gulf of Mexico. The first of them opened in 2016 — at Sabine Pass, Louisiana.[74] Its owner, Cheniere Energy, has been shipping LNG worldwide, including to Poland and Lithuania. By 2020, the US could become the world's third largest LNG exporter, after Qatar and Australia.

Since 2015, Poland has been advocating a Three Seas Initiative that would promote imports of US LNG in place of Russian gas. The initiative, strongly supported by Washington, would unite Central and Eastern European countries between the Baltic, Adriatic and Black Seas through regional trade and infrastructure. At a Three Seas summit in Warsaw in July 2017, President Trump asserted the initiative would transform the region, and he congratulated Poland on receiving its first shipment of US LNG.[75] He didn't want to see Poland and its neighbours ever again "held hostage to a single supplier of energy."[76]

Whether or not US gas proved competitive with Russian gas (a moot point), the new American law had the potential to nix Nord Stream 2 and shoehorn in American gas. The petroleum rivalry is acute — it smacks of economic warfare.

South Stream was another joint venture, this time planned to go under the Black Sea to Bulgaria and on to Austria, passing through Serbia, Hungary and Slovenia. The offshore section was to be built and operated by a joint venture of Russia's Gazprom and French, German and Italian companies; and the onshore section by joint ventures of Gazprom and local companies.

The project was first announced in 2007, when Italy's ENI and Russia's Gazprom signed a memorandum of understanding to build the pipeline. In 2009, the gas companies of Russia, Bulgaria, Greece, Italy and Serbia agreed to take part in the pipeline. The agreements predated the European Union's Third Energy Package by a few months. Construction was set to start in 2014. South Stream received its first batch of offshore pipes in May and planned to have a pipe-laying vessel start work in the autumn at the Bulgarian port of Burgas. On May 27, Bulgaria awarded construction of its onshore section to a consortium of local firms and Russia's Stroytransgaz. Then geopolitics intervened.

On June 3, the European Commission questioned whether Bulgaria had complied with EU procurement law[77] and, pending answers, requested

Bulgaria to suspend work.[78] The Commission also questioned South Stream's overall compliance with the EU's policies embodied in its Third Energy Package. In contrast, the Commission had granted the rival Trans-Adriatic Pipeline a 25-year exemption from the Third Energy Package.[79] The exemption meant Gazprom could not require Trans-Adriatic Pipeline to carry Russian gas to market.[80]

Bulgaria initially balked. Five days later, on June 8, 2014, US Senator McCain and colleagues turned up in Sofia and met with Bulgaria's Prime Minister Oresharski. One hour later, Bulgaria announced a halt to construction works and promised they would resume only after consultations with Brussels.[81]

The US is not a member of the European Union but takes a strong interest in European energy policy and collaborates with the European Commission. The US and EU have a joint Energy Council that has met annually since 2009. At its seventh meeting in May 2016, Secretary of State John Kerry said the Council was created because energy was "an issue of strategic importance to the United States." The US State Department has a Special Envoy and Coordinator for International Energy Affairs. Many other officials at the State Department follow energy developments all over the world, intervening to help countries the US deems to be friends and stymie other countries seen as enemies or non-supporters of US interests.

When South Stream was put on hold at such a late date in the planning timetable, Russia interpreted it as an event orchestrated by the European Union and the United States. A Russian diplomat called it "an underhanded economic sanction thrust on Russia by the West."[82] Russian leaders visited South Stream countries, who declared continued support for the project. They were too late. With no resolution in sight, Russia took a new approach.

Turkish Stream became Russia's fourth attempt to develop a pipeline bypassing Ukraine. In December 2014, at a press conference in Ankara with Prime Minister Erdoğan, President Putin announced the cancellation of the South Stream project. Instead, Russia would reroute the pipeline across the Black Sea to Turkey.[83]

The project, Turkish Stream, envisioned two parallel lines — one for the Turkish market and the other for export to Europe — with a total of 32 BCM.

Map 22. South Stream and Turkish Stream Projects

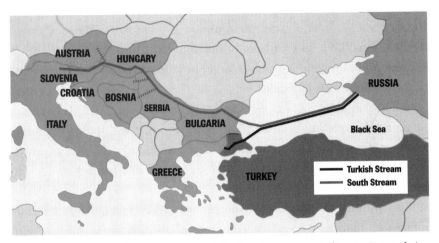

EU opposition forced the cancellation of the South Stream pipeline project to bring Russian gas under the Black Sea to the Balkans and Central Europe. Instead, Russia is building Turkish Stream to bring gas to Turkey, with potential links to Southern Europe via Greece or Bulgaria.

They would terminate at a gas hub to be built in Turkey at the Greek border. Russia and Turkey also agreed to expand capacity of the existing Blue Stream gas pipeline from 16 to 19 BCM. Blue Stream already traverses the Black Sea to provide natural gas to Turkey.

Simultaneously, Russia announced its gas exports through Ukraine would cease in 2019. Russia would continue to supply Ukraine's domestic market, but Southern Europeans would have to import via Turkey. In accordance with EU policy, they would have to build their own pipelines to connect with the hub in Turkey. Turkey does not belong to the EU, so Turkish Stream is affected only indirectly by EU regulations such as the Third Energy Package.

Turkish Stream was scorned in Brussels and Washington. The European Commission Vice-President for Energy Union Maroš Šefcovic said, in February 2015, Turkish Stream was not viable. "We will have to come back to a more rational debate on what should be the economically viable solutions for this project, and for overall gas cooperation between Gazprom and the European countries."[84] In May 2015, US Special Envoy for International

Energy Affairs Amos Hochstein told Greek media: "It's important to focus on what projects are on the table today and that is TAP (Trans-Adriatic Pipeline), that will interconnect to the Azerbaijani pipeline … Turkish Stream doesn't exist."[85] Brussels and Washington supported the existing routes through Ukraine and the Southern Gas Corridor.

Conflict interrupted negotiations on Turkish Stream when, on November 24, 2015, Turkey shot down a Russian Su-24 over Syria.[86] Russia responded with an embargo on agricultural imports from Turkey and a ban on Russian tourism to Turkey, both measures severely impacting the Turkish economy. Turkey's action was another blow to Russian efforts to export gas to Europe. For many months Russian-Turkish relations looked dim, though Russia continued to supply gas to Turkey across the Black Sea via Blue Stream.

Then came the attempted coup by a Turkish military faction on July 15–16, 2016. President Putin immediately phoned President Erdoğan to convey his support. The two leaders met on August 9 in St. Petersburg and agreed to restore relations. It was a stark contrast to the sudden chill between Turkey and Western countries, who Erdoğan hinted had backed the attempted coup.[87] Russia lifted its ban on tourism and agriculture, and the two countries resumed planning of the Turkish Stream pipeline and construction of Turkey's nuclear power plant at Akkuyu.

* * *

The Petroleum Game affects not only transit pipelines from Russia to Europe but also pipelines within Europe receiving Russian gas. The Third Energy Package, promulgated in 2009, is central to this particular Petroleum Game.

Gas received from Nord Stream is delivered to two transmissions systems, North European Gas Link (NEL) and the Baltic Sea Pipeline Link (OPAL), both owned jointly by Gazprom and Germany's Wintershall. The NEL pipeline runs westward across northern Germany towards the Netherlands. It operates at almost 100 per cent annual capacity of 20 BCM. In compliance with European Union regulations, it delivers gas auctioned by Gazprom to independent suppliers.[88]

The OPAL pipeline runs south through Germany and connects with lines to Poland and the Czech Republic. Until 2017, the pipeline had operated at only 50 per cent of its annual capacity of 35 BCM because of EU restrictions. Here's the story. The Third Energy Package stipulated that a gas transmission company cannot both own the pipeline and the gas transported through it and must allow any gas supplier access to the pipeline (third-party access).[89] The European Commission exempted OPAL from rules of third party access on half the line's capacity, which Gazprom could use freely. The other half was reserved for independent suppliers.

Since none had ever used the line, the capacity reserved for independent suppliers (50 per cent) looked absurd. In October 2016, the European Commission reduced it to about ten per cent.[90] After an appeal from Poland, in December 2016 the European Court of Justice provisionally suspended the Commission's ruling.[91] In July 2017, however, the Court lifted the suspension pending its definitive judgement, anticipated in 2019.[92] It found Polish gas suppliers would suffer no harm from increased gas delivery via the OPAL pipeline before 2019, as they had two contracts lasting until 2020 and 2022 for Russian gas via another route.

As regards Nord Stream 2, gas would be transported by a new pipeline running parallel to OPAL through Germany to the Czech Republic. It would also be a joint venture of Gazprom and Wintershall. It would have an enormous 51 BCM capacity, with much of the gas destined for Eastern and Southeast Europe. It would make Germany the key European transit and trading hub. This inland pipeline, of course, was contingent on Nord Stream 2 being built.

The Turkish Stream project comprises two parallel lines — one for the Turkish market and the other for export to Europe. Pipe-laying of the first line began offshore in May 2017 and was expected to be completed in 2019. Meanwhile, Russia was negotiating with European countries about the entry point of the second line. There were two proposals for entry point: Greece and Bulgaria.[93] At an EU Summit in December 2015, Prime Minister Borissov of Bulgaria envisioned the line across Bulgaria being 100 per cent Bulgarian-owned (not a joint venture with Russia), thereby complying with the Third Energy Package.[94] For its part, Greece backed a pipeline project named Poseidon to deliver Russian gas across Greece and the Adriatic Sea to Italy. Three companies — Gazprom, Greece's Public Gas Corporation (DEPA) and the Italian company Edison SpA — signed a cooperation agreement to that effect in June 2017.[95] They planned to use work already done by Edison and DEPA in an unsuccessful bid to build the Trans-Adriatic Pipeline, which is part of the Southern Gas Corridor.[96] Will the European Commission approve the new project? The geopolitics run deep.

Four countries — Greece, Macedonia, Serbia and Hungary — also proposed a route across the Balkans to Central Europe. It would pass through Serbia and Hungary, terminating in Austria at Baumgarten, a suburb of Vienna. Baumgarten is the Central European hub for gas imports from Ukraine and Nord Stream. Hungary's Prime Minister Orbán said: "We are convinced that locking Russia out of Europe is not rational ... Whoever thinks that ... energy security can exist in Europe without the energy that comes from Russia, is chasing ghosts."[97]

The weak links in the chain were Greece and Macedonia. Greece and Russia envisaged a joint company for the Greek section, with Russia financing the project and Greece repaying its share afterward.[98] Greek Energy Minister Panagiotis Lafazanis revealed the EU was "continuing to pressure, attempting to stop the pipeline project."[99] Greece, economically ruined, was financially in the hands of the European Troika — the triumvirate of the European Commission, European Central Bank and the International Money Fund. The Republic of Macedonia announced a Russian company would build the Macedonian section.[100] However, Macedonia had experienced ethnic unrest, political turmoil and paralysis since 2015. Did outsiders precipitate this situation? Some observers believed so.

For its part, the European Commission has worked with Balkan countries to build connections to the Southern Gas Corridor. Bulgaria, Greece and Romania agreed in 2015 to build a north-south line, the Vertical Gas Corridor, to tap into the Southern Gas Corridor.[101] As well, a Slovakian initiative envisaged a project named Eastring (confirmed in 2017) to link Slovakia, Hungary, Romania and Bulgaria. It would deliver gas on behalf of any supplier from anywhere.[102]

* * *

There are winners and losers in pipeline projects. So much depends on the major players acting in good faith. As Hamlet said, "Aye, there's the rub." Since political leaders are so deeply involved in negotiations for pipelines, it can be no surprise that ambassadors and ministers are knowledgeable about pipeline politics. They interact regularly with representatives of national and private petroleum companies. Military and intelligence leaders know the game, too, though their involvement may be hidden.

Much has changed in petroleum geopolitics since 1991, when the Soviet Union broke up. Ukraine has remained the main pipeline transit route between Russia and Europe, as of 2018, but Ukraine's corruption and payment difficulties have led Russia to seek alternate routes. Since Nord Stream became operational in 2011, Russia has proposed additional pipelines to Europe. Each has had a stormy history. Meanwhile Europe has offered exceptions to its competition rules for the Southern Gas Corridor, a partially built pipeline from Azerbaijan; it has the support of the UK and US governments and could incorporate gas from the Eastern Mediterranean.

What can be sleuthed from public information may be only the tip of the iceberg, but it is enough to show that pipeline rivalry exists. The rivalry extends far beyond the borders of Ukraine, as various countries use both diplomacy and force to jockey for pipelines in their own best interests. The money spent and the effort expended are enormous because the stakes are high.

CHAPTER 9
ECONOMIC SKIRMISHES AND PRESSURES — WHOSE OIL IS IT?

"First of all the Georgian silver goes, and then all that nice furniture that used to be in the salon. Then the Canalettos go."

—Harold Macmillan, former Prime Minister of Britain, on
privatization, November 8, 1985

When I was visiting Wisconsin a few years ago, I met a young man who was a mid-level civil servant in the state government. Apparently he had been told I knew something about petroleum because suddenly, out of the blue, he asked me what I thought of Hugo Chávez, then president of Venezuela, a major oil-exporting country. I had been warned to avoid discussions of politics that evening, so I turned the question around and said, "What do you think?"

His reply astonished me. He said, "We can't have Chávez in charge of *our* oil." I realized I was in dangerous territory but I couldn't resist a comment. I replied, "The Venezuelans might feel it's *their* oil."

This incident has come to mind often. It reflects a sense of entitlement that I've encountered in high-level officials within powerful countries. I didn't expect to find it in ordinary citizens. In 1956, Prime Minister Anthony Eden denounced the Suez Canal nationalization, saying he would not allow Egypt's President Nasser to "have his thumb on our windpipe."[1] US leaders have promoted such attitudes by calling foreign leaders "Bad Guys" when they fail to adopt American economic preferences. Talking

193

about Iraq, Donald Trump told NBC News in 2016: "It used to be to the victor belong the spoils ... There was no victory. But I always said, take the oil."[2] In the same vein, former New York Mayor Rudy Giuliani commented on ABC News: "Of course it's legal. It's a war ... That oil becomes a very critical issue."[3] Indeed, whose oil is it? Who calls the shots — the electorate, the government, foreign investors, Washington or supra-national entities such as the World Bank and International Money Fund?

ECONOMIC TOOLS: THE WASHINGTON CONSENSUS AND TRADE DEALS

A fundamental issue facing many countries today is sovereignty. As regards the energy sector, who is in charge of the natural resources? The pendulum has swung remarkably from public ownership post-World War II to privatization in the 1990s and private ownership as of 2018. The push to privatize public sector companies took place slowly, relentlessly and with good intentions. Privatization became the new way of doing things and many countries adopted it willingly. It's a change that boosts the rights of private companies, particularly international companies. In the petroleum sector, it often helps the haves more than the have-nots.

The new policies were embodied in what became known as the Washington Consensus, a term coined in 1989 by economist John Williamson. He listed economic policies on which the US government, International Money Fund and World Bank had consensus. They included privatization, deregulation and liberalization of trade and investment. For some people, the Washington Consensus is a synonym for neoliberalism — a market-oriented approach eliminating price controls, deregulating capital markets, lowering trade barriers and privatizing the public sector as much as possible. Neoliberalism owes much to economists Friedrich Hayek, Milton Friedman and Ayn Rand. It was implemented big-time by Ronald Reagan in the United States and Margaret Thatcher in Britain.

The Washington Consensus has had a profound effect on much of the world. The world seemed to revolve around Washington in the twentieth century, as it had around London in the nineteenth century. The Washington Consensus' nerve centre is the US Treasury, adjacent to the White House. Two of its key instruments, the International Money Fund and World Bank, are catalysts for economic change in much of the world.

The International Money Fund monitors economic and financial development with a view to preventing crises, makes balance-of-payments loans to countries in financial difficulty and provides technical assistance to improve financial management. The World Bank provides longer-term loans and assistance to developing nations for their economic advancement. Both institutions were created in 1944 at an international conference held at Bretton Woods, New Hampshire. Not surprisingly, both are headquartered in Washington, DC. Most countries around the world belong to the two institutions. Their staff are international, drawn from member countries.

Since the shareholding and voting power of the International Money Fund and Bank are determined by members' population and economic size, the more powerful countries call the shots. The largest shareholder in both institutions is the United States. The US Treasury represents Washington's shareholding. It ensures they accord with Washington's economic thinking. By convention, the International Money Fund's managing director is always a French official acceptable to Washington, and the Bank's president is always an American.

When I worked at the Bank in the 1960s and 1970s, the president was Robert McNamara. As former US Secretary of Defense during the Vietnam War and former CEO of the Ford Motor Company, he inspired awe and respect. His grasp of statistics was formidable. He was known to phone staff for clarification of minute details in draft reports, for example in paragraph three of page seven in Appendix D.

Four regional development banks were created later to provide additional financial and technical assistance to developing countries. They are the African Development Bank (AfDB), Asian Development Bank (ADB), European Bank for Reconstruction and Development (EBRD) and Inter-American Development Bank (IDB). Like the World Bank, they are multilateral banks, with shares held by countries both inside and outside the region, and voting powers a careful balance of lending and borrowing countries. Often the regional banks work with the World Bank on major projects. Not surprisingly, the more powerful countries call the shots — notably the United States through its Treasury Department. Essentially, the Washington Consensus promotes an economic system that is advantageous to rich, powerful countries and companies.

Another tool comprises trade and investment deals. A hallmark of the Obama Administration was three negotiations that would lock Europe, Asia and the Pacific into the Washington Consensus. China and Russia were noticeably excluded. The negotiations were secret, with only big corporations privy to their terms. When WikiLeaks managed to publish part of their drafts, people in many countries became concerned about the impact of these deals on national sovereignty. President Trump's election became a game-changer. He opposed the deals. Asserting "America First," he withdrew the US from the Trans-Pacific Partnership. He put the Trade in Services Agreement and the Transatlantic Trade and Investment Partnership on ice.

A precursor to the three deals is the 1994 North American Free Trade Agreement (NAFTA) between Canada, Mexico and the US. Before his election, Donald Trump termed the trade deal the worst in history and affirmed his intention to renegotiate it "to get a better deal for our workers."[4] Renegotiations began in August 2017. NAFTA includes petroleum. US objectives, published prior to the talks, were vague on petroleum but officials hinted at changes. NAFTA includes a proportionality clause under which, in times of scarcity, Canada must share its oil and gas supply with the United States.[5] In other words, Canada cannot favour Canadians in the event of energy supply disruption. Prior to NAFTA, it only allowed exports of oil and gas if they were surplus to domestic requirements. Mexico, currently exempt, may be pressured into a similar obligation. When it signed NAFTA, its petroleum sector was state-owned and inviolable but this is no longer so. In 2013, Mexico opened petroleum exploration and production to foreign companies.

Canada and the European Union signed their own trade deal in 2016, the Comprehensive Economic and Trade Agreement (CETA). The agreement required the signature of all 28 EU countries; and Belgium, under its federal constitution, required the approval of all five regional governments.[6] Two regions, Wallonia and Brussels, objected strongly to a proposed court system for settling disputes between foreign investors and governments. In the compromise solution, Belgium signed the deal subject to a ruling from the European Court of Justice on whether the proposed investor-state mechanism is compatible with EU law. Some parts of CETA were provisionally applied in 2017 but others, including the investor court system, await ratification by all 28 member parliaments.

Wallonia and Brussels were not alone. The negotiations caused a furor in Europe. A common feature in all these deals is an investor-state dispute settlement (ISDS) provision. This grants a foreign investor the right to sue a government for damages, including lost future profits, in an international arbitral tribunal. Foreign investors love this mechanism. Opponents argue it makes governments reluctant to legislate on such issues as health and environmental protection, labour rights and human rights. It also discriminates against domestic investors, who must bring disputes to their national courts of justice — not to international arbitration. Awards to foreign investors can be enormous. A Canadian study in 2015 tracked all known cases worldwide to the spring of 2014 and found 45 awards exceeding US$10 million each. They totalled US$6.5 billion, including pre-award interest. The largest award was *Occidental Petroleum versus Ecuador* for US$2.4 billion. Eight awards against Argentina totalled US$1.5 billion.[7]

The International Centre for Settlement of Investment Disputes (ICSID) is the leading institution for the resolution of international investment disputes.[8] It is an arm of the World Bank group. ICSID cases are decided by arbitrators who are meant to be independent and impartial. The ICSID caseload has ballooned in the past 15 years, partly reflecting the increasing number of investment agreements that include ISDS provisions. Why do countries join the ICSID? They may feel little choice if they are to attract foreign investment. In 2007, Bolivia became the world's first country to withdraw from the ICSID, which President Morales said had consistently favoured multinational corporations. Ecuador followed suit in 2009 and Venezuela in 2012. Some, like Brazil, never joined.

The ISDS mechanism results *de facto* in an irreversible commitment to private sector ownership of infrastructure and energy. What government is willing to nationalize a foreign enterprise if it has to compensate not only for the loss of fixed assets but also for loss of future profits? How do you calculate loss of profits for an oil company — at what oil price and for how many years? It's a control mechanism for the Washington Consensus — a deterrent to nationalizations such as those of the Anglo-Iranian Oil Company in 1951 and the Suez Canal in 1956.

BACKSTORY: SHIFT TO PRIVATIZATION

The multilateral development banks borrow funds on excellent triple-A terms in the world's capital markets. They also receive low-interest funds from richer member countries. They lend to other countries and state-owned enterprises, on terms far better than commercial banks can offer. They originally financed public sector projects. In the 1950s and 1960s, many newly independent countries flocked to join the International Money Fund and the World Bank. A number of these countries had nationalized the assets of colonial companies, as in Egypt and Indonesia, and sought World Bank financing for their new state-owned enterprises.

In those days, energy sector lending was for electricity — not petroleum. Even so, the World Bank wanted to understand the economic impact of petroleum on countries (oil importers and exporters alike) to whom it lent money. It still does. It tracks the global oil scene — the outlook for world oil supply and demand — and shares perspectives with member countries. That was my task there in the 1970s.

The 1973–74 oil embargo (discussed in Chapter 1) triggered shock-waves of oil price increases around the world. OPEC countries seized the opportunity to increase government revenue from oil resources. The World Bank formed a task force to study the impact of these oil price increases on developing countries — both those exporting and those importing oil. Country economists throughout the Bank analyzed the impact on their countries. This was a highly sensitive issue, with some countries the winners and others the losers, and deliberations within the Bank were confidential. We were advised to be careful on the phone, as our lines might be bugged. Nevertheless, excerpts from the report ended up in the *Wall Street Journal*. Our team had a leaker, though I never learned who it was. This was the first of the Bank's annual *World Development Reports* distributed to member countries. The series was continuing as of 2018.

The World Bank created a large Energy Department. It initiated a lending program promoting oil exploration in developing countries where international companies might not invest the time and effort.[9] It administered an

Energy Sector Management Assistance Program, funded primarily by the UNDP.[10] The Bank began collaborating with capital-surplus Gulf States, which had recently created development funds, such as the Kuwait Fund for Arab Economic Development and the OPEC Fund for International Development. For several years, UN agencies, regional development banks and bilateral agencies supported a range of energy programs. In some countries, they were tripping over themselves to find projects to support, as I witnessed in Bangladesh, Nepal, Somalia and Tanzania.

During the 1980s, International Money Fund and World Bank policies shifted to privatizing infrastructure and promoting structural adjustment — policies that included fiscal austerity, free trade and deregulation. Private sector development was the new gospel. The multinational development banks were ready to finance the private sector, separately or in partnership with commercial banks. The International Finance Corporation (the World Bank's private sector arm) expanded its lending program; the IDB, ADB and AfDB expanded their private sector windows for Latin America, Asia and Africa respectively; and the EBRD opened in 1991 for private sector projects in Eastern Europe and the former Soviet Union.

The Washington Consensus extends worldwide. It's instructive to see how it worked in Russia (the West's current *bête noire*) and in Latin America (which the US sees as its exclusive backyard).

RUSSIA

After World War II, the world was divided into two major blocs of countries, with restricted contact between the two. Exxon used the term Free World to encompass Western and Third World countries, Shell dubbed it WOCA (World Outside the Communist Area) and the World Bank referred to the world excluding CPEs (Centrally Planned Economies). For Bank staff, the CPEs were like the moon; we didn't go there. This global division gradually dissolved, with China joining the Bank in 1980, Eastern Europe joining in the 1980s and Russia in 1992.

The Iron Curtain melted in 1989. One Eastern European country after another threw over its communist regime; the Berlin Wall came down; and Germany was reunified the next year. The Warsaw Pact was dissolved in March 1991, and the Soviet military withdrew within its own borders. In

December 1991, the Soviet Union itself was dissolved and numerous countries became independent.

The US moved immediately to co-opt Russia and other countries from the former Soviet Union into the Washington Consensus. The newly independent countries joined the International Money Fund, World Bank and the new EBRD. Those in Central Asia also joined the ADB. The world was no longer bipolar; it played by Washington's rules.

The West went into high gear to restructure and open up the economies of Eastern Europe, the Caucasus, Central Asia and Russia itself. Structural adjustment was the order of the day. The International Money Fund and World Bank made a series of structural adjustment loans. Disbursements were conditional on the borrower making policy changes such as new laws and privatizations that accorded with the Washington Consensus. The Bank followed up with adjustment loans to specific sectors such as infrastructure and energy. Bilateral agencies such as USAID and the Canadian International Development Agency (CIDA) plunged in, financing a host of Western economists, financial experts, lawyers, management consultants and investment bankers to help reshape the former Soviet Union countries to Western economic specifications.

As well, Washington funded democratic reform programs through such quasi-private foundations as the National Endowment for Democracy, International Republican Institute and National Democratic Institute. It financed Colour Revolutions in one country after another, such as Georgia (Rose Revolution, 2003), Ukraine (Orange Revolution, 2004) and Kyrgyzstan (Tulip, 2005). Some commentators called them regime change efforts — working to change governments so they became favourable to US interests and the Washington Consensus. Russia banned the National Endowment for Democracy in 2015 as an undesirable international NGO.

During Boris Yeltsin's presidency (1991–1999), Russia received the full shock treatment of the Washington Consensus. Wholesale privatizations at fire-sale prices created instant billionaires, the so-called oligarchs. Much of their wealth was invested in foreign safe havens such as ritzy buildings in London's Belgravia and yachts on the French Riviera. The City of London banking district was a large beneficiary. Yeltsin was popular in

US President Bill Clinton greeted Russian President Boris Yeltsin at White House, 1994. Through the Washington Consensus, firesale privatizations looted the Russian economy, including petroleum.

Western corridors of power. In 1997, Russia was invited to join the Group of Seven (G7), making it the Group of Eight (until 2014).[11] However, the Russian economy was looted. Corruption, unemployment and poverty were widespread. Russia lost its pride and self-respect. The process is described in Naomi Klein's book *Shock Doctrine*.

The privatizations included the petroleum sector. New oil companies emerged, of which the largest five were Gazprom, Transneft, Rosneft, Lukoil and Yukos (now part of Rosneft). Gazprom is Russia's state-owned natural gas monopoly. It is the world's largest gas exploration and production company. Transneft, state-owned, is Russia's oil pipeline monopoly and the world's largest oil pipeline company. Rosneft is an integrated oil company, 50 per cent owned by Rosneftegaz (a state-owned company), 19.75

201

per cent by BP, 19.5 per cent jointly by the Qatar Investment Authority and Glencore (a Swiss company), and other shares in free float.[12] Lukoil is a privately owned oil company, engaged in oil exploration, production, refining and distribution worldwide.

The privatizations took place in two waves. In the first (1992–1994), the government gave vouchers to all Russian citizens, vouchers that could be exchanged for shares in any state-owned company. The idea was to avoid the open sale of state-owned assets, which might result in ownership by political appointees and the Russian mafia. Even so, insiders managed to acquire most of the assets, buying vouchers cheaply from people who did not understand their worth.

One such insider was Bill Browder, an American/British financier who co-founded Russia's largest foreign investment bank, Hermitage Capital Management, and made a fortune. His tax accountant was Sergei Magnitsky, who was prosecuted for corporate tax evasion and died controversially in a Russian prison. The *Magnitsky Acts* in the USA and Canada are named after him.[13] There are two narratives of what happened. The Western version is given in Bill Browder's book *Red Notice* (2015). A rebuttal is given in Alex Krainer's *Deconstructing Bill Browder's Dangerous Deception* (2017).

Whatever the truth, the legislation has been a useful rod with which to beat Russia. Upon enacting it in November 2017, Canada promptly sanctioned 52 Russians, Venezuelans and South Sudanese. Foreign Minister Chrystia Freeland said the law showed "Canada takes any and all necessary measures to respond to gross violations of human rights and acts of significant foreign corruption." President Putin accused Canada of playing "unconstructive political games."

In the second privatization wave (1995–1996), the Russian government — in dire financial straits — adopted a loans-for-shares scheme. It auctioned shares in state enterprises (including oil companies Lukoil and Yukos) to Russian banks as collateral for their making loans to the government. The banks bid knock-down prices and kept the shares or sold them to wealthy insiders. The government defaulted on the loans and forfeited the shares to the banks.

Yukos illustrated how this worked. A bank owned by Russian oligarch Mikhail Khodorkovsky acquired Yukos in the mid-1990s through a loans-for-shares auction. He bought it for a song (US$309 million). In the next few years, Yukos became one of Russia's biggest companies. In 2003, its assessed value was US$45 billion, and it produced 1.7 million b/d of oil. That was 20 per cent of Russia's total output and roughly the same as Algeria, Libya or Kuwait. Khodorkovsky became the richest man in Russia and the sixteenth richest in the world.

In 2003, Khodorkovsky was sentenced to nine years in prison for fraud and tax evasion. Yukos's assets were auctioned to pay for back taxes and were acquired by Rosneft. Khodorkovsky was pardoned in 2013 and moved to Zurich and London. He alleged the charges were politically motivated, and the Western media depicted him as an example set to break oligarchs with political ambition. Certainly, his Open Russia initiative promoting civil society was an unwelcome challenge to the government. The oligarchs were potential threats like the barons of medieval England. President Putin had made clear they should stay out of politics.[14]

How did foreign investors enter the Russian petroleum sector? Excluded from the voucher privatizations and the loans-for-shares auctions, they entered into joint ventures with Russian companies, production-sharing agreements and direct equity participation.[15] While restricted to minority interests in Russian companies, companies such as BP, ConocoPhillips, ExxonMobil, Shell and Total came rushing in.[16] By 2015, private ownership of the oil sector was about 20 per cent but the gas sector stayed in public hands.

As of 2018, the biggest foreign player has been BP. In the 1990s, it teamed up with four oligarchs to form a joint venture called TNK-BP, headquartered in Moscow. TNK-BP became Russia's third largest oil producer and ranked among the world's ten largest private oil companies. In 2013, TNK-BP was acquired by Rosneft. BP benefited from the deal, receiving US$12 billion in cash and 19.75 per cent of Rosneft's shares. In 2015, BP's share of output was 1 million b/d (one-third of its worldwide oil production). It earned 22 per cent of its worldwide pre-tax profit from its share in Rosneft — despite the sanctions against Russia. With the ruble undervalued, BP had the lowest average operating costs among the world's major oil companies.[17]

Vladimir Putin served as President of Russia from 2000 to 2008, then became prime minister under President Dmitry Medvedev, and was re-elected president in 2012 and again in 2018. As president, Putin has respected existing private ownership but limited wholesale application of the Washington Consensus.

Hopes for a new era of integration and friendship between Russia and Western countries dwindled as one Eastern European country after another joined NATO, right up to Russia's borders. The West dangled the prospect of NATO membership to Azerbaijan, Georgia, Ukraine — all formerly part of the Soviet Union. Russia became a handy foe to justify NATO build-up on Russia's borders. After having hopes of becoming a normal country, Russia saw itself encircled and threatened.

Russia is a petro-state. Its oil and gas resources are vital to its economy and to government finances. According to BP's 2018 *Statistical Review*, Russia has the world's largest gas reserves, is the second largest gas producer (after the US) and is the world's leading gas exporter. It has the world's sixth largest oil reserves; it is the third largest oil producer — just below the US and Saudi Arabia. In 2013, oil and gas accounted for 68 per cent of Russia's total export revenues and more than 50 per cent of its government revenue. Clearly, Russia is a giant in the world of petroleum.

Europe is a vital energy market for Russia. The US saw this as a wedge issue to be exploited. US Special Envoy for Eurasian Energy Richard L. Morningstar told Congress in 2011: "We want to assist Europe in its quest for energy security. We want to help Caspian and Central Asian countries find new routes to market."[18] Washington has been pushing Europe to diversify away from its long-standing energy ties to Russia. NATO marches to the same drum as Washington. Its secretary general, Anders Fogh Rasmussen, told the Brussels Energy Forum in 2014: "We must make energy diversification a strategic transatlantic priority and reduce Europe's dependency on Russian energy."[19] Of course, Russian energy would be replaced by energy from countries closely allied with the United States.

In 2014, Washington went for the jugular, imposing sanctions on specific Russian enterprises and individuals. The stated reasons were Russian annexation of Crimea and aggression in Eastern Ukraine, both issues having alternative interpretations (discussed in Chapter 8). The European Union went along with Washington, despite objections from several countries in Southeast Europe. Old Europe (Britain, France, Germany) and Poland ruled the roost, and no country appeared willing to defy Washington. The sanctions prohibited Western companies from selling goods or services to Russian companies for deepwater, Arctic offshore and shale projects that had potential to produce oil.[20] The gas sector was not sanctioned. The world was awash in oil, but Europe needed Russian gas.

As a result, ExxonMobil, Shell and Total withdrew from joint ventures with Russian oil companies in the Arctic and Siberia. ExxonMobil said it will return to the Arctic once the sanctions are lifted.[21] Meanwhile, it continues business as usual in a multinational consortium with Rosneft and others, producing oil and gas offshore Sakhalin Island in the Russian Far East.

The EU sanctions have rested more lightly on European companies operating in Russia, as they allow pre-existing contracts to continue.[22] ENI (Italy) and Statoil (Norway) received approval from their home governments to continue in joint ventures with Rosneft. Shell continued to invest in Russia. It partners in the Sakhalin-2 joint venture with Gazprom and Japanese firms, producing and exporting crude oil and LNG, and plans a major expansion.[23] Shell's CEO said in 2015 the company's "interests in Russia stay significant ... Sanctions do not mean absence of investment opportunities."[24] Other Western oil companies clearly think the same. Top officials from Western oil companies attended the 2016 St. Petersburg International Economic Forum, including the CEOs of BP, ExxonMobil,[25] Royal Dutch Shell and Total. US authorities had beforehand advised American businesses against attending the Forum.[26]

Yet Brussels and Washington exert pressure on Europe to continue the sanctions and curtail oil and gas imports from Russia. So Russia is perforce diversifying into the Chinese market, which has huge potential. It is building the Power of Siberia pipeline to bring 38 BCM per year of gas from eastern Siberia to northeast China. It is negotiating the Power of Siberia-2 pipeline to bring 30 BCM annually from western Siberia to northwest China.[27] China is also a fast growing market for Russian oil from eastern Siberia. By 2030, Russia's Eastern markets may exceed the Western. That will require vast capital expenditures, which both countries are evidently willing to make. The two countries will trade in rubles and yuan instead of the US dollar — a challenge to the petrodollar.

Map 23. Pipelines from Russia to China

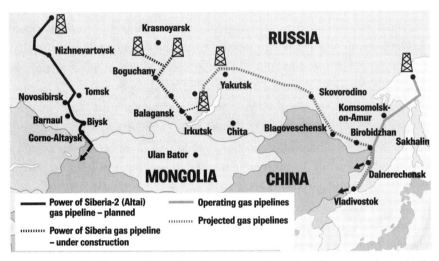

Russian pipelines bring oil from Siberia to China. Pipelines for gas are being built or planned.

Western politicians and media have snubbed, rubbished and demonized President Putin. He is the latest "Bad Guy." Meeting at the 2014 G20 Summit in Brisbane, Canada's Prime Minister Stephen Harper told President Putin: "I guess I'll shake your hand but I have only one thing to say to you, you need to get out of Ukraine." According to a Kremlin spokesman, Putin replied: "That's impossible because we are not there."

Despite these vicissitudes, Putin remains highly popular in Russia, exceeding 80 per cent ratings in opinion polls.[28] This popularity comes in part from improved conditions in Russia after limitations were placed on privatization and foreign government attempts to reshape Russia. A pragmatist, he has red lines as evinced in Georgia, Ukraine, Crimea and Syria. At the 2016 Valdai Conference (Sochi, Russia), he said the "mythical" Russian military threat was "a profitable business that can be used to pump new money into defence budgets at home, get allies to bend to a single superpower's interests, expand NATO and bring its infrastructure, military units and arms closer to our borders." He added Russia has no intention of attacking anyone: "it is unthinkable, foolish and completely unrealistic. And yet they use these ideas in pursuit of their political aims."[29] Putin is

206

highly articulate and logical from a Russian viewpoint, defending Russia's interests and wanting Russia to be respected.

During his election campaign, Donald Trump promised to reach out to Russia, and Putin welcomed rapprochement. Since his election, Trump has been under intense political pressure to distance his Administration from Moscow.

LATIN AMERICA

During the 1990s, restructuring and privatization were appealing to numerous governments in Latin America and fashionable in Latin intellectual circles. Chile led the way and became a model for the region. Argentina, Colombia and Mexico followed suit. The smaller, impoverished countries of Central America fell into line, except Costa Rica. The momentum for change was palpable. Public utilities were suffering from poor cash-flow, low frozen tariffs, subsidies, under-investment, featherbedding and strapped government budgets. In some countries, retail oil prices and electricity tariffs were controlled and their change required political approval. Latin Americans had endured military dictatorships in the 1970s and stagnant economic growth in the 1980s. In contrast, North America and Europe prospered during the 1980s. Britain's Prime Minister Margaret Thatcher dramatically transformed her nation's economy with wholesale deregulation and privatization. Many Latinos were impressed.

The instruments for assisting the transformation in Latin America were the International Money Fund, World Bank and IDB. The International Money Fund and World Bank are located near one side of the White House and Treasury, and the IDB is located near the other side. I spent 23 years in Washington, DC, working first at the World Bank and later at the IDB. At the World Bank, we went on missions to developing countries. At the IDB we were *misionarios* — the same word ("missionaries") used to describe people promoting religious tenets.

The IDB is influential in Latin America, though little known outside the region. It was created in 1962 as an initiative under President Kennedy's Alliance for Progress and, not surprisingly, is a trade-off between regional and US interests. Latin American and Caribbean countries have a shareholding slightly larger than 50 per cent, but the US has the single largest shareholding (30 per cent). Canada has just over four per cent and ranks third largest of the non-borrowing countries. European countries and Japan account for the balance. The IDB president is always a Latin American, and its executive vice-president an American. The institutional culture reflects the Latin camaraderie of the region. Entering its building in Washington, I was immediately in Latin America, my colleagues speaking Spanish or Portuguese more than English.

In the 2000s, some countries started to resist the Washington Consensus, with Venezuela in the lead and Argentina, Bolivia, Brazil, Ecuador and Nicaragua close behind. They all, except Nicaragua, have petroleum resources. Until 2014, high oil prices gave them the wherewithal to resist Washington pressures and implement programs of health, education and poverty reduction. The poor in these countries were thrilled; the well-to-do, antagonized. Since 2014, with collapsed oil prices, the economic pressures have been severe. The political pendulum has swung again in Argentina, Brazil and Ecuador, with new governments returning to the Washington Consensus. Venezuela faces one political crisis after another, and pressures mount on Bolivia. The US government has been active behind the scenes, backing Latin politicians who support the Consensus.

Latin America has a long history of national oil companies, created to take over from foreign companies the exploration, production and refining of domestic oil resources. Petroleum resources were viewed as a national patrimony, too important to be left exclusively in foreign hands. Foreign companies could operate under contractual arrangements with the national oil company but without ownership of the resources. Washington wanted to re-open the petroleum sector to foreign private investment. In the early 1990s, the World Bank helped Argentina and Bolivia privatize their state-owned petroleum companies. Foreign companies were waiting in the wings to acquire the assets, and investment banks were waiting to facilitate privatization and earn huge transaction fees. The specific experiences of four petroleum-rich countries — Argentina, Bolivia, Brazil and Venezuela — illustrate what happened.

* * *

Argentina is a proud nation with strong European roots. Its capital, Buenos Aires, is an elegant city. After a period of stagnation and hyper-inflation in the 1980s, Argentineans elected Carlos Menem as president in 1989. During his ten years in office, Argentina became the darling of the Washington Consensus. Finance Minister Domingo Cavallo abruptly ended hyper-inflation, launched neoliberalism and pegged the Argentinean new peso to the US dollar. With support from the World Bank and the IDB, he downsized the public sector with wholesale restructuring, deregulation and privatization. Included were the petroleum and electricity sectors.

Argentina's national oil company, Yacimientos Petrolíferos Fiscales (YPF), is the nation's largest oil producer. It dates back to 1922 — the world's first state-owned oil company outside the Soviet Union. It was restructured and privatized with World Bank assistance in 1993 and acquired in 1999 by Spain's Repsol.

I was on the IDB team supporting the restructuring of the electricity sector and visited Buenos Aires several times. In Buenos Aires, we found the Argentineans knew exactly what they wanted to do. In 1992, they restructured and unbundled the sector into stand-alone generation, transmission and distribution functions. Generation was auctioned off to the private sector; transmission and distribution became regulated private monopolies; and private generation companies supplied electricity to a competitive wholesale market. It was a made-in-Argentina program, building on previous privatizations in Britain and Chile. To support the restructuring, the IDB made a US$300 million sector adjustment loan. The loan was disbursed in tranches upon predetermined actions being achieved, such as bringing specific power stations to point of sale. Argentina used the proceeds to finance employee redundancy packets.

For over a decade, Argentineans endured increasing unemployment and austerity, imposed in defence of the exchange rate pegged to the US dollar. In 2003, they elected change — choosing Néstor Kirchner as president. He ended the straitjacket of austerity, promoted strong economic growth and restructured the public debt burden with overseas bondholders. In 2007, Cristina Fernández de Kirchner, his spouse, was elected president and continued these policies. Argentina's relations with the United States were strained.

As regards petroleum, the government partially renationalized YPF by purchasing a 51 per cent shareholding from the Spanish owner Repsol. The government accused Repsol of under-investing in exploration and development, excessive dividends and asset stripping. Repsol blamed the decline in exploration and production on government controls on export volumes and domestic oil and gas prices. For many years, Argentina had produced enough oil and gas to meet the domestic market. But it became a net energy importer in 2011, the first time since 1987. In 2014, the government agreed to pay US$5 billion compensation to Repsol, which had taken the dispute to the International Centre for Settlement of Investment Disputes for arbitration.

In 2015, the political pendulum swung back with the election of President Mauricio Macri. With economic doldrums, rising unemployment and high inflation, the electorate voted for change. The business elite and right wing were ecstatic.[30] Macri had a market-oriented stance and reached out to Washington. He cut government spending, raised interest rates and settled a festering dispute with two American "vulture" hedge funds. Washington expressed pleasure. The US government lifted its block on World Bank and IDB loans to Argentina, imposed in 2013 for financial "misconduct." President Obama congratulated Macri and visited Argentina in March 2016, back-to-back from his historic visit to Cuba. Argentina was back in the fold of the Washington Consensus.

* * *

Bolivia has more natural gas than oil. It has large gas reserves, mostly in the eastern region and exports 80 per cent of its production by pipeline to Argentina and Brazil. Its national oil company, Yacimientos Petrolíferos Fiscales Bolivianos (YPFB), dates from 1937. YPFB was created upon the nationalization of Exxon's local holdings and became a symbol of national sovereignty. In the 1990s, like many other countries, Bolivia implemented far-reaching programs of restructuring and privatizing public enterprises. It privatized YPFB in 1994, with World Bank assistance. The privatization was politically contentious. When President Evo Morales came to office in 2006, one of his first actions was to renationalize YPFB and grant formal ownership of Bolivia's oil and gas reserves to YPFB. Foreign exploration and production companies now operate under joint venture and service contracts with YPFB.[31]

Bolivia is the largest exporter of natural gas in South America. Export pipelines deliver the gas to Argentina and Brazil. The Bolivia-Brazil pipeline is the longest gas pipeline in South America, stretching 3,150 kilometres from Bolivia's eastern fields to markets in Brazil's southeast region. Having been a dream for more than 40 years, it was commissioned in 1999 — a complex mixture of public and private capital. In Bolivia, the gas sector had just been restructured. Two joint venture companies were created to build, own and operate the pipeline. For the Bolivian section, the main partners were Shell and ill-fated Enron. For Brazil, the lead firm was the federally owned Petrobras with several international partners. To help finance the pipeline, the World Bank, IDB and other development banks made loans to Petrobras, with Brazilian government guarantee.[32] Their presence gave the private firms confidence to invest in the project. I participated in the IDB appraisal team, a memorable experience.

Bolivia's population is 55 per cent of indigenous ancestry (Indio). Evo Morales is Bolivia's first indigenous president, loved by the Indios and not by the right-wing elite or Washington. In 2002, US Ambassador Manuel Rocha threatened US aid to Bolivia would be cut off if Morales's Movement for Socialism party were ever elected to office.[33] In fact, USAID continued operations. It spent more than US$97 million from 2002 to 2008 promoting decentralization and regional autonomy and supporting opposition parties in Bolivia."[34] It did so through USAID's Office of Transition Initiatives, whose mandate is to help "local partners advance peace and democracy" by providing short-term assistance "targeted at key political transition and stabilization needs."[35]

In 2008, violent unrest broke out in Bolivia's eastern provinces, where the elite strove for regional autonomy.[36] The US embassy was caught providing covert assistance to the opposition movement,[37] and President Morales ordered the US ambassador, Philip Goldberg, to leave the country.[38] Tit-for-tat, the US government expelled the Bolivian ambassador to Washington.

Difficulties between the United States and Bolivia were exacerbated in 2013 because of an incident involving President Morales's airplane.

Washington was seeking to capture Edward Snowden, who had released a trove of data on NSA spying and been forced to take refuge in Moscow airport when Washington revoked his US passport. The US suspected Snowden might be onboard the presidential flight returning from Moscow to La Paz. As the plane approached Western Europe, France, Spain and Portugal denied air transit. Eventually, it had to refuel in Austria, and was delayed 14 hours while Austrian officials demanded to inspect the aircraft. Eight Latin American countries protested jointly to UN Secretary-General Ban Ki-Moon, who said heads of state and their aircraft enjoy immunity and inviolability.[39] The US admitted it had contacted other nations about potential flights involving Snowden, but would not comment if it had made specific representations about President Morales's flight.[40] Spain's foreign minister told media "they told us they were sure ... he was on board," without indicating who "they" were.[41]

In February 2016, Bolivia held a referendum on modifying the constitution to allow a president to be re-elected twice instead of once. A majority voted in favour, allowing President Morales to stand again for office in 2019. Defenders of the old order were bitterly opposed to the referendum, and the United States was at their service. The US embassy reportedly paid US$200,000 to groups opposing the referendum.[42] Bolivia expelled the US Vice Consul in December 2015, claiming he was a CIA agent meeting secretly with social movement leaders.[43] Indeed, the US National Endowment for Democracy has vigorously financed opposition activities. Between 2003 and 2014, it disbursed US$7.7 million to 20 Bolivian institutions for political objectives.[44] Bolivia illustrates the political skirmishes and pressures from Washington on non-conforming countries.

* * *

Brazil is the largest country in South America and the world's ninth largest economy. In the 1970s, Brazil was seen as an economic miracle. Its economic success, however, was accompanied by growing inequality, making Brazil one of the world's most unequal societies. Brazil relied heavily on foreign borrowing. In the early 1980s, with world interest rates rapidly rising, this reliance caused severe economic problems. When the 21-year military dictatorship finally ended in 1985, the problems were passed to the civilian government. Inflation soared, and various economic measures failed to solve it. The next president, Fernando Collor de Mello, made privatization an integral part of his economic policies. An underlying reason was to raise revenues to alleviate huge fiscal deficits. His government privatized 33 state-owned enterprises in the early 1990s, including steel, petrochemicals and fertilizers. Alas for him, he was impeached by Congress in 1992 on grounds of corruption and forced to resign.

The incoming president in 1993, Itama Franco, inherited a severe economic crisis and hyper-inflation. His Finance Minister Fernando Henrique Cardoso introduced an economic plan that continued the privatization program and successfully stabilized the economy and ended the inflation. In 1995, Cardoso himself became president, staying two terms until 2002. He oversaw a deeper wave of privatization. Petrobras, Brazil's largest state enterprise, remained outside the privatization program. In 2000 and 2001, the government made two public offerings of Petrobras shares but kept majority control of the corporation, allowing a minority of private shareholders. Cardoso was also the first president to start a program to address the inequality issue in Brazil.

Lula da Silva of the Workers' Party was a very different president (2003–2010). Brazil rose to become the world's tenth largest oil producer, and da Silva used the oil wealth to improve health, education and employment, especially for the poor. He was democratically succeeded in 2010 by his chief aide, Dilma Rousseff, who continued his policies.

Petrobras, created in 1953, had a petroleum monopoly (except in wholesale and retail operations) until 1997, when private companies were allowed to explore and develop oil and gas fields under concessions or production-sharing contracts. With the discovery of giant offshore fields, oil production quadrupled between the mid-1980s and 2017, reaching 2.7 million b/d. Having been an oil importer, Brazil became a net oil exporter in 2011. Until the 2014 oil price collapse, the petroleum sector was Brazil's strong engine of economic growth. As of 2018, there were more than 50 companies engaged in oil exploration. Even so, Petrobras has grown to become the world's fourth largest oil company, measured by market capitalization. Its shares are held 54 per cent by the federal government, 5 per cent each by the Brazilian Development Bank and Sovereign Wealth Fund, and 36 per cent by the general public.

Brazil is a new oil frontier. Offshore fields have huge potential for further expansion, but they are deep and high-cost. The offshore potential includes "pre-salt" reservoirs buried below 4,000 metres of rock and salt. They are being developed by consortia of Petrobras and private companies. Government regulations required that Petrobras have a minimum 30 per cent interest and be the operator in each consortium.[45] Foreign companies and their governments wanted to see Petrobras' favoured status overturned. The pre-salt reservoirs are of enormous interest to them. Why else would the US NSA be monitoring phone calls and emails of Petrobras, and Canada's Communications Security Establishment be monitoring computers at Brazil's Ministry of Mines and Energy? Thus reported *The Guardian*[46] and the *Globe and Mail* in 2013.[47]

In 2014, Petrobras became mired in a vast corruption scandal, the largest in Brazil's history. A federal police investigation, named Operation Car Wash, found prominent politicians and businessmen, including some Petrobras directors, were overcharging contracts with Petrobras and using part of the money to pay for bribes and electoral campaigns. When Petrobras' auditors failed to sign off on third quarter accounts in 2014, the value of its assets plummeted. Several of those charged with wrongdoing went to jail.

Brazilian President Dilma Rousseff, who had chaired the board of Petrobras from 2003 to 2010, denied knowledge of any wrongdoing. But her political enemies saw an opportunity to oust her. In 2016, Brazil's Lower House of Congress voted to impeach her for manipulating the federal budget and sent the removal process to the Senate. One day later, a key opposition senator, Aloysio Nunes, flew to Washington for undisclosed meetings with US politicians and officials.[48] Brazil's Senate initiated impeachment proceedings, suspended Rousseff from office and appointed Vice-President Michel Temer as interim president. A few days later, May 22, Planning Minister Romero Jucá resigned when a secretly taped call came to light. In the call, he said Rousseff must be removed to quash the Petrobras corruption investigations implicating him and others in the Interim Cabinet.[49] Whatever the underlying motivation, the Senate impeached Rousseff and removed her from office on August 31.

The US State Department gave Washington's blessing, saying Brazil had acted within its constitutional framework. In contrast, leaders around Latin America questioned the process and expressed support for Rousseff. The politician who spearheaded the impeachment, Eduardo Cunha, was himself expelled from Parliament and was arrested on corruption charges related to the Petrobras scandal. Dilma Rousseff called the impeachment a political coup.

Following Rousseff's impeachment, Vice-President Temer became president pending new elections in 2018. He promised to revive the economy by reversing Rousseff's policies, and he talked of privatization, deregulation and fiscal discipline. Corruption scandals continued to swirl around Temer's cabinet and party, but Brazil returned to the Washington Consensus. In November 2016, President Temer signed a bill giving private companies a larger role in exploring the massive deepwater pre-salt reservoirs off the southern coast. The bill removed the requirement that Petrobras must be the operator and have a minimum 30 per cent share in any pre-salt project.[50] Shell expressed immediate interest, saying the deepwater fields were among the highest-quality assets in its global portfolio. Shell was the second largest participant after Petrobras.[51]

In the general elections scheduled for October 2018, the front-runner presidential candidate was Lula da Silva. He headed the Workers' Party and had been Brazil's president twice before (2003–2010). His campaign came to naught in April, when the Brazilian Supreme Court of Brazil upheld a lower court sentencing him to 12 years' imprisonment on charges of fraud. He was accused of receiving an apartment and renovations from a construction company in order to get contracts from Petrobras. US journalists Glenn Greenwald[52] and Mark Weisbrot[53] separately commented the evidence was basically non-existent and the case looked politically motivated. With Lula out of the race, Brazil's right wing and the Washington Consensus were relieved.

* * *

Venezuela illustrates a country that has been resistant to the Washington Consensus, preferring to keep its petroleum within Venezuelan control. It is the number one petro-state in the world with larger proven oil reserves than any other country. Foreign oil companies rushed in when oil was first discovered in 1914. By the late 1930s, Venezuela was the world's largest exporter and third largest producer of crude oil. Production peaked in 1970 at 3.8 million b/d. The main producing fields are beside and under Lake Maracaibo in the west and in the nation's east. In addition, a vast belt of heavy oil exists along the Orinoco River. Much like bitumen in Canada, the heavy oil is costly to produce and refine.

In 1976, the government nationalized the oil industry. Unlike Iran's nationalization in 1951, this was not a cataclysmic event. It took place just after the 1973–74 oil price shock when OPEC countries sensed their newfound power. Kuwait, Saudi Arabia, UAE and Qatar had just acquired 60 per cent participation in local subsidiaries of foreign oil companies and were poised to acquire 100 per cent, and Libya and Iraq had just nationalized oil assets as well. In Venezuela, corporate concessions were due to expire and revert to the state in 1983–84, as a result of which companies had little incentive to invest in and maintain the oilfields.[54] There was a surge of economic nationalism — a belief that natural resources were a strategic national patrimony, different from oranges and lemons.

Venezuela created a holding company, Petróleos de Venezuela S.A. (PDVSA), with four main subsidiaries each retaining the nationalized assets of the previous companies: Lagoven (previously Exxon), Maraven (Shell), Meneven (Gulf Oil), Corpoven (others). The subsidiaries signed service contracts with several previous parent companies, such as Shell, to provide specific services. Later, the subsidiaries were merged into PDVSA itself. The government appointed technocrats and economists to the board of directors to ensure PDVSA operated in the national interest. On a World Bank economic mission soon after the nationalization, my task was to understand the nationalization and its ramifications for the economy. It appeared well prepared and executed.

Twenty years later, in 1995, Venezuela reopened the door to foreign investors in exploration and production. It offered three new arrangements with PDVSA: operating services agreements, risk/profit-sharing agreements and strategic associations.[55] The agreements were successful in attracting foreign investment and increasing production.[56] PDVSA signed 32 operating service agreements with 22 companies, handing over much of its fields to private investment. In Spanish, the policy shift was called the *Apertura Petrolera* (Petroleum Opening). The context was a severe economic crisis. Rafael Caldera had just been elected president and, election promises to the contrary, was forced by the crisis to seek International Money Fund assistance. The government implemented a tough economic program as required by the International Money Fund, including devaluation, fuel price and interest rate hikes, and privatizations.

Four years later, in 1999, Hugo Chávez was elected president and reversed these policies. He introduced a new constitution, which was easily approved in a national referendum. Chávez had immense charisma. He championed the poor, those living in the barrios tumbling down the city hillsides. He was heartily disliked by the business elite, the well-to-do and private media owners. Chávez tapped Venezuela's oil wealth to improve living standards, health and education. His 2001 Hydrocarbons Law raised royalty rates and required foreign investment in petroleum to be made in joint venture with PDVSA.

The success was dramatic. According to one study, poverty was reduced from 71 per cent in 1996 to 21 per cent in 2010 and extreme poverty from 40 per cent to just 7 per cent in 2010.[57] Infant mortality halved in the 20 years 1990 to 2010; the number of doctors tripled; 96 per cent of the population now had access to clean water. Illiteracy was eliminated. Education was no longer restricted to the well-to-do. It was made free from daycare to university, with 85 per cent of school-age children attending school, and ten new universities were created.

In December 2001, oil industry executives led a strike, and called for Chávez's resignation. By March 2002, the strikes and protests were almost daily. That month, Washington appointed a new ambassador, Charles Shapiro. He had an interesting background. He had served in Chile when President Salvador Allende was ousted from power, in El Salvador during its brutal civil war and in Washington as coordinator for Cuban Affairs. He was widely suspected of prior knowledge of the 47-hour coup which took place a month later.

On April 11, a huge rally was held at PDVSA's headquarters in Caracas, calling for Chávez's ouster. Leading the rally were the Confederation of

Labour Unions, the Chamber of Commerce (Fedecamaras) and senior military officers. The rally marched toward the Miraflores presidential palace. Outside the palace was an opposing rally of pro-Chávez supporters. Snipers opened fire from buildings overlooking the people below. Pro-Chávez supporters on a bridge next to the palace fired back. Dozens of supporters in both rallies were killed.

A Venevision television crew filmed the pro-Chávez shooters. The station claimed they were firing at "peaceful opposition protesters."[58] The images went viral. The media blamed Chávez, calling for his removal from power. The incident was remarkably similar to the sniping 12 years later in Kiev's Maidan that was blamed on Ukraine's President Yanukovych and led to his removal. History sometimes repeats in mysterious ways.

The military arrested Chávez and sequestered him in a military base on a remote Venezuelan island. The head of Fedecameras, Pedro Carmona, was sworn in as president on April 12. The same day, Washington endorsed his presidency. US Assistant Secretary of State for Western Hemisphere Affairs Otto Reich summoned Latin America's ambassadors and announced the US would support Carmona's government, saying Chávez's removal was not a rupture of democratic rule as he had resigned and was responsible for his fate. *The Observer* newspaper (UK) learned from officials at the Organization of American States in Washington that Reich had previously met several times with Carmona and other coup leaders and discussed plans in detail.[59]

Chávez's supporters from the barrios took to the streets in immense number, surrounded the Miraflores palace and demanded his return to power. On April 14, military loyalists restored him to office. It was a 47-hour coup. Chávez accused the United States of involvement, which President George W. Bush denied. Later, declassified documents showed CIA and US officials did have advance knowledge. Activist lawyer Eva Golinger also obtained evidence from the US National Endowment for Democracy that it spent US$2.2 million from 2000 to 2003 on training and financing anti-Chávez organizations.[60]

Following the failed coup, opposition leaders unsuccessfully sought to force a new presidential election. Just eight months after the coup, they began a general strike. It lasted from December 2002 to February 2003 and paralyzed the nation. PDVSA was central to the strike. Its management imposed an oil lockout, bringing oil production to a standstill.

PDVSA's marine captains stopped work, too, bringing the 13-ship fleet to a halt. On December 4, the captain of the tanker *Pilín León* (named after a Venezuelan beauty queen) anchored it in the Lake Maracaibo shipping channel and refused to move. The tanker remained there 17 days until troops seized it and a replacement crew took over, working two days to restart the ship. According to one source, the departing crew "had sabotaged the ship, leaving behind hard-to-notice traps in the computer system and elsewhere that could set off an explosion."[61]

The government finally prevailed and dismissed 18,000 PDVSA employees, 40 per cent of the company's workforce, for dereliction of duty. Oil production was restored to its pre-strike level by April 2003. Chávez took control of the petroleum sector. In 2005, he transformed exploration agreements (except for heavy oil) into joint ventures with PDVSA, and in 2007 restructured Orinoco heavy oil projects to give PDVSA a majority interest. He declared: "The owner will be PDVSA and the business will be in the hands of Venezuelans."[62] While most foreign companies acceded and Petro-Canada withdrew, ExxonMobil and ConocoPhillips filed for arbitration with the ICSID. In 2014, the ICSID ruled the expropriation of ExxonMobil assets was legal and required PDVSA to pay US$188 million in compensation. ExxonMobil had hoped for US$10 billion.[63]

ConocoPhillips claimed much more, US$31 billion. In September 2013, an ICSID tribunal ruled Venezuela's expropriation was illegal. On appeal, a subsequent tribunal ruled (two arbitrators to one) that it lacked authority to reconsider the earlier decision. By April 2018, the ICSID had not announced the amount of award against Venezuela.

After Argentina, Venezuela tops the world for investor-state dispute claims — at least 37 up to 2014, though some were dismissed, discontinued or settled.[64] ConocoPhillips' claim is the largest by far. In 2012, Venezuela pronounced enough-is-enough and withdrew from the ICSID Convention and several bilateral investment treaties, starting with the Netherlands. In 2007, ConocoPhillips had transferred its Venezuelan holdings to a new Dutch subsidiary, which sued Venezuela under the Dutch bilateral investment treaty. Alas for Venezuela, the treaty gave investors the right to arbitration until 2023.[65]

Within Latin America, Chávez developed close links with the presidents of like-minded countries: Cuba's Fidél Castro, Bolivia's Evo Morales, Ecuador's Rafael Correa and Nicaragua's Daniel Ortega. At his initiative, they created a new intergovernmental entity, the Bolivarian Alliance for Peoples of America (ALBA), to promote the integration of their countries. In 2005, ALBA established Petro-Caribe, which sells oil under concessionary (discounted) terms to Caribbean member countries. Venezuela reached out as well to the Southern Cone countries. In 2012, it joined the Mercosur trading bloc, comprising Argentina, Brazil, Paraguay and Uruguay.

Since 2010, Venezuela's oil exports to the United States — its biggest market — have been hit by competition from US fracked oil and Canadian bitumen oil. Venezuela was also hit by US sanctions. Production plunged from 3.0 million b/d in 2010 to 2.1 million b/d in 2017.

In 2013, President Chávez died of cancer at the young age of 58. He was mourned especially by the Venezuelan poor, who had benefited greatly from his policies. His successor, President Nicolás Maduro, continued Chávez's policies. However, the 2014 oil price collapse triggered a profound economic crisis. Venezuela is reliant on oil for 95 per cent of its export earnings and for almost half of government revenues. In April 2014, right-wing opponents of President Maduro staged a revolt in Caracas. It took place in the upper-class districts of Altamira and Palo Grande. The working class remained staunchly loyal, the revolt was put down and its leaders imprisoned.[66]

American antipathy to Venezuela continued. In March 2015, President Obama declared Venezuela a security threat and ordered sanctions against seven Venezuelan officials for their alleged role in human rights abuses during 2014 anti-government protests.[67] President Maduro submitted a petition with 10 million signatures calling on the US to reverse its stance. President Obama appeared to back down, telling the media: "We do not believe that Venezuela poses a threat to the United States, nor is the US a threat to the Venezuelan government."[68] Nonetheless, he renewed the Executive Order in March 2016.

With the deep economic crisis, popular discontent mounted. Elections for the National Assembly in December 2015 resulted in a heavy defeat for the ruling coalition. For many electors, it was a protest vote.[69] Since then, governance has been paralysed in a stand-off between the presidency and the National Assembly. All the while, the nation has experienced severe economic crisis and anti-government violence. Attempting to break the political gridlock, in mid-2017 President Maduro established an *ad hoc* National Constituent Assembly to draft a new constitution, which he promised to put to a referendum for approval. A general election was held for representatives to the new Constituent Assembly. The working class and poor voted in huge numbers. The opposition boycotted the election, held violent street rallies, attacked government institutions and called for general strikes. The opposition-controlled National Assembly expressed hostility to any constitutional change and alleged President Maduro was moving toward a dictatorship.

Washington sought regime change. Just before the election, the White House imposed sanctions on various government officials, military officers and PDVSA executives. CIA Director Mike Pompeo said he was hopeful there could be "a transition in Venezuela and the CIA is doing its best to understand the dynamic there."[70] Immediately after the election, the White House imposed sanctions on President Maduro himself, calling him a dictator for attempting to crush his country's opposition.[71]

Two weeks later, on August 11, President Trump threatened military intervention, telling reporters: "The people are suffering and they are dying. We have many options for Venezuela including a possible military option if necessary." The South American trade bloc Mercosur rejected the use of force, saying dialogue and diplomacy were the only acceptable means to promote democracy in Venezuela.[72] Mercosur had suspended Venezuela's membership a few days earlier.

On August 25, the White House imposed severe sanctions on Venezuela's oil sector.[73] It prohibited US financial institutions from dealings in new debt or equity issued by the Venezuelan government or PDVSA. It prohibited dealings in bonds owned by the Venezuelan public sector, as well as dividend payments to the government of Venezuela. The White House exempted oil exports and imports involving Citgo, PDVSA's large US subsidiary, but restricted it from remitting dividends to Venezuela. US National Security Advisor H.R. McMaster said the US would continue to increase pressure on Venezuela until its citizens' "rights and democracy are fully restored." The White House said the measures were "carefully calibrated to deny the Maduro dictatorship a critical source of financing to maintain its illegitimate rule."

Responding to Washington's financial sanctions, President Maduro took action. In September, he announced in future Venezuela will trade in oil, gas and gold using currencies other than the US dollar, including the Chinese yuan, Japanese yen, Russian ruble and Indian rupee. In December, he announced the creation of El Petro, a crypto-currency backed by oil reserves, to circumvent Venezuela's need for US dollars. Venezuela became the fourth oil country — after China, Russia and Iran — to move away from petrodollar dependence.

Ottawa lined up with Washington. In September, Foreign Minister Chrystia Freeland announced sanctions on 40 senior Venezuelan officials, including President Nicolás Maduro. The intent, she said, was "to send a clear message that their anti-democratic behaviour has consequences." Canada would "not stand by silently as the Government of Venezuela robs its people of their fundamental democratic rights." In November, Canada targeted 19 Venezuelans under the new *Magnitsky Act*, again including President Maduro. Dare it be said, Washington's squeeze on Venezuelan oil exports to US refineries greatly benefited Canadian exporters of bitumen oil.[74]

China and Russia both spoke against outside interference and unilateral sanctions, which would only worsen Venezuela's situation. Venezuela has drawn closer to both countries diplomatically and economically in recent years, in part because of American pressures, and both have invested big-time in Venezuela's energy and infrastructure. China and Russia have lent billions of dollars to Venezuela, much through oil-for-loan deals that require oil shipments to be used to service those loans.[75] Russia's Rosneft has invested heavily in joint ventures with PDVSA to develop Orinoco heavy oil fields and offshore gas fields. In 2016, Rosneft acquired a 49.9 per cent interest in Citgo as collateral for a $1.5 billion loan to PDVSA. With its collateral now put at risk, Rosneft is looking to exchange its stake in Citgo for joint ventures in Venezuela.[76]

These latest measures by the US and Canada against Venezuela appear to contravene the Charter of the Organization of American States, of which the United States, Canada and Venezuela are members. Article 19 stipulates that "no State or group of States has the right to intervene ... in the internal or external affairs of any other State." Article 20 stipulates: "No State may use or encourage the use of coercive measures of an economic or political character in order to force the sovereign will of another State." Powerful countries do not have the right to flout the OAS Charter, although the US clearly did so in the 2002 coup attempt against President Chávez.

Will US sanctions bring down the Venezuelan government or bring it yet closer to China and Russia? In 2018, Venezuela remained independent and in charge of its own oil, still outside the Washington Consensus, but was weakened and under siege.

CANADA

Petro-Canada was created as a Crown Corporation in Canada in 1975. Its headquarters were initially in Ottawa but moved shortly to Calgary, into a building dubbed Red Square by the local citizenry. In the 1970s, national oil companies were being created all over the world, except the United States. They were well established in Latin America. Even BP was then owned 51 per cent by the UK government, thanks to Winston Churchill's actions in 1913. Canada, too, had a long history of state enterprises, known as Crown Corporations.

In Canada, the 1970s were the heyday of economic nationalism. Foreign ownership had increased rapidly since World War II, with multinational companies owning branch plants in Canada. Concerns rose because of key corporate decisions being made in head offices outside Canada; the dearth of research and development by branch plants; manipulation of import and export transfer prices detrimental to branch plant balance sheets and tax obligations; and US assertion of legal jurisdiction over branch plants.

The government of Prime Minister Pierre Trudeau shared these concerns. It established the Foreign Investment Review Agency (FIRA) in 1973 to review proposals for foreign acquisitions and the creation of foreign-owned businesses in Canada. It created Petro-Canada in 1975 as a window on the industry and a catalyst for investment. Alberta's reserves of light crude oil appeared to be on the decline. Major oil companies became increasingly interested in developing Canada's petroleum resources in tougher places — the Alberta oil sands, offshore Newfoundland, offshore Nova Scotia, the

High Arctic. Petro-Canada became a major player in these activities. It grew rapidly through corporate acquisitions.

Petro-Canada was a company reporting to the federal government in Ottawa and not to corporate headquarters in Houston or London. It had to undertake research in-house that would otherwise be done in head offices abroad. It teamed up with Venezuela's PDVSA to conduct research in heavy oil technology for the Orinoco and Athabasca deposits — two national oil companies holding hands. It did the same for economic studies of world oil prospects. The big question was: would oil prices sustain the viability of frontier projects which the companies were considering? Confronting that question was my role at Petro-Canada, working with PDVSA's Francisco Parra, a distinguished oil economist and OPEC's first secretary general.

Petro-Canada became popular outside of Alberta — an emblem of Canadian pride. But it was a red flag in Alberta, with cries of creeping social-ism and unfair advantages. Alberta saw the petroleum as *theirs*, a provincial matter. Bumper stickers surfaced with the slogan "Let the Eastern bastards freeze in the dark." The Progressive Conservatives, led by Albertan Joe Clark, were strongly opposed to the company.

Nor was it popular in Washington, DC, where I experienced this opposi-tion first hand. I had gone to the Canadian Embassy for a brief update on the US energy scene. After our discussion, the diplomat asked: "Are you free to stay a bit? My next meeting is with two US officials. I'd like you to witness." When the men from US Treasury arrived, I was introduced as an economist with Petro-Canada. They asked no questions. Instead, they launched into a 30-minute harangue, a monologue berating Canadian oil policy, including Petro-Canada. We simply listened respectfully. As they were leaving, the Canadian diplomat thanked them courteously for sharing their views. Afterward, we shared a moment of silence. Then the diplomat said: "That's what I have to put up with on a regular basis." As I left the embassy, I thought about the harangue. We were Canadians — friends and neighbours. How would they treat people in other countries who chose an independent path?

In Canada, energy was a major preoccupation. In 1980, the Liberal govern-ment under Pierre Trudeau launched its National Energy Program (NEP). It was controversial for its oil and gas policies, which contained tax provisions favouring Canadian over foreign companies, and made-in-Canada crude oil prices below world levels. These measures went over like a lead balloon in Alberta. But the NEP was broader than petroleum and contained a raft of interesting ideas for electricity, renewable energy and energy conservation. Spooked by the NEP, some foreign oil companies began selling their assets in Canada.[77] The NEP was slammed by critics as nothing more than a gigantic "revenue grab."[78] In 1984, Pierre Trudeau made his famous walk in the snow and retired from politics.

In the ensuing general election, the Progressive Conservatives under Brian Mulroney swept into power. They dismantled the NEP in 1985; and Canadian governments since then, both Liberal and Conservative, have remained committed to market-based oil and gas prices. Mulroney's government negotiated free trade deals with the United States, first the 1988 Canada-United States Free Trade Agreement and then, with the addition of Mexico, the 1994 North American Free Trade Agreement (NAFTA). Free trade includes petroleum. In times of scarcity, Canada would have to share its oil and gas supply with the United States.

In 1990, Mulroney's government began privatizing Petro-Canada and gradually reduced its shareholding to 19 per cent. In 2004, the Liberal government under Jean Chrétien sold the remaining shareholding. In 2009, Petro-Canada was acquired by Suncor Energy, an independent Canadian company. It was the end of an era. Canada swung from economic nationalism to neoliberalism and came into line with the Washington Consensus.

* * *

The experiences of Russia, Argentina, Bolivia, Brazil and Venezuela illustrate the pressures to conform to the Washington Consensus, the use of international financial institutions to implement change, and US efforts to promote privatization in the petroleum sector. Any country that balked or refused was subject to pressures of one kind or another, even Canada.

Since 2014, economies depending on petroleum revenue have been badly hurt by the fall in oil prices. The Russian economy has been further hurt by Western sanctions; tit-for-tat, so has European agriculture. In

Latin America, widespread unrest has pitted rich against poor, big business against reformers. Is the pendulum swinging back toward the Washington Consensus? In three countries, Argentina, Brazil and Ecuador, that appears so. Venezuelan leaders are in Washington's crosshairs — the recipient of US sanctions and media wrath. Canada, too, has issued sanctions against Russia and Venezuela.

The ebb and flow of pressures to privatize are likely to continue. Sovereignty has become a delicate balancing game. It was always fragile, only the game itself moved from colonialism to the use of international institutions to effect change. Economic skirmishes illustrate how countries are nudged or pressured to conform to the Washington Consensus.

CHAPTER 10
THE PETROLEUM GAME — NEW REALITIES

"Ten years from now, twenty years from now, you will see: oil will bring us ruin ... Oil is the Devil's excrement."

—Juan Pablo Pérez Alfonzo, Venezuelan diplomat and politician

Pérez Alfonzo's words about oil bringing ruin have come down through the decades and become famous. Born in 1903 to a patrician family in Venezuela, he became a lawyer, politician and diplomat, having an extraordinary influence on petroleum policy during his lifetime. As Venezuelan Minister of Mines and Hydrocarbons, he initiated innovative petroleum policy both within Venezuela and internationally. Through his collaboration with countries in the Middle East, he founded and became the first president of the OPEC in 1960.

When I went to Venezuela as part of a World Bank economic mission a decade later, he was still an influential figure. Though retired, he agreed to meet our team at his home for discussions on petroleum. He was an affable and genteel man, with a warm smile. As we sat on his patio, shaded from a hot sun, we looked out over tree-lined streets to the valley of Caracas. In that lovely setting, I heard him utter those famous words: "Oil is the Devil's excrement."

Oil is both a benefit and a curse. It is a highly convenient fuel. It is easily transportable. It fuels modern economies worldwide. Petroleum exports provide government revenues and help with balance of payments, but they can force up the exchange rate and hobble other productive sectors.

This had happened in Venezuela. It also happened in the Netherlands with North Sea gas. In reality, the petroleum market is a rollercoaster. Price fluctuations affect the economies and politics of both importing and exporting countries. When prices are high, exporting countries receive abundant revenue and become accustomed to it. When the price drops, they face hard times. The reverse is true for importing countries.

The effects of petroleum are even broader. Petroleum's association with enormous wealth and power make it a highly sought commodity, a worthwhile target of intrigues, rivalry and conflict. Petroleum is also intricately linked with climate change and the destruction of life itself — a dilemma that has so far defied solution. Amid new economic realities affecting the world oil scene and new geopolitical realities emerging, the challenges are complex, interrelated and still unfolding.

THE PATTERN AROUND CONFLICT AND PETROLEUM

Pérez Alfonzo's words about petroleum bringing ruin could apply to recent conflicts. In Iraq, Libya and Syria, both destruction and loss of life have been widespread. In many other countries, ruin is extensive. Both the attacked and the attacker have suffered in many ways. And huge amounts of money have been spent through defence departments, intelligence agencies and special forces, money that might have been spent in other ways. Yet petroleum issues and international rivalry are rarely discussed in public fora. Again and again, interventions, sanctions and pressures have been applied to countries with petroleum resources or transit routes with no mention of their petroleum significance.

Where did all these conflicts come from? In a 2007 speech, US General Wesley Clark recounted an experience he had in 2001, a few weeks after 9/11.[1] He had just retired and was visiting a senior officer in the Pentagon. The officer showed him a memo from the Secretary of Defense's office, indicating the US was going to attack and destroy the governments in seven countries in five years — starting with Iraq, and moving on to Syria, Lebanon, Libya, Somalia, Sudan and Iran.

Clark said the aim was "to destabilize the Middle East, turn it upside down, make it under our control."

What transpired is consistent with the policy coup that Clark heard about just after 9/11. The coup was being engineered by neoconservatives — Cheney, Rumsfeld, Wolfowitz and others from the think-tank Project for the New American Century. Five of the countries in the memo — Iraq, Libya, Sudan, Somalia, Syria — are destabilized as of 2018; and Iran has been the target of immense pressure. The conflicts of recent years were planned at the highest levels of the US government.

Looking at each conflict in turn reveals patterns. For example, one so-called Bad Guy after another has been accused of threatening peace or stifling freedom and democracy. It's a long list: bin Laden, the Taliban, Hussein, Gaddafi, Assad, Yanukovych, Chávez/Maduro, Putin. Each narrative has promoted black-and-white thinking, creating "us" and "them." The pattern is remarkably consistent. A leader, previously tolerated, becomes a Bad Guy. Western interference begins through sanctions or assistance to rebels or proxies. The leader is demonized; horror stories spread; war begins. The Bad Guy dies or is ousted; the regime changes; chaos endures. That was the story for Afghanistan, Iraq, Libya, Somalia and Ukraine. That was the outcome sought for Syria, except its leader survived in power; so have leaders in Iran, Russia and Venezuela. A matrix illustrates the pattern for numerous recent conflicts.

Matrix: Pattern of Countries in Conflict

	Leader demonized	Sanctions	Rebels assisted	Horror stories	War begins	Leader ousted	Regime changed	Chaos endures
Iraq	/	/	/	/	/	/	/	/
Syria	/	/	/	/	/	–	–	/
Iran	/	/	/	/	–	–	–	–
Libya	/	/	/	/	/	/	/	/
Somalia	/	–	/	/	/	/	/	/
Afghanistan	/	–	/	/	/	/	/	/
Ukraine	/	–	/	/	/	/	/	/
Russia	/	/	/	/	–	–	–	–

All these countries involve petroleum, a vital commodity for economies worldwide. Iran, Iraq and Libya have vast oil reserves. Iran and Russia have the world's largest gas reserves. Other countries — Afghanistan, Syria,

Ukraine — have a strategic location for pipelines. Somalia borders strategic sea routes. Petroleum may not be the whole story but is certainly part of it. Why else would the US government have literally hundreds of people monitoring world petroleum — at the Departments of State, Energy, Defense and Commerce, the CIA and National Security Council? Other countries monitor world petroleum, too, though not on this scale. The geopolitics is like a chess game — for mastery and power. Wars for resources are illegal under the UN Charter, yet each of these countries in conflict has a petroleum dimension.

Was the pattern orchestrated? The memo described to Wesley Clark in 2001 identified a motive — the intention to bring the Middle East under US control. The Middle East is the world's energy heartland, a region extending into Central Asia. American policy sees both regions as requiring America's exclusive defence umbrella. Regional governments are meant to toe the line. Washington deplored Russian assistance to President Assad in Syria. It was irked at Chinese efforts to build up economic and diplomatic links with the Middle East and Central Asia. It contested Iran's influence as a regional power.

Henry Kissinger, when US National Security Advisor and Secretary of State in the 1970s, reportedly said: "If you control oil, you control entire nations; if you control food, you control the people; if you control money, you control the entire world." As of 2018 he was an unofficial adviser to President Trump on foreign affairs.

Donald Trump gave a clear signal of petroleum's importance to his presidency by appointing Rex Tillerson, previously CEO of the world's largest oil company, ExxonMobil, as secretary of state. Trump declared in 2017: "Our country is blessed with extraordinary energy abundance ... We have nearly 100 years' worth of natural gas and more than 250 years' worth of clean, beautiful coal. We are a top producer of petroleum and the number-one producer of natural gas ... With these incredible resources, my administration will seek not only American energy independence ... but American energy dominance. We will export American energy all over the world."[2] His America First Energy Plan expresses commitment to "energy independence from the OPEC cartel and any nations hostile to our interests" and "to develop a positive energy relationship with our Gulf allies ... as part of our anti-terrorism strategy."[3] His allies exclude Iran.

When the US prefers to use its military rather than diplomacy in foreign policies, conflict and outright war ensue. The Pentagon has a far larger budget than State Department. As the military takes over, the petroleum game fades out of sight. But it is still there, even though politicians may assert there's no oil motivation in one intervention after another.

In 2018, Venezuela was singled out for new attention. In February 2018, Secretary Tillerson made a tour of South America, pressing for increased regional attention to the crisis in Venezuela. Starting at the University of Texas at Austin, he cited Venezuela's Constituent Assembly as illegitimate and asserted the US believed there would be regime change. He said, "in the history of Venezuela ... oftentimes it's the military that handles that."[4] Later in his tour, he indicated the US might prohibit the sale of Venezuelan oil to the United States.[5] Are US threats about Venezuela's system of government? Or are they because Venezuela has the world's largest reserves of petroleum under state control?

The United States projects military and cyber power. It spends more on its military than the rest of the world combined. It has roughly 1,000 military bases worldwide in 130 countries on every continent, except Antarctica. The US is less adroit at diplomacy. It tends not to understand local cultures and is surprised when others have different viewpoints and motivations.

The US scholar and retired colonel Andrew Bacevich says the US has developed an over-reliance on military power to achieve its foreign policy aims. In his view, romanticized images of war in popular culture produce a highly unrealistic, dangerous notion of what war is really like.[6] His 2016 book *America's War for the Greater Middle East* points to ignorance and hubris in US military policy: "A succession of American leaders ... has persisted in the belief that the determined exercise of US military power will somehow get things right. None have seen their hopes fulfilled."

The wars have generated enormous antipathy to Westerners. The late Chalmers Johnson, professor emeritus of the University of California, San Diego, and long-time adviser to the CIA, warned against blowback, "retaliation for the numerous illegal operations we have carried out abroad that were kept totally secret from the American public."[7] After he left office, US General McChrystal, commander of Joint Special Operations Command (2003–2008), spoke to the BBC about the impact of drones. There is "a perception of helpless people in an area being shot at like thunderbolts from the sky by an entity that is acting as though they have omniscience and omnipotence ..." Among the population affected, this creates enormous resentment.[8] The 2017 use of the Mother of All Bombs in Afghanistan would have had the same effect.

In every war, there are winners and losers. Winners include defence departments, militaries and NATO; all require enemies to justify their budgets and existence. Winners are also politicians, security and intelligence establishments, arms manufacturers, even the media. Losers include taxpayers, non-military spending on infrastructure, health and education, the dead and their families, the wounded and all that is destroyed.

Wars are costly. A 2013 study by Linda Bilmes at Harvard's Kennedy School of Government found that the Iraq and Afghanistan wars, taken together, will be the most expensive in US history, somewhere between US$4 to $6 trillion. The estimate includes long-term medical care and disability compensation for veterans and families.[9] In 2015, US military expenditures totalled about US$600 billion, or 54 per cent of the federal government's total discretionary budget.[10] These figures exclude big-ticket items such as nuclear weapons, veterans' benefits and the interest on debt from the Afghan-Iraq wars.[11] In addition, undisclosed black budget spending by US intelligence agencies is estimated at about US$52 billion annually.[12]

What about the cost to the losers? According to a 2016 World Bank study, in four war-torn countries — Iraq, Libya, Syria and Yemen — every aspect of people's lives — home, clinic, school, work, food, water — has been affected by the fighting, with some 46 million people needing humanitarian aid. The Syrian war has displaced more than 12 million people, or half its population, both internally and externally. In Iraq and Yemen, another 6.5 million have been internally displaced.[13] The Bank study does not add the huge numbers of dead and injured.

Some analysts see what's going on as energy wars — for control of world energy reserves, pipelines and chokepoints. US scholar Michael Klare argues that wars will increasingly "be fought not over ideology but over access to dwindling supplies of precious natural commodities."[14] He asserts that global competition over energy will be "a pivotal, if not central, feature of world affairs for the remainder of the century."[15] Of course, wars for resources are illegal under the UN Charter. That's why they are described by terms that sound innocuous, such as humanitarian missions. The links between conflict and petroleum are long-standing but largely hidden in the day-to-day evolution of conflict.

The Petroleum Game is part of the American push for hegemony. Since the collapse of the Soviet Union, the United States has seen itself as a unipolar nation. The US asserts its good intentions, emphasizing freedom and democracy. In his 1997 book *The Grand Chessboard*, Zbigniew Brzezinski described America as standing at the centre of an interlocking world, in which power originated ultimately from a single source: Washington, DC.[16]

Chalmers Johnson saw the US as an empire, with its huge defence budgets, large standing armies, continuous wars and massive military-industrial industries.[17] He argued convincingly that democracy and empire were incompatible. If the US continued to pursue empire abroad, it would lose its democratic traditions at home.

TOOLS TO IMPLEMENT HEGEMONY

For years, the United States has sought to involve other countries in its plans. US leaders constantly refer to the "international community," as if all other countries agreed. In fact, many countries do not agree or may accede reluctantly. Do Canadian leaders always agree with the United States, or do they go along because it is the price of remaining on good terms with Canada's largest trading partner? Agreeing with the United States means a loss of national sovereignty. Disagreeing can be perilous, as France discovered after it declined to join the invasion of Iraq. Many smaller countries feel obligated, even if they can only provide a few soldiers. Canada, Europe, Australia, New Zealand and Japan are locked in through military alliances, intelligence sharing, trade deals such as NAFTA and supra-governmental institutions like the European Commission. For example, the intelligence services of US, Canada, Britain, Australia and New Zealand are inextricably bonded together as the Five Eyes.

The military-industrial complex has grown enormously over time and especially in recent years. In the United States, the defence budget for 2017 amounted to $594 billion, including overseas contingency operations for war. For 2018, it was US$53 billion higher. The Defense Department's budget, excluding overseas contingency operations, grew by 31 per cent between 2000 and 2014.[18] William Hartung, an expert on US military spending at the US Center for International Policy, notes the increase is larger than the defence budgets of Britain, Germany or Japan.[19]

Military expenditure data for 2016, published by the Stockholm International Peace Research Institute, show the United States as the world's largest spender at US$611 billion (36 per cent of the world total). US totals dwarfed military spending by China and Russia. In second place, China spent US$215 billion (13 per cent of the world total). In third place, Russia spent US$69 billion (4 per cent of the total). NATO's collective spending was US$881 billion (52 per cent of the total), 12 times more than Russia's. The United States and NATO are way ahead in the arms race. By comparison, Canada's military spending amounted to US$15.5 billion.

The system has become entrenched. Only a far-reaching public outcry is likely to change or cut back the military-industrial complex — and those who are part of the system are unlikely to protest. The huge investment in preparation for war and the enormous wealth generated by selling weapons to other countries promote the likelihood of war, either accidentally or on purpose.

Are US enemies real? Or are they phantoms, created to support the continuation of enormous expenditures in the military-industrial complex? The vested interests are widespread in both federal and state governments. Military and intelligence agencies, defence contractors and well-heeled lobbyists are immensely powerful. Military bases exist in every state of the union. Major defence contractors have manufacturing plants in most US states. Canada's defence contractors benefit, too, from government largesse and export sales, mostly to the Pentagon. Several of the biggest Canadian contractors are US-owned branch plants, including General Dynamics, Lockheed Martin, Raytheon and Boeing. When armament sales are important to economic prosperity, pressures exist for their continuation and expansion.

* * *

Perception management is a term used in government and intelligence circles. It means offering a limited version of what's going on to sell a policy agenda. Yves Engler, a Montreal writer, describes the process in a new book, *A Propaganda System — How Governments, Corporations, Media and Academia Sell War and Exploitation*. During World War II, allied governments practised deception against the enemy. Today, they practise deception against their own voters and are aided by the mainstream media. For instance, during the build-up to the 2003 Iraq War, the *New York Times* published repeated articles reporting weapons of mass destruction. Secretary of State Colin Powell alleged their existence at the UN Security Council. It was all false — there were none. The US and UK governments were promoting war. They were exaggerating threats, demonizing foreign leaders and ridiculing any media that failed to follow their messages.

Governments engage in perception management as an instrument of military warfare. The Pentagon and NATO both do so. They call it *strategic communications*, which they conduct via public diplomacy, civilian and military public affairs, information operations and psychological operations. Strategic communications are an essential component of NATO operations.[20]

In 2014, seven NATO countries — Britain, Estonia, Germany, Italy, Latvia, Lithuania and Poland — established a Strategic Communications Centre of Excellence in Latvia.[21] Though outside NATO's command structure, the Centre is a NATO-accredited international military organization and its mission is to contribute to NATO's strategic communications capability. It holds conferences and seminars, conducts training and issues publications. Fake news, of course, is assumed to be propagated by the other people, not Western governments.

The Ghouta chemical attacks in Syria are illustrative of perception management or strategic communications. After media reports surfaced, Western governments claimed immediately they knew who was responsible, even though no evidence was yet available. Initial language asserted the belief that President Assad was responsible, or called it an "alleged chemical attack," but soon — after a barrage of media coverage — Assad's responsibility was assumed, still without evidence. When evidence emerged to the contrary, it failed to get similar attention. Virtually ignored were photos suggesting staging, analysis showing the rocket's trajectory must have come from rebel forces and analysis of the sarin itself indicating rebel sources.

Failure to correct the record of widespread coverage in 2013 left people and news media ready to quickly accept the assertion that Assad had attacked with chemical weapons in 2017 and again in 2018. No investigation was made immediately. Yet US assertions were accepted as fact and media quickly offered photos apparently shot in a hospital, supporting the US view. Ignored was the question: who benefits? A chemical attack could not benefit Assad, who at this point was defeating the rebels. It could benefit rebels, by providing an excuse for outsiders to intervene on their behalf. Without prior investigation, President Trump fired missiles both times, in contravention of international law.

Western media tend to promulgate the official narrative on foreign affairs. The publishers are patriotic; they support the home team. Journalists stay within the box — it's safer there. The corporate media cannot afford to antagonize their advertisers or government sources. Some media companies are part of large conglomerates benefiting from war. General Electric (GE), for example, owns the NBC network in the United States. Most Americans associate GE with its consumer products, a minority of its sales. A bigger part of GE's business is with the US Defense Department — jet engines, for example — and war is a profitable opportunity. Does this affect the way management at NBC reports the news?[22]

As governments and media promote only one way of looking at things, citizens, too, develop group-think. In his novel *Nineteen Eighty-Four*, George Orwell illustrated how group-think happens and how it operates. He coined the words Newspeak and Thoughtcrime. In the twenty-first century, governments and media have encouraged group-think as they demonize leaders, promote single-minded views without evidence and undertake action on the basis of manufactured crises.[23] In 2017, Raytheon stock surged after its Tomahawk missiles were used by the US to attack Syria, adding about $1 billion to the company's market value. The attack used 59 missiles at an estimated cost of $1.4 million each.

When leaders play disinformation games and the media fail to uncover them, taxpayers are taken for suckers. After all, it is taxpayers who fund the governments and the wars, while the manufacturers of armaments and accoutrements of war get rich. Simple fact-checking can reveal powerful interests are at stake. When a crisis erupted in Mali in 2016, it was easy to discover that Mali has huge deposits of gold and uranium, both high-value commodities. Canadian mining investments there were estimated at more than $1 billion. Mali's uranium fuels France's nuclear power and weapons. Canada and France were monitoring their national interests.

Who will talk truth to power? With the growth of the Internet, various online news sites are willing to think outside the box. They have become a major challenge to governments and media. In 2016, the US government launched an effort to discredit websites that critique their narratives. Mainline media supported this effort by publishing articles of dubious provenance castigating online sites. For instance, the *Washington Post* carried an article in November 2016 lauding two anonymous research groups for examining "Russian propaganda efforts to undermine American democracy and interests."[24] One of them, PropOrNot (Is it Propaganda or Not?), had posted a list of more than 200 websites that purportedly published or echoed Russian propaganda.[25] The list included many progressive US news sites that dared to question the official narrative.[26]

Many Americans fear a new McCarthyism to quell freedom of speech. In December 2016, with US officials alleging Russia was disseminating fake news through agencies such as RT News, President Obama signed the *Countering Foreign Propaganda and Disinformation Act*.[27] The *Act* created a centre within State Department to disseminate fact-based narratives countering propaganda and disinformation aimed at the United States and allies.[28] Some wits renamed it George Orwell's Ministry of Truth. Across the Atlantic, the European Parliament resolved that the EU likewise develop strategic communication mechanisms to counter disinformation and propaganda from Russia.[29]

Our media incessantly mention Russia as a source of fake news. Nobody addresses the misinformation or omissions of information by Western governments. To promote their own aims, Western countries have a long record of using false stories and half-truths. In essence, it is propaganda which leads to misleading interpretations of world events and an overemphasis on military actions. Hopefully, exposure and discussion can encourage a critical examination of all views.

* * *

International organizations provide fora for the exercise of power and for encouraging support of US political goals. The United States exerts economic power through the International Money Fund, World Bank and regional development banks, as well as through development assistance, including USAID and US non-governmental organizations (NGOs). One mode of assistance is democracy promotion. It includes support for opposition groups in selected countries in order to encourage acceptance of the US world view. Actions of organizations such as the National Endowment for Democracy in Bolivia, Ukraine and Venezuela are illustrative.

Since the mid-1980s, the Washington Consensus has profoundly affected much of the world, with deregulation and privatization. Some countries pushed back, like Bolivia, Ecuador and Venezuela. Countries that take an independent line can move overnight from friend to foe. That was the fate of Iraq, Iran, Libya and Syria. Influence may also be exerted through UN agencies, by ensuring that top jobs go to people sympathetic to US policies. An example is the UN International Atomic Energy Agency (IAEA). It played a key role in the search for nuclear weapons in Iraq prior to the 2003 invasion and in Iran prior to the 2016 nuclear deal. Its director general from 1997 to 2009 was Mohamed ElBaradei, an Egyptian law scholar and diplomat. He and the IAEA were jointly awarded the Nobel Peace Prize in 2005. The US wanted him ousted because he said repeatedly the IAEA had found no clear evidence of a nuclear weapons program. Such statements were unhelpful to the US agenda. In 2009, Yukiya Amano, a Japanese diplomat, was elected director general. Amano offered nuanced comments more helpful to the US agenda. According to a US diplomatic cable revealed by Wikileaks, Amano had assured the US ambassador he "was solidly in the US court on every key strategic decision, from high-level personnel appointments to the handling of Iran's alleged nuclear weapons program." Former high-level IAEA officials accused Amano of pro-Western bias, over-reliance on unverified intelligence and sidelining of skeptics.[30]

NATO has become a prime tool for co-opting allies into support for US geopolitical goals — and foreign adventures. NATO was established in 1949 to defend Western Europe against military invasion by the Soviet

Union. With the collapse of the Soviet Union in 1991, NATO lost its reason for existence. Some European voices called for its replacement by an EU defence force, but the United States was strongly opposed. Instead, NATO expanded its membership into Eastern Europe and extended its activities outside the NATO region — first to Bosnia and Serbia, then Afghanistan, and the western periphery of Russia as of 2018.

While NATO is governed by its 29 member countries, there is no voting or decision by majority. In concept, each nation retains sovereignty and responsibility for its own decisions. In reality, pressures to conform to Washington's will are immense. The US has key leadership roles and the biggest military by far. The two strategic commanders of military operations are both senior US military officers. The US makes the biggest contribution to NATO's budget, about 70 per cent. Compared to other NATO countries, it also dedicates the largest percentage of GDP to military spending, 3.6 per cent in 2016. Only four other countries reached the NATO target of 2 per cent: Britain, Estonia, Greece and Poland.[31] For its part, Canada stood at 1 per cent.

The EU cooperates closely with NATO. This is hardly surprising, as the EU and NATO have 22 members in common. As well, the 2007 Lisbon Treaty requires new EU members to align their military and economic policies with the EU's Common Security and Defence Policy. NATO is the key to Washington's control over Europe.

Donald Trump's election to the US Presidency rattled European leaders. During his campaign, he pronounced NATO to be obsolete and said the US might not come to the aid of countries that did not meet the defence spending target — 2 per cent of GDP.[32] After his election, Trump mollified the Europeans, saying he was fully behind NATO. But he insisted on their meeting the 2 per cent target. This, of course, would be a bonanza for US arms sales and the European military-industrial complex. He made the same pitch at the Brussels NATO Summit in May 2017, where he harangued NATO countries to "contribute their fair share and meet their financial obligations." He said 23 member nations were still not paying what they were supposed to be paying for their defence, and this was "not fair to the people and taxpayers of the United States." He omitted the customary presidential commitment to shared defence under NATO's Article 5 (an attack on one member is an attack on all).[33]

Countries took note. Prime Minister Justin Trudeau immediately affirmed Canada continued to be "a strong and reliable ally, now and into the future" and was leading a multinational NATO battle-group that would soon deploy to Latvia.[34] Twelve days later, Foreign Minister Chrystia Freeland, addressing Parliament on Canada's foreign policy priorities, promised the government would make the necessary investments in the Canadian military to "redress years of neglect and under-funding."[35] Asking rhetorically "why do we spend billions on defence if we are not immediately threatened?", she pointed to North Korea, Syria, Daesh [Islamic State], Ukraine and "Russian military adventurism and expansionism." The next day, Defence Minister Harjit Sajjan announced a new long-term defence policy with major increases in military spending.[36] It was politically inevitable.

Since 9/11, Canada has been flexing military muscle. It joined in wars on Afghanistan and Libya; as of 2018, it had sanctions on North Korea, Russia and Venezuela; as well as troops in Iraq, Latvia and Ukraine. The geopolitics is complex, and some realpolitik is inescapable in Canada for whom an open trading border with the United States is crucial. Even so, how far is Ottawa willing to go to appease Washington? The Middle East has been called the world's energy heartland — it is a tinderbox. Is Prime Minister Trudeau ready for a Middle East war? That was the question posed in 2017 by journalist Murray Dobbin, who observed putting Canadian troops on Russia's border has yielded Canada nothing in return.[37]

NATO is also a mechanism for collaborating on energy security. At the 2006 NATO Summit in Latvia, Washington sought to have NATO prevent risks in the Persian Gulf and elsewhere and alleged the unreliability of Russian gas supplies to Europe. Indeed US Senator Lugar, the Senate Foreign Relations Committee Chairman, wanted energy security to be an Article 5 commitment under the North Atlantic Treaty. But Europeans were wary of a commitment they might come to regret, and the Summit fudged the issue. Undaunted, the NATO bureaucracy marched on. In 2010, it created an Emerging Security Challenges Division to focus on terrorism, WMD proliferation, cyber defence and energy security.[38] In 2012, it opened an Energy Security Centre of Excellence in Vilnius, Lithuania[39] to provide expertise on "operational energy security."[40] These changes unfolded quietly with little public discussion in NATO countries.

The European Commission, like NATO, is headquartered in Brussels. It is the EU's secretariat, a huge bureaucracy drawn from all member countries. The European Commission and US Administration are fully in accord on European energy policy. The European Commission overtly collaborates with Washington on energy policies designed to reduce dependence on Russian oil and gas. Addressing the Atlantic Council in 2015, EU Energy Commissioner Miguel Arias Cañete praised EU-US cooperation. He said: "We already have achieved so much, but we could still achieve so much more."[41] He singled out EU-US cooperation on Ukraine, "from reform measures in Ukraine, to sanctions against Russia; from reverse gas flow from Slovakia to Ukraine, to integration of South East Europe in the EU's energy market."

In 2015, the EU created an Energy Union, with common laws and rules, to ensure member countries march to the same drum on energy policy. The European Council president, Donald Tusk, pointed to Russia as Europe's dominant supplier. He asserted "gas contracts should ... not be used as political weapons ... and should not negatively impact Europe's energy security."[42] The European Commission wanted to scrutinize gas deals with non-EU countries before they were signed, to ensure they complied with EU laws. Not all member countries were happy with this proposal. In 2015, Hungary's Prime Minister Orbán declared the EU was "heading into an energy union that hinders national sovereignty."[43] In 2017, Germany opposed European Commission pressure for a mandate to negotiate with Russia a legal framework for the Nord Stream 2 pipeline.

During his 2016 election campaign, Trump indicated his "desire to live peacefully and in friendship with Russia and China."[44] That triggered an extraordinary effort to taint him as unpatriotic — a Russophile — and force his presidency back into the traditional fold. The intelligence agencies weighed in, producing no concrete evidence, but alleging Russian interference in the election on Trump's behalf. The barrage continued unremittingly, with a special counsel appointed to investigate the Administration's alleged ties with Russia, and Senate hearings on Russia's alleged interference in the election. The allegations were repeated day after day, and soon the fact that they were only allegations was dropped. Critics and media began referring to Russian influence as if it were the truth. (The media failed to mention well-documented information on US interference in many foreign elections, even an election in Russia.) The White House adjusted course and US foreign policy began to look like a continuum from earlier days.

In recent decades the US has pushed for hegemony through military ventures, perception management and exertion of power within international organizations. In spite of all these many efforts, the world is changing and pushback against US hegemony is accelerating. New geopolitical realities are changing the Petroleum Game.

NEW GEOPOLITICAL REALITIES

Although unipolar thinking persists in Washington, the world is becoming increasingly multipolar. Before his death in 2017, Brzezinski recognized the change: "The United States is still the world's politically, economically, and militarily most powerful entity but, given complex geopolitical shifts in regional balances, it is no longer the globally imperial power."[45]

No country can challenge US military power, but several have joined hands to stave off US pressures. These pressures have brought China and Russia into a close relationship strategically, militarily, economically — including energy cooperation. Russia is vulnerable to US-EU efforts to reduce European dependence on Russian oil and gas. China, the world's largest oil importer, is vulnerable to potential closure of sea routes and chokepoints: the Strait of Hormuz, Strait of Malacca, South China Sea. To mitigate these vulnerabilities, the two countries have agreed to dramatic increases in petroleum exports overland from Russia to China. Russia has become China's top source of imported oil. It is building a huge gas pipeline from eastern Siberia to northeast China and is planning another from western Siberia to northwest China. All this requires vast capital expenditures, which both countries are making.

While the US has roughly 1,000 military bases worldwide in 130 countries, China has just one base abroad, in Djibouti, and plans another in Pakistan, both servicing Chinese naval vessels patrolling the strategic route from the Middle East to China. Russia has bases in nine countries. Of these, two are in Syria, and one is in Vietnam. The other seven are located in former Soviet republics: Armenia, Belarus, Georgia (peacekeeping in Abkhazia and South Ossetia), Kazakhstan, Kyrgyzstan, Moldova (peacekeeping in Transnistria), Tajikistan.

Russia and China are trading in rubles and yuan instead of the US dollar — a challenge to the petrodollar system for world oil trading. Iran and Venezuela, too, require payment for oil exports in yuan or euros. In 2018, Pakistan announced measures to promote the use of Chinese yuan in bilateral trade and investment with China. All five countries have experienced US economic sanctions or policies of containment. In 2018, China created a yuan-denominated oil futures contract backed by gold. That meant oil exporters to China could receive payment in yuan and convert it into gold. At the time, China was the world's largest importer. Would Arab Gulf oil exporters be willing to accept such payment terms? For the time being, it seemed unlikely as they would put the whole petrodollar system at risk and incur US wrath. The longer term is another matter.

The use of non-US currencies is a serious challenge to the petrodollar system. In the early 2000s, Iraq and Libya wanted to trade in euros or other currencies and soon faced military attacks. Was this coincidental? Gaddafi, Libya's leader, also wanted to return to the gold standard, and he proposed an African Investment Bank and an African Monetary Fund to undermine Western hegemony. He had the wherewithal to move forward on these proposals. Western accusations and attacks intervened. When he died, his plans died with him. Libya and Iraq both continued to trade in US dollars.

China takes an economic, non-military approach to trade and investment worldwide. It is the Middle East's largest investor and oil purchaser. It purchased more than half Iraq's crude oil by 2018. It became Africa's largest trading partner and its third largest investor.[46] It was investing big-time in Latin America and was the largest trading partner of Argentina, Brazil, Chile and Peru.

China's One Belt One Road initiative is a multi-billion dollar strategy to integrate Asia and Europe by land and sea — through trade and infrastructure. To finance the initiative, China created the Asian Infrastructure Investment Bank. Sixty-four countries joined, including Canada. The United States remained aloof. Another banking initiative is the New Development Bank, headquartered in Shanghai and established in 2015 by the BRICS countries — Brazil, Russia, India, China, South Africa. These new banks were created to provide an alternative source of financing to the World Bank and existing regional development banks. The new banks will facilitate a multipolar world with different economic models.

China and Russia have also been developing strategic associations with non-NATO countries. The Shanghai Cooperation Organization — comprising China, Russia, Kazakhstan, Kyrgyzstan, Tajikistan and Uzbekistan — was expanded at its 2017 Summit to include India and Pakistan. It encompassed roughly half the world's population and a quarter of the world's GDP. The Summit announced it would consider extending membership to Iran, which currently has observer status. In addition, China and Russia promoted new regional trading blocs. Russia's is the Eurasian Customs Union. China's is the Regional Comprehensive Economic Partnership — an alternative to Washington's moribund Trans-Pacific Partnership.[47]

Russia is becoming a major player in the Middle East petroleum sector. For instance, in 2017 Rosneft bought a 60 per cent stake in Iraqi Kurdistan's oil export pipeline and agreed to invest in five exploration blocks.[48] Rosneft and the National Iranian Oil Company agreed to work together on strategic oil and gas projects in Iran totalling US$30 billion.[49] In 2018, Russian and Saudi energy ministers signed a cooperation memorandum envisioning 23 projects, including Arctic LNG.[50] They also envisaged Russian investment in the upcoming Initial Public Offering (IPO) of Saudi Aramco shares. The IPO is a linchpin of Crown Prince Mohammed bin Salman's plan to transform the Saudi economy.[51]

The American trade deficit with China is a major White House preoccupation. In recent years, US companies have transferred much of their manufacturing from the United States to China, shipping raw materials there and bringing back finished goods into the United States. In his election campaign, President Trump promised to bring back jobs to American workers. In March 2018, he ordered severe tariffs on a range of imports from China, saying, "this is the first of many" trade actions. China immediately retaliated with plans to raise tariffs on various American goods. Observers presaged the outbreak of a trade war between the United States and China.

US power is being challenged. Its wars have failed, and the world is becoming multipolar again. Washington has not taken kindly to this new reality. It has put Moscow in its crosshairs, attributing to it one incident after another — the MH-17 downing, annexation of Crimea, aggression in eastern Ukraine, destruction of East Aleppo, Olympics doping, hacking into Democratic Party computers, the poisoning of two Russians in the United Kingdom. The information provided was always interpretative and unsubstantiated. NATO needs an enemy to justify its existence, and the military-industrial complex needs an adversary to justify sales and budgets. Washington has never liked the idea of Russia integrated into Europe — a threat to US leadership. It sought to break links between Europe and Russia, to isolate and weaken the Russian Bear. Not surprisingly, powerful US interests have felt threatened by Trump's overtures to Russia.

The New Cold War intensified in early 2018. President Trump shifted his inner circle of advisers, signalling a toughening of Trump's America First policy and setting off alarm bells in foreign capitals and media.[52] President Putin disclosed new hypersonic missiles capable of outmanoeuvring the United States' latest missile-defence systems and first-strike nuclear capability.

Europe has traditionally been an ally of the United States, but President Trump's imposition of tariffs on European and Canadian exports shattered expectations. At the June 2018 G7 Summit in Québec, leaders confronted Trump's outlier positions. Further, a tug-of-war exists within Europe between those reaching out to Russia as a normal European country and those spurning it and reaching out to the United States. With short-lived glitches, trade between Europe and Russia flourished for more than 50 years. After the upheavals of 2014 in Ukraine, Washington imposed sanctions on Russia for alleged aggression in Crimea and the Donbass. European governments lined up with Washington. Russia retaliated with sanctions on agriculture. Sanctions hurt the economies of both Russia and Europe, barely affecting the United States.

The European Union was under strain as never before. Britain was negotiating Brexit. Old Europe (France, Germany) and New Europe (Poland, the Baltic countries) were increasingly at loggerheads on investment and trade with Russia and the continuance of sanctions. Since Trump became president, some European governments have spoken more freely, expressing concerns about his pulling the United States out of the climate accord, and exasperation with new legislation that could sanction Europeans

Western leaders confront President Trump at G7 Summit, Québec, June 9, 2018.

participating in joint energy projects with Russia, notably Nord Stream 2. Washington's Russophobia looked increasingly self-serving and surrealistic. So did its sanctions imposed on one country after another — Iraq, Iran, Libya, North Korea, Russia, Syria, Venezuela.

The *cause célèbre* in March 2018 was the poison attack on Russian ex-double agent Sergei Skripal and his daughter Yulia in Salisbury, England. British statements indicated the poison was "of a type developed by Russia." Russian responsibility was assumed even though several countries were capable of creating the poison. The condemning of Russia without waiting for a proper investigation was reminiscent of earlier allegations against Iraq, Libya and Russia to justify war or sanctions. Other NATO countries — including Canada — joined in expelling diplomats. The media leapt aboard, but some politicians and observers were unconvinced. UK Labour Party leader Jeremy Corbyn, former UK Ambassador Craig Murray and others called for evidence. Once recovered, the Skripals remained incommunicado, unavailable to reveal what happened. The big question as always was *cui bono*, who benefited from the poisoning and its aftermath? Was the incident a Russian attack or an example of information warfare? It was altogether a strange affair, with facts and allegations changing daily.

In Western countries, public lack of trust in government statements has increased because of the Iraq War, the 2008 financial crisis, the disappearance of jobs. In their very different ways, President Trump, Britain's Jeremy Corbyn and France's Marine Le Pen have championed this popular discontent. With governments failing to level with the public and elites out of tune with large sections of the electorate, many voters have reflected their discontent at the ballot box.

THE PETROLEUM GAME CONTINUES

Both the world petroleum scene and the geopolitical situation have changed in the twenty-first century. The links between petroleum and conflict have unfolded in one country after another. As the US pursued hegemony, it drew in other countries to form coalitions and drop bombs on Afghanistan, Iraq, Libya, Syria and Yemen. It continued to impose non-nuclear and banking sanctions on Iran, then jettisoned the nuclear deal and reimposed oil sanctions. It encouraged regime change in Ukraine and promoted sanctions against Russia, North Korea and Venezuela. It stymied energy trade between Europe and Russia and expanded its own energy exports to Europe. NATO has built up its maritime strength to dominate strategic waterways.

What has happened as a result of this massive show of force? Instead of bringing countries under US control, conflict has continued, and millions of refugees have fled their countries to populate camps and swamp Europe. Terrorist incidents have expanded into Europe. Instead of falling into line, some countries have rejected Western advances and struggled to retain sovereignty. American leadership is being confronted. Its efforts to expand its own petroleum markets at the expense of other countries are being challenged. Countries in the Middle East are increasingly tied to Russia and China to counterbalance US control. Iran is highly skilled at diplomacy. Like other countries, it understands the US game and US strengths and weaknesses, and manoeuvres cautiously to its own advantage, always trying to avoid war.

In Europe, US policy has been self-serving and damaging to European economic interests. Trump's withdrawal from the Iran deal, including the threat of secondary sanctions on European firms that continue business with Iran, shocked Europe. His strong words to Europe to increase spending on defence were seen as another way to benefit US arms manufacturers.

His rough words to Germany to stop spending billions on Russian gas were seen as another way to benefit US LNG exporters.

With the rise of China and the renaissance of Russia, the world is shifting from a unipolar order dominated by the United States to a multipolar order. Europeans are evincing war fatigue and are sick of leaders who pursue war and austerity and neglect people's basic needs. The blowback from recent and ongoing wars led to the flood of refugees to Europe, the rise of anti-immigrant movements, the increase in terror incidents in Europe. Western interventions have expanded conflicts. Western support for Syrian rebels has not toppled Assad, and regime change in Kiev failed to bring peace. The Afghan war goes on and on. Cooperation is needed with Russia and others to achieve political solutions.

The world is so interconnected there cannot be winners and losers as before. It's either win-win or lose-lose. New economic and geopolitical realities are beginning to filter into Western public awareness, but significant omissions occur. Many people in non-NATO countries have a different legitimate outlook. Their perspectives can be read online, are written in English and are available to those who look for them. Understanding the whole picture enables critical thinking about who gains and who loses.

Petroleum is the biggest game in the world. Efforts to control petroleum resources and their trade routes figure in numerous conflicts. With the military its main tool of choice, the United States spends inordinate sums of money attempting to control the world's resources and supply routes. It draws other countries into its plans through NATO and encourages them to spend more, too. These plans need an adversary, and Russia and China fit the bill. The history of recent conflicts is dismal — a legacy of death and destruction that will persist for many generations. With climate change looming, humanity is on a collision course that hegemony over petroleum will only exacerbate.

The Petroleum Game will continue in its present destructive ways as long as Western media under-report it and the public remains unaware. It matters whether people know what's going on. It matters whether the public speak up to their politicians. In the 1930s, Albert Einstein observed: "Peace cannot be kept by force. It can only be achieved through understanding." In foreign affairs, the public deserves to understand much more about what's going on, not just the part governments want us to know.

Pérez Alfonzo uttered his famous words about petroleum bringing ruin decades ago. He was prescient regarding not only economic vicissitudes but also the part petroleum plays in conflicts and climate change. New thinking, incorporating a broader understanding of petroleum issues, is needed.

The twenty-first century is proving to be a tumultuous time. The balance of power is changing politically, economically, militarily. Adjusting to these changes will challenge all countries in coming years. Many are reacting to the recent patterns of invasion and interference. There are hopeful signs. The 2017 decision of China and the Philippines to jointly share oil and gas found in their disputed areas of the South China Sea removes a reason for intervention. Russian and South American warnings against interference in the internal affairs of Venezuela may ward off military action. Cooperation and diplomacy can reduce Western interventions, but each new crisis brings challenges.

As a new multipolar balance of power emerges, geopolitics, power and petroleum remain inseparable. Petroleum retains its extraordinary economic and strategic importance. The connections between geopolitical rivalry and conflict deserve widespread attention as the Petroleum Game continues.

ACKNOWLEDGEMENTS

At an all candidates meeting in Kingston before the 2008 Canadian election, I positioned myself to ask a question: "There are long-standing plans to build a gas pipeline through Afghanistan from Central to South Asia. American diplomats admit this is a US goal. Are our troops in Kandahar to protect the pipeline route?" Candidates from all four parties consulted their briefing notes and earnestly assured the audience that was not Canada's goal. I expected that response; the question had been raised in newspapers three months earlier. What surprised me was the spontaneous applause from the audience before the candidates said a word. Apparently, my fellow Kingstonians were concerned about Canada's presence in Afghanistan. They sent a strong message to the candidates that voters cared about Canada's participation in armed conflict. It was remarkable because foreign affairs had scarcely been mentioned in election debates.

I want to thank that audience and the many others who have probed foreign affairs with me and urged me to share my understandings with others. When I began my research, I had no plans to write a book. I wanted only to understand what was going on. Many people exhorted me to write — my father David Foster, Stephen Staples at the Rideau Institute, Bruce Campbell at the Canadian Centre for Policy Alternatives and others. I am indebted to them for their persistence. Many others — friends, kith and kin — cheered me on, especially family in Vancouver (Katrina and Dan) and Toronto (Margery, Dean, Joanna). They wanted to learn more.

My first efforts to share occurred in small group discussions on foreign affairs, which my wife and I organized as an activity of the Kingston Unitarian Fellowship. Later, I tested my findings in larger fora in Kingston, Ottawa and across Canada. They included Later Life Learning in Kingston, the Group of 78, Canadian Centre for Policy Alternatives and Rideau Institute in Ottawa and the Canadian International Council across Canada. I thank all those whose questions and feedback encouraged me to dig deeper. I especially appreciate the early encouragement of Brian Osborne, Paul Dewar, Daphne Mayne, Elaine Harvey, Jean Purvis and Kathy Sage. Thanks to author Wayne Grady for reviewing an early version of the manuscript. And thanks to my publisher, James Lorimer and Company, Ltd., for having faith in my book and bringing the manuscript to publication.

My wife Millie Morton was an integral part of this book's creation — my collaborator. She listened patiently a zillion times to my thoughts, shared the research with me and helped conceptualize and structure the manuscript. She introduced many ideas to strengthen the analysis. Our daily breakfast dialogues will undoubtedly continue. My gratitude is endless.

Finally, I acknowledge the independent thinkers whose books, articles and blogs have deepened my understanding, and the many people I've known worldwide who, wittingly or not, stimulated me to think outside the box and broadened my comprehension of this world in which we all live. Of course, responsibility for the conclusions in this book remains my own.

ENDNOTES

Foreword
1. Hansard, 39th Parliament, Ottawa, 2nd Session, Number 074, April 8, 2008.
2. John Foster, "A Pipeline through a Troubled Land: Afghanistan: Canada, and the New Great Energy Game." Ottawa: Canadian Centre for Policy Alternatives, June 2008.
3. Shawn McCarthy, "Pipeline Opens New Front in Afghan War," *The Globe and Mail*, June 19, 2008.

Chapter 1
1. *The Guardian*, "Among friends at 'Blair Petroleum'," November 9, 2001.
2. Dick Cheney, "Remarks at IP Autumn Lunch," Institute of Petroleum, 1999.
3. World Trade Organization, "International Trade Statistics 2016," Geneva, Switzerland.
4. Peak load is the maximum load on an electrical power-supply system.
5. Gordon Laxer, "If We're Renegotiating NAFTA, Let's Be Ready to Walk Away," *The Globe and Mail*, August 31, 2016.
6. Environment and Climate Change Canada, "Canadian Environmental Sustainability Indicators: Greenhouse Gas Emissions," April 2017.
7. Syria Civil Defence, "The White Helmets, Our Partners."
8. Syrian Observatory for Human Rights.
9. OAPEC was founded in 1968 by Kuwait, Libya and Saudi Arabia, and later joined by Algeria, Bahrain, Egypt, Iraq, Qatar, Syria, Tunisia and United Arab Emirates. It coordinates energy policies among oil-producing Arab nations.
10. The Organization of Petroleum Exporting Countries (OPEC) was founded in 1960 by Iran, Iraq, Kuwait, Saudi Arabia and Venezuela, and later joined by Qatar, Indonesia, Libya, United Arab Emirates, Algeria, Nigeria, Ecuador, Gabon and Angola. It aims to coordinate member countries' petroleum policies.
11. The Seven Sisters were British Petroleum; Gulf Oil; Royal Dutch Shell; Standard Oil of California (now Chevron); Texaco (later merged with Chevron); Standard Oil of New Jersey (Esso, Exxon) and Standard Oil Company of New York (Socony, Mobil, now part of ExxonMobil).
12. International Energy Agency (IEA), "What Is Energy Security?", Paris, France.
13. *Atomic Insights*, "US State Department Bureau of Energy Resources Input on Energy and Climate at Central Europe's Tatra Summit," November 5, 2015.
14. President Jimmy Carter, "State of the Union Address," Washington DC, January 23, 1980.
15. Zbigniew Brzezinski, *The Grand Chessboard: American Primacy and Its Geostrategic Imperatives* (New York: Basic Books, 1997).
16. Ron Suskind, "Faith, Certainty and the Presidency of George W. Bush," *The New York Times*, October 17, 2004.
17. Sotto voce, Kagan's spouse is Victoria Nuland, who masterminded US policies for Ukraine as assistant secretary of state in the Obama Administration.
18. Project for the New American Century, "Rebuilding America's Defenses: Strategy, Forces and Resources for a New Century," Washington, DC, September 2000.
19. "The National Security Strategy of the United States of America," White House, Washington, DC, March 2006, p. 23.
20. Obama Administration Says Goodbye to 'War on Terror.' US Defence Department Seems to Confirm Use of the Bureaucratic Phrase 'Overseas Contingency Operations,' *The Guardian*, March 25, 2009.
21. President Barack Obama, "Remarks by the President in Address to the Nation on Syria," White House, Washington, DC, September 10, 2013.
22. Daniel Lazare, "Hillary Clinton's Exceptionalist Warpath," *Consortium News*, September 3, 2016.
23. President Vladimir Putin, "A Plea for Caution from Russia," *The New York Times*,

September 11, 2013.

24. President Barack Obama, "Address to the United Nations General Assembly," White House, Washington, DC, September 24, 2013.

25. *McClatchy*, "WikiLeaks Cables Show that It Was all about the Oil," Washington, DC, May 16, 2011.

26. *The Guardian*, "NSA Accused of Spying on Brazilian Oil Company Petrobras," Rio de Janeiro, September 9, 2013.

27. *The Guardian*, "Brazilian President Postpones Washington Visit over NSA Spying," Rio de Janeiro, September 17, 2013.

28. *The Globe and Mail*, "Charges that Canada Spied on Brazil Unveil CSEC's Inner Workings," Toronto, October 7, 2013.

29. Glenn Greenwald, Roberto Kaz and José Casado, "Espionagem dos EUA se espalhou pela América Latina," *O Globo*, Brazil, July 9, 2013.

30. President Dilma Rousseff, "Statement at Opening of General Debate of the 68th Session of the United Nations General Assembly," New York, September 24, 2013.

31. *The Globe and Mail*, "Brazil Is Tip of the Iceberg on Canadian Spying, U.S. Journalist Says," Toronto, October 7, 2013.

32. Fracking employs two new techniques — horizontal drilling and hydraulic fracturing. Wells are angled horizontally along the shale formation, and a mix of water, sand and chemicals is injected down the well to create small fractures in the rock and force oil and gas to the surface.

33. Other major gas-producing basins are Eagle Ford and Permian in Texas; Haynesville in Louisiana, Arkansas and Texas; Niobrara in Colorado and Wyoming; and Utica in Ohio.

34. US Energy Information Administration, "How Much Oil Consumed by the United States Comes from Foreign Sources?"

35. President Barack Obama, weekly address, "Taking Control of America's Energy Future," White House, Washington, DC, November 16, 2013.

36. LNG is natural gas refrigerated into liquid form at the loading port for ease of tanker transportation. It takes up about 1/600th the gas volume at standard temperature and pressure. It is re-gasified at the delivery terminal.

37. US Energy Information Administration, "US Liquefied Natural Gas Exports Quadrupled in 2017," Washington, DC, March 27, 2018.

38. J. David Hughes, "Tight Oil: A Solution to US Import Dependence?", *Geological Society of America*, Denver, Colorado, October 28, 2013.

39. David Suzuki, "What's the Fracking Problem with Natural Gas," *David Suzuki Foundation*, September 13, 2012.

40. BP, "Statistical Review of World Energy 2018," London, June 2018.

41. BP, "2017 Energy Outlook,", London, January 2017.

42. Kevin Taft, *Oil's Deep State* (Toronto: Lorimer, 2017).

43. David Hughes, "Will the Trans Mountain Pipeline and Tidewater Access Boost Prices and Save Canada's Oil Industry?", Canadian Centre for Policy Alternatives, May 2017.

44. Robyn Allan, "4 Reasons the Oil to Tidewater Argument Is Bunk," *DeSmog Canada*, March 20, 2017. Bruce Campbell, *Public Betrayal, Justice Denied: The Lac-Mégantic Rail Disaster* (Toronto: Lorimer, 2018).

45. Bruce Campbell, *The Lac-Megantic Rail Disaster: Public Betrayal, Justice Denied* (Toronto: Lorimer, 2018).

46. "A Crude Awakening: The Oil Crash," documentary, Lava Productions AG, Switzerland, 2006.

47. *The Guardian*, "Military Experts Say Climate Change Poses 'Significant Risk' to Security," September 14, 2016.

48. Two books addressing climate change are: Donald Gutstein, *The Big Stall: How Big Oil and Think Tanks Are Blocking Action on Climate Change in Canada* (Toronto: Lorimer, 2018); and Tony Clarke, *Getting to Zero: Canada Confronts Global Warming* (Toronto: Lorimer, 2018).

Chapter 2
1. US General (ret'd) John P. Abizaid, "Courting Disaster: The Fight for Oil, Water and a Healthy Planet," video (minute 21:17), 2007 Roundtable at Stanford University, October 13, 2007; Matt Corley, "Abizaid: 'We've Treated the Arab World as a Collection of Big Gas Stations'," *Think Progress*, October 17, 2007; *Huffington Post*, "Of Course It's about Oil," Washington, DC, October 15, 2007.
2. "Greenspan Clarifies Iraq War, Oil Link," *Reuters*, September 18, 2007.
3. *The New York Times*, "Clinton Says Some G.I.'s in Iraq Would Remain," March 2007.
4. Data include production in northeast Iraq (Kurdistan).
5. *Washington Post*, "Papers Detail Industry's Role in Cheney's Energy Report," July 18, 2007.
6. National Energy Policy Development Group, "National Energy Policy Report," Washington, DC, May 2001.
7. *Judicial Watch*, "Cheney Energy Task Force Documents Feature Map of Iraqi Oil Fields," Washington, DC, July 17, 2003.
8. *Judicial Watch*, "Maps and Charts of Iraqi Oil Fields," Washington, DC, July 17, 2003.
9. Future of Iraq Project, "Report of the Oil and Energy Working Group," State Department, Washington, DC, April 20, 2003.
10. Michael Smith, "The Secret Downing Street Memo," *Sunday Times*, London, May 1, 2005.
11. *The New York Times*, "Bush Was Set on Path to War, British Memo Says," March 27, 2006.
12. Wolf Blitzer, "Interview with Condoleezza Rice," CNN, September 8, 2002.
13. US Secretary of State Colin Powell, "Remarks to the United Nations Security Council," New York, February 5, 2003.
14. "Bush Comment on Policy," *Associated Press*, January 21, 2003.
15. The Guardian, "Alastair Campbell Had Iraq Dossier Changed to Fit US Claims," January 10, 2010.
16. Greg Muttitt, *Fuel on the Fire: Oil and Politics in Occupied Iraq* (London: Bodley Head, 2011).
17. BBC News, "Australia 'Has Iraq Oil Interest'," July 5, 2007.
18. CNN, "Rumsfeld on Looting in Iraq: 'Stuff Happens'," April 12, 2003.
19. Erik Leaver and Greg Muttitt, "Slick Connections: US Influence on Iraqi Oil," Foreign Policy in Focus, July 17, 2007.
20. Antonia Juhasz, "Whose Oil Is It, Anyway?," *The New York Times*, March 13, 2007.
21. *The Independent*, "Blood and Oil: How the West Will Profit from Iraq's Most Precious Commodity," January 7, 2007.
22. In production-sharing contracts, the government retains ownership of oil in the ground. The company explores for and produces oil on behalf of the government, receiving "cost oil" in recovery of operating and capital expenses, and "profit oil" as a percentage share of net earnings. The government or its national oil company retains the remainder of the earnings.
23. In service contracts, the state always owns the resource and pays the contractor a service fee per barrel produced.
24. Andrew Kramer, "Deals with Iraq Are Set to Bring Oil Giants Back," *The New York Times*, June 19, 2008.
25. "Pickens Says US Firms 'Entitled' to Iraqi Oil," *Reuters*, October 22, 2009.
26. BBC News, "Iraq Oil Capacity 'to Reach 12m Barrels per Day'," December 12, 2009.
27. "Iraq Cuts Output Targets in Revised Oil Deals with BP, CNPC," *Reuters*, September 4, 2014.
28. Margaret MacMillan, *Paris 1919* (New York: Random House, 2001).
29. Peter Sluglett, *Britain in Iraq: 1914–1932* (London: Ithaca Press, 1976).
30. Helmut Mejcher, *Imperial Quest for Oil: Iraq 1910-1928* (London: Ithaca Press, 1976).
31. Office of the Historian, "The 1928 Red Line Agreement," State Department, Washington, DC.

32. Jeffrey Frank, "Twenty-Five Years after Another Gulf War," *The New Yorker*, July 16, 2015.
33. "Madeleine Albright Says 500,000 Dead Iraqi Children Was 'Worth It,' Wins Medal of Freedom," May 12, 1996.
34. Andrew J. Bacevich, *America's War for the Greater Middle East* (New York: Random House, 2016).
35. Jeremy Scahill, "Beyond That Memo: Bush Wanted al-Jazeera Gone," *Anti-War.com*, November 24, 2005.
36. Committee of Privy Counsellors chaired by Sir John Chilcot, "Executive Summary," The Report of the Iraq Inquiry, London, July 6, 2016.
37. *The Guardian*, "Chilcot Report: Key Points from the Iraq Inquiry," July 6, 2016.
38. Patrick Cockburn, "What Tony Blair Has Learned about the Middle East: Absolutely Nothing," *CounterPunch*, June 13, 2016.
39. Patrick Cockburn, "Rise of Islamic State: Isis and the New Sunni Revolution," *Verso*, February 2015.
40. "Iraq's Oil Exports Hit Record High so Far in June," *Reuters*, June 17, 2015.
41. Producing companies are DNO (Norway), Gulf Keystone (UK), Genel (UK) and MOL Group (Hungary), operating under production-sharing contracts.
42. The state-owned North Oil Company contracted BP in 2013 to rehabilitate the field but temporarily had to suspend work.
43. "How Kurdistan Bypassed Baghdad and Sold Oil on Global Markets," *Reuters UK*, November 17, 2015.
44. *Toronto Star*, "Canada Suspends Military Aid to Iraqi, Kurdish Forces amid Outbreak of Hostilities," October 27, 2017.

Chapter 3
1. Open Society Initiative, "Globalizing Torture: CIA Secret Detention and Extraordinary Rendition," New York, 2013.
2. "Arab Gas Pipeline to Extend to Turkey," *MEED*, London, March 24, 2006.
3. "Presidents Al-Assad / Gül Press Conference," Damascus, Syria, May 15, 2009.
4. Tamsin Carlisle, "Qatar Seeks Gas Pipeline to Turkey," *The National*, Abu Dhabi, August 26, 2009.
5. *Tehran Times*, "Iran, Iraq, Syria Sign Major Gas Pipeline Deal," November 28, 2011.
6. *Financial Times*, "Qatar Bankrolls Syrian Revolt with Cash and Arms," London, May 16, 2013.
7. Christof Lehman, "NATO Special Forces in Syria Now Official," MSNBC, June 4, 2012.
8. *Israel National News*, "Syria: Seven Police Killed, Buildings Torched in Protests," March 21, 2011.
9. *Voice of America*, "Clinton Says Syria's Assad 'Not Indispensable'," July 10, 2011.
10. "Statement by President Obama on the Situation in Syria," White House, Washington, DC, August 18, 2011.
11. Catherine Ashton, High Representative for Foreign Affairs, "Declaration on EU Action Following the Escalation of Violent Repression in Syria," European Union, Brussels, August 18, 2011.
12. Council of the European Union, "Council Bans Import of Syrian Oil," Brussels, September 2, 2011.
13. *Arab Weekly*, "Syria's War Sends Oil Output Crashing to Almost Nothing," May 5, 2015.
14. *The Guardian*, "Syria Intervention Plan Fuelled by Oil Interests, not Chemical Weapon Concern," August 30, 2013.
15. *Syriana Analysis*, "Hamad Bin Jassim: We Supported Al-Qaeda in Syria," *YouTube* interview, October 27, 2017; and *Tyler Durden*, "In Shocking Viral Interview, Qatar Confesses Secrets behind Syrian War," *Zero Hedge*, October 29, 2017.
16. *Charlie Rose*, interview with Sheikh Hamad Bin Jassim Al-Thani, *YouTube* and transcript, June 12, 2017.

17. Haid Haid, "How the Gulf Crisis Could Spill over into Rebel Rivalry in Syria," *Middle East Eye*, June 26, 2017.
18. "Unfolding the Future of the Long War," RAND Corporation, 2008.
19. "Ratline" is the official military term used by the US Department of Defence to describe an organized, clandestine effort to move personnel or material across a denied border.
20. Seymour M. Hersh, "The Red Line and the Rat Line. Obama, Erdoğan and the Syrian Rebels," *London Review of Books*, April 17, 2014.
21. BBC News, "Turkey Jails Cumhuriyet Journalists Can Dundar and Erdem Gul," May 6, 2016.
22. US House of Representatives, "Select Committee on Benghazi Releases Proposed Report," Washington, DC, May 2016.
23. *Judicial Watch*, "2012 Defense Intelligence Agency Document."
24. Salafism is a fundamentalist conservative movement within Sunni Islam.
25. *Levant Report*, "2012 Defense Intelligence Agency Document: West Will Facilitate Rise of Islamic State 'in Order to Isolate the Syrian Regime'," May 19, 2015.
26. *Politics Forum*, "Leaked: Russian-Saudi Meeting Report, and More," September 1, 2013.
27. *As-Safir*, "Russian President, Saudi Spy Chief Discussed Syria, Egypt," Beirut, August 22, 2013.
28. United Nations, "United Nations Mission to Investigate Allegations of the Use of Chemical Weapons in the Syrian Arab Republic," December 13, 2013.
29. al Jazeera, "Kerry: Syria Gas Attack a Moral Obscenity," August 26, 2013.
30. *Washington Post*, "More Than 1,400 Killed in Syrian Chemical Weapons Attack, US Says," August 30, 2013.
31. *The Guardian*, "US Set for Syria Strikes after Kerry Says Evidence of Chemical Attack Is 'clear'," August 31, 2013.
32. John Kerry, Secretary of State, "Remarks with Russian Foreign Minister Sergey Lavrov after Their Meeting," State Department, Washington, DC, September 13, 2013.
33. "Remarks by President Obama in Address to the United Nations General Assembly," White House, Washington, DC, September 24, 2013.
34. Mother Agnes Mariam of the Cross, "The Chemical Attacks on East Ghouta Used to Justify a Military Intervention in Syria," September 17, 2013.
35. Richard Lloyd and Theodore A. Postol, "Possible Implications of Faulty US Technical Intelligence in the Damascus Nerve Agent Attack of August 21, 2013," MIT Science, Technology, and Global Security Working Group, Washington, DC, January 14, 2014.
36. Seymour M. Hersh, "Whose Sarin?", *London Review of Books*, December 19, 2013.
37. *RT News*, "Turkish MP Faces Treason Charges after Telling RT ISIS Used Turkey for Transiting Sarin," December 16, 2015.
38. *Institute for Advanced Strategic and Political Studies*, "A Clean Break: A New Strategy for Securing the Realm," 1996.
39. *The Guardian*, "Isis 'Controls 50% of Syria' after Seizing Historic City of Palmyra,"May 21, 2015.
40. BBC News, "Islamic State: Where Does Jihadist Group Get Its Support?", September 1, 2014.
41. *Middle East Eye*, "US Commandos Aid Kurdish-led Push on Islamic State's Syrian Stronghold," London, May 26, 2016.
42. *IB Times*, "ISIS Fight 2016: French Special Forces Advise Syrian Rebels, Defense Ministry Official Confirms," June 9, 2016.
43. "German Special Forces Arrive in Northern Syria: Report," AMN, June 14, 2016.
44. "French Jets Bomb Syria in the ISIS Stronghold of Raqqa," CNN, November 15, 2015.
45. "UK Drops First Bombs in Syria after MPs Approve Air Strikes," France 24, December 3, 2015.
46. *Bloomberg*, "Obama and Putin Agree on Bombing Islamic State's Oil Pipeline," November 19, 2015.
47. "Russia Says It Has Proof Turkey Involved in Islamic State Oil Trade," *Reuters*, December 2, 2015.

48. *The Independent*, "Russia Unveils 'Proof' Turkey's Erdoğan Is Smuggling Isis Oil across Border from Syria," London, December 4, 2015.

49. US Energy Information Administration, "Energy Overview," 2015.

50. Yezid Sayigh, "The War Over Syria's Gas Fields," Carnegie Middle East Centre, Beirut, June 8, 2015.

51. The pipeline, built in 1952, was shut by Syria during the Iraq-Iran War (1980–1988) and badly damaged in Iraq by US bombing (2003). It remains closed, though Iraq and Syria have on occasion discussed rebuilding or replacing it.

52. "US, Russia Clinch Syria Deal, Aim for Truce from Monday," *Reuters*, September 10, 2016.

53. *The Guardian*, "Vladimir Putin Questions US Commitment to Syria Ceasefire Deal," The 17, 2016.

54. *Democracy Now*, "Raytheon Stocks Surge after Chemical Attack, Personally Benefiting Trump," April 10, 2017.

55. *RT News*, "Low Efficiency: Only 23 Tomahawk Missiles out of 59 Reached Syrian Airfield, Russian MoD Says," April 7, 2017.

56. National Security Council, "Declassified US Report on Chemical Weapons Attack," Washington, DC, April 11, 2017.

57. *The New York Times*, "White House Accuses Russia of Cover-up in Syria Chemical Attack," April 11, 2017.

58. Theodore A. Postol, "An Assessment of the White House Intelligence Report about the Nerve Agent Attack in Khan Shaykhun, Syria," April 13, 2017.

59. Seymour Hersh, "Trump's Red Line," *Welt am Sonntag*, June 25, 2017.

60. Hersh published his article in the German newspaper Welt am Sonntag. He said his previous publisher, the *London Review of Books*, had accepted and paid for it, but declined to publish, concerned they could be criticized for siding with the Syrian and Russian governments. Interview: Dirk Laabs, "The Fog of War," *Welt am Sonntag*, June 25, 2017.

61. Organization for the Prohibition of Chemical Weapons, "OPCW Fact-Finding Mission Confirms Use of Chemical Weapons in Khan Shaykhun on 4 April 2017," The Hague, Netherlands, June 30, 2017.

62. Organization for the Prohibition of Chemical Weapons, "Report of the Fifty-fourth Meeting of the Executive Council," The Hague, Netherlands, April 20, 2017.

63. Organization for the Prohibition of Chemical Weapons, "Status Update of the OPCW Fact-Finding Mission in Syria Regarding a Reported Incident in Khan Shaykhun, 4 April 2017," The Hague, Netherlands, May 18, 2017.

64. Scott Ritter, "Ex-Weapons Inspector: Trump's Sarin Claims Built on 'Lie'," *American Conservative*, June 29, 2017.

65. Governments have been known to go to inordinate lengths to deceive their opponents. Many examples exist of UK operations in World War II. In Operation Mincemeat, documents placed on a dead body washed ashore in Spain falsely suggested the Allies planned to invade Greece and Sardinia, when the real target was Sicily. The extensive efforts to achieve the deception are documented in a book by the same name by journalist Ben Macintyre. They make fascinating reading.

66. Technical Secretariat, Organization for the Prohibition of Chemical Weapons, "Report of the OPCW Fact-Finding Mission in Syria Regarding an Alleged Incident in Khan Shaykhun, Syrian Arab Republic, April 2017," The Hague, Netherlands, June 29, 2017.

67. MK Bhadrakumar, "The Scramble for Control of Syrian-Iraqi Border," *Indian Punchline*, June 4, 2017.

68. *MK Bhadrakumar, "The Scramble for Control."*

69. Peter Korsun, "Syria's Cauldron: One Step Away from Major Showdown," Strategic Culture Foundation, June 7, 2017.

70. *The New York Times*, "Trump Ends Covert Aid to Syrian Rebels Trying to Topple Assad," July 17, 2017.

71. *Wall Street Journal*, "Israel Gives Secret Aid to Syrian Rebels," June 18, 2017.
72. *Times of Israel*, "Major Oil Reserve Said Found on Golan,"October 7, 2016.
73. Robert Fisk, "Western Howls of Outrage over the Ghouta Siege Ring Hollow — We Aren't Likely to Do Anything to Save Civilians," *The Independent*, February 21, 2018.
74. Ambassador Nikki Haley, US Permanent Representative to the United Nations, "Remarks at a UN Security Council Briefing on Syria Ceasefire Implementation," New York City, March 12, 2018.
75. Sharmine Narwani, "Terrorist Capabilities Laid Bare in an Eastern Ghouta Chemical Lab," *RT News*, March 16, 2018.
76. *RT News*, "US Plans to Remain in Syria 'for a Long Time, If not Forever' — Lavrov," March 14, 2018.
77. "US Preparing Strikes on Syria, Carrier Strike Groups Set up in Mediterranean — General," *TASS*, March 17, 2018.
78. Rex Tillerson, US Secretary of State, "Press Availability with Kuwaiti Foreign Minister Sheikh Sabah al-Khalid al-Sabah," Kuwait, February 13, 2018.
79. *Washington Post*, "Trump Tells Turkish President U.S. Will Stop Arming Kurds in Syria," November 24, 2017.
80. Pepe Escobar, "The New Silk Road Will Go through Syria," *CounterPunch*, July 14, 2017.

Chapter 4
1. President George W. Bush, "State of the Union Address," White House, Washington, DC, January 29, 2002.
2. "EU and Iran to Start Negotiations on Trade and Cooperation Agreement," Brussels, December 12, 2002.
3. Jonathan Freedland, "Patten Lays into Bush's America," *The Guardian*, February 9, 2002.
4. BBC News, "Germany Warns US against Unilateralism," February 12, 2002.
5. John Le Carré, "The United States of America Has Gone Mad," *The Times*, reprinted in Common Dreams, January 15, 2003.
6. Patrick Foy, "The Iran Nuclear Straw Man," *CounterPunch*, July 17, 2015.
7. Greg Bruno, "Iran's Nuclear Program," Council on Foreign Relations, New York, March 10, 2010.
8. BBC News, "Israeli PM Netanyahu 'Ready' to Order Strike on Iran," November 6, 2012.
9. *Times of Israel*, "Ya'alon: Israel 'not Responsible (for Iran Nuke Scientists' Lives. Defense Minister Hints Assassinations May Resume, Says Israel Considering Air Strikes against Nuclear Facilities," August 7, 2015.
10. David Sanger, "Obama Order Sped Up Wave of Cyberattacks against Iran," *The New York Times*, June 1, 2012.
11. Latest Iran Safeguards Report Circulated to IAEA Board, UN IAEA, Vienna, Austria, February 22, 2008.
12. Joshua Rovner, "Why US Intelligence Is Right about Iran," *Washington Post*, April 13, 2015.
13. President Barack Obama, "State of the Union Address," White House, Washington, DC, January 24, 2012.
14. Richard Lachmann, Michael Schwarz and Kevin Young, "Why They Hate the Deal with Iran." *CounterPunch*, July 15, 2015.
15. Jonathan Steele, "Lost in Translation," *The Guardian*, June 14, 2006.
16. al Jazeera, "Dan Meridor: We Misquoted Ahmadinejad," April 16, 2012.
17. Ironically, all five permanent members have nuclear weapons themselves.
18. Conversation with John Kerry, "Assessing the Iran Nuclear Accord," Council on Foreign Relations, July 24, 2015.
19. Federica Mogherini, "The Iran Agreement Is a Disaster for Isis," *The Guardian*, July 28, 2015.
20. William Beeman, "Iran Won the Vienna Accords by Agreeing to Stop What It Never Was Doing," *New American Media*, July 14, 2015.

21. Stephen Kinzer, *All the Shah's Men: An American Coup and the Roots of Middle East Terror* (Hoboken, NJ: John Wiley & Sons, 2007).
22. In service contracts, the state always owns the resource and pays the contractor a fee per barrel produced.
23. President Jimmy Carter, "State of the Union Address," Joint Session of Congress, Washington, DC, January 23, 1980.
24. Robert Parry, "Missing US-Iraq History," *Consortium News*, February 27, 2003.
25. "Executive Order 12613 — Prohibiting Imports from Iran," White House, Washington, DC, October 29, 1987.
26. Jeff Reed, "Troubled Waters: Recalling the Iran-Iraq Tanker War," *OilPro.com*, March 12, 2015.
27. "Executive Order 12957 — Prohibiting Certain Transactions with Respect to the Development of Iranian Petroleum Resources," White House, Washington, DC, March 17, 1995.
28. "Executive Order 12959 — Prohibiting Certain Transactions with Respect to Iran," White House, Washington, DC, May 9, 1995.
29. Herman Franssen and Elaine Morton, Middle East Economic Survey, "A Review of US Unilateral Sanctions against Iran, Nicosia, Cyprus," August 26, 2002.
30. Glenn E. Curtis and Eric Hooglund, "Iran: A Country Study," US Library of Congress, Washington, DC, 2008.
31. *Financial Times*, "Iran Fulfils Pledge to Raise Oil Production," London, May 24, 2016.
32. *Sputnik*, "Iran's De-Dollarization of Oil Is about Business, Not Politics," February 12, 2016.
33. "Iran Eyes $185 Billion Oil and Gas projects after Sanctions," *Reuters*, July 23, 2015.
34. *Bloomberg*, "Iran Plans Foreign Oil Deals within Months as Sanctions Ease," June 12, 2016.
35. *RT News*, "Russia & Iran Sign Oil-for-Goods Trade Agreement," May 25, 2017.
36. *Business Insider*, "Europe Risks Losing Iran to China and Russia," August 5, 2015.
37. *GB Times*, "Iran, China Plan a Massive Boost in Trade," January 25, 2016.
38. US Treasury, "Treasury Sanctions Those Involved in Ballistic Missile Procurement for Iran," Washington, DC, January 17, 2016.
39. "Iran's Leader Says Never Trusted the West, Seeks Closer Ties with China," *Reuters*, January 23, 2016.
40. *The Guardian*, "US Aircraft Sales to Iran Blocked by House, Jeopardising $25bn Boeing Deal," July 9, 2016.
41. "European Banks' Reluctance to Lend to Iran," *Reuters*, May 14, 2016.
42. MK Bhadrakumar, "Iran Trade Is not Vulnerable to US Sanctions," *Indian Punchline*, February 28, 2018.
43. Patrick Cockburn, "We Know What Inspired the Manchester Attack, We Just Won't Admit It," *CounterPunch*, May 26, 2017.
44. Qatar hosts Al Jazeera, which reports critically on Middle Eastern skullduggery and has incurred the wrath of Saudi, US and other leaders.
45. al Jazeera, "Arab States Issue List of Demands to End Qatar Crisis," June 23, 2017.
46. The North Dome gas field is Qatar's part of the giant Persian Gulf reservoir, shared with Iran.
47. William Engdahl, "Has Washington Lost the Middle East after Qatar?" *New Eastern Outlook*, June 24, 2017.
48. IRNA News Agency, "Export of Gas to Neighbours, India on Agenda: Deputy Petroleum Minister," Tehran, July 7, 2017.
49. Express Tribune, "IP Project in Jeopardy: US Threatens Curbs If Pakistan Pursues Iran Deal, Says PM," Pakistan, August 5, 2013.
50. BBC News, "US Cautions Pakistan over Gas Deal with Iran," June 21, 2010.
51. M. Fazal Elahi, "Sanctions over IP Gas Pipeline," *Pakistan Observer*, October 14, 2013.
52. Pepe Escobar, "Pipelineistan — The Iran-Pak-China Connection," *Asia Times*, August 14, 2015.

53. *Daily Times*, "Russia Ready for North-South Gas Pipeline with Pakistan," Pakistan, August 6, 2015.
54. *Business Recorder*, "Pipeline Project Shelved," Karachi, June 15, 2017.
55. *Washington Post*, "Piling on Pressure over Safe Havens, U.S. Suspends Military Aid to Pakistan," January 4, 2018.
56. MK Bhadrakumar, "Why Businessman Trump Is Upset with Pakistan," *Indian Punchline*, January 6, 2018.
57. *ZeroHedge*, "China Is Building Its Second Foreign Military Base in Pakistan amid US Diplomatic Scandal," January 6, 2018.
58. *The Times of Israel*, "Full Text of Donald Trump's Speech to AIPAC," March 22, 2016.

Chapter 5
1. Alex Newman, "Gadhafi's Gold-money Plan Would Have Devastated Dollar," *New American*, November 11, 2011.
2. BBC, "Libya Protests: Tripoli Hit by Renewed Clashes," February 21, 2011.
3. al Jazeera, "Libya Protests Spread and Intensify," February 21, 2011.
4. *RT News*, "'Airstrikes in Libya Did not Take Place' — Russian Military," March 1, 2011.
5. "Libya Oil Production Grinding to a Halt," CNN, February 23, 2011.
6. *Xinhua News*, "35,860 Chinese Evacuated from Unrest-torn Libya," March 3, 2011.
7. United Nations, "In Swift, Decisive Action, Security Council Imposes Tough Measures on Libyan Regime, Adopting Resolution 1970 in Wake of Crackdown on Protesters," February 26, 2011.
8. *Euronews*, "Libya: Timeline of the Conflict," August 29, 2011.
9. BBC News, "Libya Unrest: Foreign Ministers Urge End to Violence," February 28, 2011.
10. Prime Minister's Office, "Prime Minister's Statement on Libya," London, February 28, 2011.
11. CTV News, "Gadhafi Stashed More than $2 Billion in Canada," February 28, 2011.
12. *Daily Mail*, "Proof We Are Winning: MoD Release Footage of Airstrikes Wiping out Gaddafi's Guns as Coalition Planes 'Fly Free over Libya'," March 25, 2011.
13. *The Guardian*, "NATO Will not Put Troops on Ground in Libya," August 24, 2011.
14. *New York Times*, "C.I.A. Agents in Libya Aid Airstrikes and Meet Rebels," March 30, 2011.
15. UN Security Council, Resolution 1973, New York, March 17, 2011.
16. "Remarks by the President on Libya," White House, Washington, DC, March 19, 2011.
17. Prime Minister's Office, "Prime Minister: Libya – 'The Time for Action Has Come'," London, March 19, 2011.
18. Newman, "Gadhafi's Gold-money Plan."
19. Micah Zenko, "The Big Lie about the Libyan War," *Foreign Policy*, March 22, 2016.
20. "Remarks by the President in Address to the Nation on Libya," White House, Washington, DC, March 28, 2011.
21. *Financial Times*, "Oil Companies Fear Nationalisation in Libya," London, March 20, 2011.
22. Micah Zenko, "The Big Lie about the Libyan War," Foreign Policy,March 22, 2016.
23. BBC News, "Libya Conflict: Black African Migrants Caught in Backlash," September 18, 2011.
24. BBC News, "Libya: Cameron and Sarkozy Mobbed in Benghazi," September 15, 2011.
25. *The Guardian*, "Cameron and Sarkozy Meet Libya's New Leaders in Tripoli," September 15, 2011.
26. United Nations, "After Much Wrangling, General Assembly Seats National Transitional Council of Libya as Country's Representative for Sixty-Sixth Session," New York, September 16, 2011.
27. CBS News, "Clinton on Qaddafi: 'We Came, We Saw, He Died'," September 20, 2011.
28. "Statement by the President on the Declaration of Liberation in Libya," White House, Washington, DC, October 23, 2011.

29. Anders Fogh Rasmussen, "NATO Secretary General Statement on End of Libya Mission," October 28, 2011.
30. BBC News, "Hague Welcomes Libyan Liberation," October 23, 2011.
31. *Levant Report*, "New Hillary Emails Reveal Propaganda, Executions, Coveting Libyan Oil and Gold," Texas, January 3, 2016.
32. *Levant Report*, "New Hillary Emails."
33. *Middle East Eye*, "Sorted by MI5: How UK government Sent British-Libyans to Fight Gaddafi," May 25, 2017.
34. John Pilger, "Terror in Britain: What Did the Prime Minister Know?" *CounterPunch*, May 31, 2017.
35. Pilger, "Terror in Britain."
36. Patrick Cockburn, "We Can't Let Britain Become a Vast ISIS Recruiting Station," *CounterPunch*, May 30, 2017.
37. Tom Bowman, "For Reagan, Gadhafi Was a Frustrating 'Mad Dog'," NPR, March 4, 2011.
38. Ronald Bruce St John, "Libya and the United States: Elements of a Performance-based Roadmap," Middle East Policy Council, Washington, DC, Fall 2003.
39. *Arms Control Association*, "Chronology of Libya's Disarmament and Relations with the United States," Washington, DC, February 2014.
40. *The Guardian*, "BP Marks Return to Libya with $900m Gas Deal," May 30, 2007.
41. *Daily Telegraph*, "Blair, Gaddafi and the BP Oil Deal," May 20, 2007.
42. BBC News, "Blair Hails Positive Libya Talks," May 29, 2007.
43. International Crisis Group, "The Prize: Fighting for Libya's Energy Wealth," Brussels, December 3, 2015.
44. International Crisis Group, "The Prize."
45. Amanda Kadlec, "All Eyes on Sirte: Beating the Islamic State, but Losing Libya," War on the Rocks, June 23, 2016.
46. *The Fuse*, "Libya's Oil in ISIS' Crosshairs," January 20, 2016.
47. Kadlec, "All Eyes on Sirte."
48. "US Special Forces Take the Fight to ISIS in Libya," CNN, May 26, 2016.
49. *Daily Telegraph*, "British Special Forces Destroyed Islamic State Trucks in Libya, Say Local Troops," May 26, 2016.
50. "French Advisers Helping Libyan Forces Fight Islamic State in Benghazi: Libyan Commander," *Reuters*, February 25, 2016.
51. *OS Net Daily*, "Italian-British Special Ops Force Ambushed, Smashed by ISIS in Libya," April 29, 2016.
52. *Bloomberg*, "Libyan Oil Revival Less Likely as East-West Standoff Escalates," May 6, 2016.
53. International Crisis Group, "The Prize."
54. *ENI*, "GreenStream."
55. *Financial Times*, "Political Rivalry Puts Libya's Oil Lifeline at Risk," May 10, 2016.
56. BBC News, "President Obama: Libya Aftermath 'Worst Mistake' of Presidency," April 11, 2016.
57. *The Independent*, "David Cameron 'Ultimately Responsible' for Libya Collapse and the Rise of Isis, Commons Report Concludes," September 13, 2016.

Chapter 6
1. NATO, "Alliance Maritime Strategy," March 18, 2011.
2. United Nations Commission on Trade and Development, "Review of Maritime Transport 2015," New York and Geneva, 2015.
3. Clarkson Research, "Scaling the Heights and Plumbing the Depths," January 6, 2016.
4. BP, "Statistical Review of World Energy 2018," London, June 2018.
5. US Energy Information Administration, "World Oil Transit Chokepoints," Washington, DC, July 25, 2017.

6. Member nations of Combined Maritime Forces are: Australia, Bahrain, Belgium, Canada, Denmark, France, Germany, Greece, Iraq, Italy, Japan, Jordan, Republic of Korea, Kuwait, Malaysia, Netherlands, New Zealand, Norway, Pakistan, the Philippines, Portugal, Saudi Arabia, Seychelles, Singapore, Spain, Thailand, Turkey, UAE, United Kingdom, United States and Yemen.

7. US Energy Information Administration, "World Oil Transit Chokepoints."

8. The Sirius Star was ransomed for US$3 million, the Maran Centaurus for US$5.5 million and the Samho Dream for US$9.5 million.

9. Royal Navy, "Royal Navy Takes Charge of Pirate-hunting Force," September 10, 2013.

10. The State of Maritime Piracy in 2015, "Somali Piracy in the Western Indian Ocean Region," Oceans Beyond Piracy, Colorado, 2016.

11. *Project Censored*, "Toxic Waste behind Somali pirates," Sonoma State University, California, 2010.

12. Frans Teutscher, "Somalia's Fishery Review," Food and Agriculture Organization, Rome, November 11, 2005.

13. George Monbiot, "From Toxic Waste to Toxic Assets, the Same People Always Get Dumped on," *The Guardian*, September 21, 2009.

14. UN Environmental Programme, "Tsunami Exposes Somalia Toxic Waste," Nairobi, March 4, 2005.

15. Nick Turse, "The Stealth Expansion of a Secret US Drone Base in Africa," The Intercept, October 21, 2015.

16. *Bloomberg*, "Japan Opens Military Base in Djibouti to Help Combat Piracy," July 8, 2011.

17. *The Diplomat*, "Confirmed: Construction Begins on China's First Overseas Military Base in Djibouti,", February 29, 2016.

18. Secretary of State Rex Tillerson, "Press Availability with Djiboutian Foreign Minister Mahamoud Ali Youssouf," State Department, March 9, 2018.

19. BBC News, "Djibouti Country Profile," April 9, 2016.

20. *VOA*, "US Imposes New Sanctions on Eritrea's Navy over North Korea Links," April 8, 2017.

21. Vittorio Longhi, "Are Oil Interests at the Heart of the EU's 145m Aid Package to Eritrea?" *The Guardian*, December 18, 2015.

22. "Last Stops on the East Africa Oil & Gas Frontier: Eritrea," *Oilprice.com*, December 19, 2015.

23. United Nations Statistics Division, "National Accounts Main Aggregates Database," 2014.

24. *Los Angeles Times*, "The Oil Factor in Somalia: Four American Petroleum Giants Had Agreements with the African Nation before Its Civil War Began. They Could Reap Big Rewards If Peace Is Restored," January 18, 1993.

25. *The National*, "Why Marib Province Is Crucial to Coalition Victory in Yemen," Abu Dhabi, September 7, 2015.

26. Bureau of Investigative Journalism, "Obama Drone Casualty Numbers a Fraction of Those Recorded by the Bureau," July 1, 2016.

27. Director of National Intelligence, "Summary of Information Regarding US Counterterrorism Strikes outside Areas of Active Hostilities," Washington, DC, July 1, 2016.

28. Stanford Law School and New University School of Law, "Living under Drones Death, Injury, and Trauma to Civilians from US Drone Practices in Pakistan," September 2012.

29. Jeremy Scahill, *Dirty Wars: The World Is a Battlefield*, Nation Book, New York, 2013.

30. US Energy Information Administration, "World Oil Transit Chokepoints."

31. *International Energy Agency*, "Facts on Egypt: Oil and Gas," February 2011.

32. "Fact Sheet: The Malacca Straits Patrol."

33. BBC News, "US Calls for Land Reclamation 'Halt' in South China Sea," May 30, 2015.

34. US Department of Defense, "Joint Press Conference by Secretary Carter, Secretary Kerry,

Australian Foreign Minister Bishop and Australian Defence Minister Payne in Boston, Massachusetts," Washington, DC, October 13, 2015.

35. Ministry of Foreign Affairs, "Foreign Minister Wang Yi Meets the Press," Beijing, China, March 3, 2016.

36. Russia, too, has an interest in Myanmar. Russia supplies military equipment, and the Russian company Bashneft is exploring onshore for oil and gas.

37. Peter Lee, "Scorched Earth Ruling on S China Sea," *Asia Times*, July 14, 2016.

38. MK Bhadrakumar, "UN Award Causes No Waves in South China Sea," *Indian Punchline*, July 13, 2016.

39. ASEAN comprises Brunei, Cambodia, Indonesia, Laos, Malaysia, Myanmar, the Philippines, Singapore, Thailand and Vietnam.

40. China and Russia also seek removal of the new US anti-missile Terminal High-Altitude Area Defence (THAAD) system in South Korea, which they see as a grave threat to their strategic security.

41. "Vladimir Putin's News Conference Following BRICS Summit," September 5, 2017.

42. Alex Gorka, "Bull in a China Shop: US Announces More Unilateral Sanctions on North Korea," Strategic Cultural Foundation, February 26, 2018.

43. Mel Gurtov, "Getting to Yes with North Korea," *CounterPunch*, March 9, 2018.

Chapter 7

1. "US Mission Betrayed Afghanistan for 13 Years [Karzai]," *Zeitgeist*, September 25, 2014.

2. Jim Lobe, "Timing of Leak of Afghan Mineral Wealth Evokes Scepticism," Inter Press Service, Washington, DC, June 14, 2010.

3. *The New York Times*, "Trump Finds Reason for the U.S. to Remain in Afghanistan: Minerals," July 25, 2017.

4. CNS News, "DOD and Petraeus: US Planning Military Presence and Operations in Afghanistan Beyond 2014," Virginia, March 15, 2011.

5. Richard Boucher, US Assistant Secretary of State, South and Central Asian Affairs, "Speech at Paul H. Nitze School for Advanced International Studies," September 20, 2007.

6. George Krol, Deputy Assistant Secretary of State for South and Central Asian Affairs, "Testimony before the Senate Committee on Foreign Relations, Subcommittee on Near Eastern and South and Central Asian Affairs," December 15, 2009.

7. *Wall Street Journal*, "Pipeline Dreams: How Two Firms' Fight For Turkmenistan Gas Landed in Court," January 19, 1998.

8. "Timeline of Competition between Unocal and Bridas for the Afghanistan Pipeline," *Worldpress.org*.

9. Larry Chin, "Unocal and the Afghanistan Pipeline," Centre for Research on Globalisation, March 6, 2002.

10. Ahmed Rashid, *Taliban: Militant Islam, Oil and Fundamentalism in Central Asia*, (New Haven, CT: Yale University Press, 2001).

11. Zbigniew Brzezinski, interview, "How Jimmy Carter and I Started the Mujahideen," *CounterPunch*, January 15, 1998.

12. BBC News, "Who Are the Taliban?" May 26, 2016.

13. *Salon*, "Al-Qaida Monitored US Negotiations with Taliban over Oil Pipeline," June 5, 2002.

14. Revolutionary Association of Women of Afghanistan, "Reports from Afghanistan under the Taliban - 1997," Quetta, Pakistan.

15. Subcommittee on Asia and the Pacific, Committee on International Relations, House of Representatives, "US Interests in the Central Asian Republics," Washington, DC, February 12, 1998, pp. 37–38.

16. Executive Order 13129, "Property and Prohibiting Transactions with the Taliban," White House, Washington, DC, July 4, 1999.

17. Cary Gladstone, editor, *Afghanistan Revisited*, Nova Science Publishing, January 2003.

18. *Salon*, "Al-Qaeda Monitored US Negotiations with Taliban."
19. *The Guardian*, "Threat of US Strikes Passed to Taliban Weeks before NY Attack," September 22, 2001.
20. Julio Godoy, "US Policy towards Taliban Influenced by Oil — Authors," Inter Press Service, November 15, 2001.
21. President George W. Bush, "Address to the Nation," White House, Washington, DC, September 20, 2001.
22. Asian Development Bank, TAPI Natural Gas Pipeline Project (Phases 1 and 2), Technical Assistance Completion Report, TA 7632-REG and TA 7756-REG.
23. *The Hindu*, "Company to Be Set up Soon to Execute TAPI Pipeline Project," July 10, 2013.
24. *Express Tribune*, "TAPI Pipeline: Project Participants, ADB Fail to Agree on Advisory Fee," July 24, 2013.
25. *Express Tribune*, "TAPI Pipeline: Officials to Finalise Contract Award in Ashgabat Next Week," July 5, 2014.
26. *Express Tribune*, "TAPI Pipeline Construction: US Firms Lose out; French, Malaysian Could Win Race," November 11, 2014.
27. Asian Development Bank, "TAPI Steering Committee Endorses Turkmengaz as Consortium Leader for TAPI Gas Pipeline Project," Manila, August 7, 2015.
28. Declaration, Second Regional Economic Cooperation Conference, New Delhi, November 19, 2006.
29. "Parliamentary Secretary Obhrai to Represent Government at Second Regional Economic Cooperation Conference on Afghanistan," November 17, 2013 (PDF available).
30. "Declaration of the International Conference in Support of Afghanistan," Paris, June 12, 2008.
31. Afghanistan National Development Strategy (2008–2013), pp. 81, 143.
32. "Afghanistan-Pakistan Border Region Prosperity Initiative," Gatineau, QC, March 29, 2010.
33. "Joint Declaration on Next Steps in Afghanistan-Pakistan Comprehensive Cooperation," March 11, 2010.
34. Shawn McCarthy, "Pipeline Opens New Front in Afghan War," *The Globe and Mail*, June 19, 2008.
35. John Foster, "A Pipeline through a Troubled Land: Afghanistan: Canada, and the New Great Energy Game" (Ottawa: Canadian Centre for Policy Alternatives June 2008).
36. *Canadian Press*, "Canada not in Afghanistan over Pipeline: Mackay," CTV News, July 30, 2008.
37. Canada-Afghanistan Solidarity Committee, "Pipeline Politics in Afghanistan," UBC event, January 14, 2010.
38. Peter Klein, *The Standard*, Joy TV, Vancouver, B.C., January 25, 2010.
39. John Foster, "Afghanistan, the TAPI Pipeline, and Energy Geopolitics," *Journal of Energy Security*, Washington, DC, March 23, 2010.
40. S. Frederick Starr and Andrew C. Kuchins, "The Key to Success in Afghanistan," Central Asia-Caucasus Institute (SAIS) and Silk Road Studies Program (Stockholm), in cooperation with the Center for Strategic & International Studies, Washington, DC, May 2010.
41. Robert O. Blake, Jr., Assistant Secretary, Bureau of South and Central Asian Affairs, "The Obama Administration's Priorities in South and Central Asia," Houston, TX, January 19, 2011.
42. Hillary Rodham Clinton, US Secretary of State, "Remarks on India and the United States: A Vision for the 21st Century," Chennai, India, July 2011.
43. Hillary Rodham Clinton, US Secretary of State, "Remarks at the New Silk Road Ministerial Meeting," New York, September 22, 2011.
44. Foreign Affairs, Trade and Development Canada, "Canada Discusses New (Silk) Road Forward for Afghanistan," New York, September 22, 2011.

45. John Kerry, US Secretary of State, "Remarks on the U.S.-India Strategic Partnership," New Delhi, India, June 23, 2013.
46. *Express Tribune*, "Afghanistan to Raise 7,000-member Security Force for TAPI Project," Pakistan, December 28, 2015.
47. Gilles Dorronso, "The Taliban's Winning Strategy in Afghanistan," Carnegie Institute for International Peace, Washington, DC, June 29, 2009.
48. *Huffington Post*, "The Afghan Ethno-Tribal Army," June 19, 2016.
49. Special Inspector General for Afghanistan Reconstruction (SIGAR), "35th Quarterly Report to Congress," Arlington, VA, April 30, 2017.
50. NATO, "ANA Trust Fund," Brussels.
51. *Stars and Stripes*, "Despite Billions in US Funding, Afghan Forces Have a Problem with Boots," May 5, 2016.
52. General John W. Nicholson, Commander US Forces — Afghanistan, "Statement for the Record on the Situation in Afghanistan," Senate Armed Services Committee, Washington, DC, February 9, 2017.
53. The White House, "The Vice President Appears on 'Meet the Press' with Tim Russert," Washington, DC, September 16, 2001.
54. Prime Minister Stephen Harper, "PM Confirms Firm End to Canada's Military Mission in Afghanistan," Ottawa, May 21, 2012.
55. *The Globe and Mail*, "Afghanistan's Mounting Toll," January 5, 2017.
56. Gloria Galloway, "One in 10 Canadian Vets of Afghan War Diagnosed with PTSD," *The Globe and Mail*, January 22, 2016.
57. Watson Institute, "Costs of War," Brown University, August 2016.
58. Transparency International, "Corruption Perceptions Index 2015," Berlin, 2016.
59. Jaap de Hoop Scheffer, NATO Secretary General, "Transatlantic Leadership for a New Era, Security and Defence Agenda," NATO, Brussels, January 26, 2009.
60. "Security and Defense Cooperation Agreement between the Islamic Republic of Afghanistan and the United States of America," Kabul, September 30, 2014.
61. David Vine, "Garrisoning the Globe. How US Military Bases Abroad Undermine National Security and Harm Us All," September 13, 2013.
62. *The Independent*, "'A Complete Waste': What Trump Said about War in Afghanistan before He Dropped the $16m 'Mother of all Bombs'," April 14, 2017.
63. Lead Inspector General, Report to US Congress, "Operation Freedom's Sentinel," February 18, 2018.
64. Pentagon data for August 2017 indicated that 57 per cent of the country's 407 districts were under Afghan government control or influence, 13 per cent under insurgent control or influence and 30 per cent were contested.
65. SIGAR, Quarterly Report to US Congress, January 30, 2018.
66. "Afghanistan's Ghani Offers Talks with Taliban without Preconditions," *Reuters*, February 28, 2018.
67. Thomas Ruttig and Jelena Bjelica, "Who Shall Cease the Fire First? Afghanistan's Peace Offer to the Taleban," Afghan Analysts Network, March 1, 2018.
68. MK Bhadrakumar, "Joint Gains from Afghan Peace," *Tribune*, India, March 5, 2018.
69. Ariana News, "Taliban Announces Support for TAPI Gas Pipeline Project in Afghanistan," Kabul, February 23, 2018.
70. VOA, "Taliban Vows to Protect TAPI Gas Pipeline Project," February 24, 2018.
71. "Afghanistan's Karzai Criticizes U.N., Pakistan in Farewell Speech," *Reuters*, September 24, 2014.

Chapter 8
1. "Remarks by President Obama to the United Nations General Assembly," White House, Washington, DC, September 28, 2015.
2. UN News Centre, "In Assembly Address, Russian President Stresses National Sovereignty within Context of UN Charter," September 28, 2015.

3. USAID, "Ukraine."
4. IFC, "IFC in Ukraine."
5. World Bank, "Ukraine Country Brief," Washington, DC, July 17, 2016.
6. Victoria Nuland, Assistant Secretary, Bureau of European and Eurasian Affairs, "Remarks at the US-Ukraine Foundation Conference," State Department, Washington, DC, December 13, 2013
7. USAID, "Democracy, Human Rights and Governance," Washington, DC, 2016.
8. In February 2018, Victoria Nuland was elected to the National Endowment for Democracy's Board of Directors.
9. Carl Gershman, President, National Endowment for Democracy, "Former Soviet States Stand up to Russia. Will the US?" *Washington Post*, September 26, 2013.
10. BBC News, "EU Rejects Russia 'Veto' on Ukraine Agreement," November 29, 2013.
11. BBC News, "Russia Offers Ukraine Major Economic Assistance," December 17, 2013.
12. The first Ukrainian Eurobond matured on December 20, 2015.Though the IMF ruled the bond to be sovereign (not commercial) debt, Ukraine refused to repay Russia. Russia has bought no more bonds.
13. *The Guardian*, "John McCain Tells Ukraine Protesters: 'We Are Here to Support Your Just cause,'"December 15, 2013.
14. BBC News, "Ukraine Crisis: Transcript of Leaked Nuland-Pyatt Call," February 7, 2014.
15. "Victoria Nuland Phoning with Geoffrey Pyatt," *YouTube*, February 4, 2014.
16. BBC, "Profile: Ukraine's Ultra-nationalist Right Sector," April 28, 2014.
17. *The Guardian*, "Ukraine Opposition Leaders Sign Deal with Government," February 21, 2014.
18. *RT News*, "US 'Rudely and Insolently Cheated Russia' during Ukraine Coup — Putin," March 8, 2018.
19. President of Russia, "Vladimir Putin Answered Journalists' Questions on the Situation in Ukraine," Moscow, March 4, 2014.
20. "Estonian Foreign Minister Urmas Paet and Catherine Ashton Discuss Ukraine over the Phone," February 26, 2016.
21. Thierry Meyssan, "Ukraine: Poland Trained Putchists Two Months in Advance," *Voltaire Network*, April 19, 2014.
22. Ivan Katchanovski, "The Snipers' Massacre on the Maidan in Ukraine," University of Ottawa, Ottawa, October 1, 2014.
23. Gabriel Gatehouse, "The Untold Story of the Maidan Massacre," BBC News, February 12, 2015.
24. Christopher Black, "The Maidan Massacre: US Army Orders: Sow Chaos," New Eastern Outlook, December 15, 2017.
25. Gian Micalessin, "The Version of Snipers on the Kiev Massacre: 'Opposition Orders'," *Il Giornale*, November 15, 2017.
26. Gian Micalessin, "Quelle verità nascoste sui cecchini di Maidan," *Le Verità Nascoste*, November 16, 2017.
27. Gian Micalessin, "The Hidden Truth about Ukraine," video, Gli Occhi della Guerra, November 16, 2017.
28. International Foundation for Electoral Systems (IFES), "Public Opinion in Ukraine 2014," Washington, DC, April 30, 2014; and Voice of America, "Poll Finds Ukrainians Doubt Effectiveness of Interim Government," April 30, 2014.
29. Hashed Said, "Map: Russian Language Dominant in Crimea," al Jazeera America, March 15, 2014.
30. Andrew Lambert, "The Crimean War," BBC History, March 29, 2011.
31. The Kremlin, "Address by President of the Russian Federation," Moscow, March 18, 2014.
32. *RT News*, "Time to Grab Guns and Kill Damn Russians — Tymoshenko in Leaked Tape," March 24, 2014.
33. The Memorandum followed negotiations to dispose of Ukraine's nuclear weapons —

one-third of the former Soviet nuclear arsenal. Ukraine transferred its nuclear warheads to Russia for elimination and, in return, received compensation for the value of the warheads' highly enriched uranium plus US assistance in dismantling the missiles, silos, bombers and nuclear infrastructure.

34. Alexander Yakovenko, Russian Ambassador to the United Kingdom, "Who Undermines the Budapest Memorandum on Ukraine?" RT News, May 29, 2014.
35. *Kommersant*, "Crimea Is More Important to Russia than the Falklands to the UK," March 15, 2014.
36. Henry Kirby, "Support in Russia for Crimea Annexation Hits Two-year High, Poll Finds," *BE Inerines*, June 17, 2016.
37. Kenneth Rapoza, "One Year after Russia Annexed Crimea, Locals Prefer Moscow to Kiev," *Forbes Magazine*, March 20, 2015.
38. Ukraine became an aspirant country in 2018.
39. *AFP*, "CIA, FBI Agents Advising Ukraine Government: Report," Mint Press, May 5, 2014.
40. *Financial Times*, "Ukraine Crisis: US Extends Sanctions on Russia," April 28, 2014.
41. BBC News, "New US Sanctions Target Russian Officials and Companies," April 28, 2014.
42. *Sputnik*, "Russia Receives over 1.36 Million Ukrainians Fleeing Conflict since 2014," January 28, 2016.
43. Kyi, "Investigation of May 2014 Events in Odessa Failed to Comply with Requirements of European Human Right Convention, Says International Advisory Panel's Report," November 4, 2015.
44. BBC News, "Ukraine's Inquiry into Odessa Fire not Independent," November 4, 2015.
45. Fort Russia, "Russians Are Supportive of the Volunteers Fighting against Kiev Junta," March 31, 2015.
46. "Remarks by the Vice President at the John F. Kennedy Forum," Harvard Kennedy School, Boston, Massachusetts, October 3, 2014.
47. Lee Fang, "Hacked Emails Reveal NATO General Plotting against Obama on Russia Policy," *The Intercept*, July 1, 2016.
48. The former deputy chief of Ukrainian Railways, Nikolai Sergienko, reportedly shot himself (January 26). The former chairman of the Kharkov region government, Alexey Kolesnik, was found hanged (January 29). Stanislav Melnik, former Party of Regions parliamentarian, reportedly shot himself (February 24). The Mayor of Melitopol Sergey Valter was found hanged just before trial (February 25); a Melitopol police chief, Alexander Bordiuga, was found dead in his garage (February 26); and former Party of Regions member of parliament Alexander Peklushenko was found shot to death. Former Party of Regions parliamentarian Mikhail Chechetov fell from his seventeenth floor apartment in Kiev (February 28), and Odessa prosecutor Sergey Melnichuk fell from the ninth floor (March 14). Shot dead were journalist Sergey Sukhobok (April 13), former Party of Regions parliamentarian Oleh Kalashniko (April 14) and journalist Oles Buzyna (April 16).
49. Shaun Walker, "Pro-Russia Journalist Shot Dead in Kiev," *The Guardian*, April 2015.
50. Alexander Donetsky, "Ukraine: NATO and Political Assassinations," Strategic Culture Foundation, April 20, 2015.
51. Other provisions include pardon and amnesty of those involved in the conflict; unimpeded delivery of humanitarian aid; and restoration of pensions and banking services.
52. "Nord Stream-2 Pipeline to Kill Ukraine's Gas Transit Business - Naftogaz CEO," *Reuters*, November 6, 2015.
53. Anders Åslund, "Ukraine: What Went Wrong and How to Fix It," Peterson Institute for International Economic, Washington, DC, April 15, 2015, Chapter 10.
54. Transparency International, "Corruption Perceptions Index 2014 Brochure," 2015.
55. Global Affairs Canada, "Address by Minister Freeland on Canada's Foreign Policy Priorities," Ottawa, June 6, 2017.

56. CNN News, "US Will Provide Anti-tank Weapons to Ukraine, State Dept. Official Says," December 23, 2017.
57. Radio Canada International, "Liberals Clear Way for Weapons Sales to Ukraine," December 14, 2017.
58. *The Ukrainian Weekly*, "Canada Adds Ukraine to Automatic Firearms Country Control List," December 22, 2017.
59. Ministry of Foreign Affairs, "Comment by Foreign Ministry Spokesperson Maria Zakharova on American and Canadian Weapons Deliveries to Ukraine," Russian Federation, December 14, 2017.
60. *APA*, "UK Ambassador: Return of Azerbaijani Lands Will Prevent Loss of Life," Azerbaijan, May 4, 2016.
61. *The Hill*, "Biden: Cyprus Poised to Be Key Energy Player," Washington, DC, May 22, 2014.
62. ENGIE (French), OMV (Austrian), Uniper (German) and Wintershall (German).
63. US Secretary of State John Kerry, "Remarks with EU High Representative Federica Mogherini, Secretary of Energy," State Department, Washington DC, May 4, 2016.
64. Atomic Insights, "US State Department Bureau of Energy Resources Input on Energy and Climate at Central Europe's Tatra Summit," November 5, 2015.
65. EurActiv, "Germany-favoured Nord Stream-2 Risks Strangling Ukraine, US Says," November 5, 2015.
66. "Ten EU Nations Say Nord Stream Gas Extension not in EU Interests," *Reuters*, November 27, 2015.
67. *Sputnik International*, "Warsaw Wants Nord Stream 2 Gas Pipeline to Run through Poland," January 4, 2016.
68. Russia Beyond the Headlines, "Gazprom to Build Nord Stream 2 on Its Own after Partners Pull out," August 16, 2016.
69. "Joint Press Release of ENGIE, Gazprom, OMV, Shell, Uniper, Wintershall and Nord Stream 2 AG," Zug, Switzerland, August 12, 2016.
70. European Commission, "Energy Union: Commission Takes Steps to Extend Common EU Gas Rules to Import Pipelines," Brussels, November 8, 2017.
71. "Germany, Austria vs. US Senate: America and Europe on Collision Course," Strategic Culture Foundation, June 17, 2017.
72. Federal Chancellor's Office, "Kern und Gabriel zu einseitiger Verschärfung der Russland-Sanktionen durch die USA," Austria, June 15, 2017.
73. EurActiv, "Juncker Flexes Muscles over US Sanctions," July 27, 2017.
74. Prior to Sabine Pass, the only US LNG export facility was the Kenai plant in Alaska, opened in 1969.
75. "Remarks by President Trump at the Three Seas Initiative Summit, Warsaw, Poland," White House, Washington, DC, July 6, 2017.
76. "Remarks by President Trump to the People of Poland, Warsaw, Poland," White House, Washington, DC, July 6, 2017.
77. New Europe, "Bulgaria Should Comply with EU Requirements on South Stream Pipeline: Expert," June 10, 2014.
78. EU Business, "EU Urges Bulgaria to Suspend South Stream Pipeline Project," June 3, 2014.
79. Trans-Adriatic Pipeline, "Trans-Adriatic Pipeline Secures Third Party Access Exemption," May 17, 2013.
80. EurActiv, "TAP Pipeline Secures Exemption from Third Energy Package," April 30, 2015.
81. New Europe, "EU-US Bulgaria Squeeze Freezes South Stream," June 13, 2014.
82. *Moscow Times*, "Russia Sees Underhanded Sanctions against Russia," June 9, 2014.
83. *RT News*, "Putin: Russia Forced to Withdraw from S. Stream Project due to EU Stance," December 1, 2014.
84. EurActiv, "Šefcovic: Turkish Stream Will not Work," February 2015.
85. "US Urges Greece to Resist Russian Gas Pipeline," *Reuters*, May 8, 2015.

86. *RT News*, "Russia Halts Turkish Stream Project over Downed Jet," December 3, 2015.
87. In June 2017, the Turkish foreign minister said: "We know that a country provided $3 billion in financial support for the coup attempt in Turkey and exerted efforts to topple the government in illegal ways. On top of that, it is a Muslim country." Foreign Ministry sources identified it as UAE.
88. Matteo Villa, "Higher than You Think: Myths and Reality of Nord Stream's Utilization Rates," Italian Institute for International Political Studies, April 17, 2016.
89. European Commission, "Questions and Answers on the Third Legislative Package for an Internal EU Gas and Electricity Market," MEMO/11/125, Brussels, March 2, 2011.
90. *Wall Street Journal*, "EU Approves Increased Gazprom Use of Opal Pipeline," October 25, 2016.
91. "Gazprom Cuts Glows via Opal Gas Pipeline after Polish Challenge Upheld," *Reuters*, February 1, 2017.
92. General Court of the European Union, "President of the General Court Rejects the Applications for a Stay of Execution of the Commission's Decision that 50% of the Transport Capacities of the OPAL Gas Pipeline Are to Be Subject to a Bidding Procedure," Luxembourg, July 21, 2017.
93. Daily Sabah, "Russia Discussing Turkish Stream Entry Point with European Countries, Russian PM Says," May 22, 2017.
94. EurActiv, "'South Stream' to Become 'Bulgarian Stream'," January 14, 2016.
95. EurActiv, "Gazprom-Edison-DEPA Agreement Signed for Southern Gas Supply Route," Greece, June 2, 2017.
96. *RT News*, "Gazprom Proposes New Gas Pipeline to Southern Europe," February 25, 2016.
97. EurActive, "Putin and Orbán Contemplate Stronger Energy Ties," February 18, 2015.
98. *RT News*, "Russia, Greece Sign €2bn Deal on Deal on Turkish Stream Gas Pipeline," June 19, 2015.
99. *RT News*, "Turkish Stream Pipeline Priority for Greece, Despite EU Pressure — Ex-minister," July 20, 2015.
100. *Turkish Weekly*, "Russia's Stroytransgaz to Build Gas Pipeline in Macedonia," March 13, 2015.
101. Balkan News Agency, "Bulgaria, Greece and Romania Sign Gas Corridor Memorandum," April 23, 2015.
102. *RT News*, "Russia Awaits Slovak Offer to Join Turkish Stream Extension - Energy Minister," June 3, 2015.

Chapter 9
1. Paul Reynolds, "Suez: End of Empire," BBC News, July 24, 2006.
2. NBC News, "Trump Said 'Take the Oil' from Iraq. Can He?," September 8, 2016.
3. ABC News, "This Week Transcript: Rudy Giuliani, Gen. John Allen, and Secretary Jeh Johnson," September 11, 2016.
4. *The Hill*, "Trump Says He Will Renegotiate or withdraw from NAFTA," June 28, 2016.
5. Article 605 requires Canada or the US to export the same proportion of total supply of oil and gas (including imports) to the other country as it had during the previous three years, in the event it wants to cut production or redirect resources elsewhere. If it cuts energy exports to the other country, it must also cut supply domestically to the same extent.
6. *The Guardian*, "Belgian Politicians Drop Opposition to EU-Canada Trade Deal," October 27, 2016.
7. Gus Van Harten and Pavel Malysheuski, "Who Was Awarded Compensation in Past ISDS Awards?" March 28, 2015.
8. World Bank Group, "Background Information on the International Centre for Settlement of Investment Disputes (ICSID)," Washington, DC.
9. Two similar exploration programs were conducted for several years by Petro-Canada

International Assistance Corporation (a subsidiary of the nationally owned Petro-Canada), with funding from the Government of Canada; and by the International Energy Development Corporation (based in Geneva), with Canadian and Kuwaiti financing.

10. Energy Sector Management Assistance Program (ESMAP), Washington, DC.

11. G7 member countries are Canada, France, Germany, Great Britain, Italy, Japan and the United States.

12. In May 2018, Rosneft announced the Qatar Investment Authority would increase its stake to 18.93 per cent, leaving Glencore with 0.57 per cent.

13. In Britain, inspired by the US *Magnitsky Act*, the 2017 Criminal Finances Act allows the government to freeze assets of international human rights violators in the UK.

14. Elizabeth Zolotukhina, "Why Khodorkovsky?" Institute of Modern Russia, June 25, 2013.

15. US Energy Information Administration, "Privatization and the Globalization of Energy Markets," Washington, DC.

16. Andreas Heinrich, Julia Kusznir and Heiko Pleines, "Foreign Investment and National Interests in the Russian Oil and Gas Industry," *Post-Communist Economies*, Carfax Publishing Company, Vol. 14, No. 4, 2002.

17. *Bloomberg*, "BP Reaping Rewards in Russia Even after Sanctions Added to Risks," April 12, 2016.

18. Richard L. Morningstar, Special Envoy for Eurasian Energy, "European and Eurasian Energy: Developing Capabilities for Security and Prosperity," testimony, Subcommittee on Europe and Eurasia, House Committee on Foreign Affairs, Washington, DC, June 2, 2011.

19. Anders Fogh Rasmussen, NATO Secretary General, "A Strong NATO in a Changed World," Brussels Energy Forum, March 21, 2014.

20. US Treasury, "Announcement of Expanded Treasury Sanctions within the Russian Financial Services, Energy and Defense or Related Materiel Sectors," Washington, DC, September 12, 2014.

21. "ExxonMobil Says to Return to Russian Arctic Once Sanctions Lifted," *Reuters*, April 19, 2016.

22. *Financial Times*, "EU's Russia Sanctions Fail to Dent Oil Deals," June 14, 2015.

23. "Gazprom, Shell to Invest $13 Billion in Projects in Russia: Russian Energy Minister," June 16, 2016.

24. Ben van Beurden, Chief Executive Officer, Royal Dutch Shell, "More Oil, Less Money," Oil & Money Conference, London, UK, October 6, 2016.

25. Rex Tillerson, subsequently US Secretary of State, February 2017–March 2018.

26. *Associated Press*, "Western Leaders, CEOs Visit Russia amid Sanctions Fatigue," June 16, 2016.

27. Gazprom, "Negotiations on Western Route of Gas Supply to China Showing Good Dynamics," August 18, 2015.

28. *RT News*, "Putin Tops Russians' Trust Ratings with 80% Support," May 26, 2016.

29. Vladimir Putin, President of the Russian Federation, "Meeting of the Valdai International Discussion Club," Sochi, Russia, October 27, 2016.

30. *Mint Press News*, "Right-Wing Victories in Argentina, Venezuela Could Accelerate US Dominance in the Region," December 16, 2015.

31. BP, Exxon-Mobil, Petrobras (Brazil), Repsol (Argentina-Spain), Shell and Total.

32. Brazil's Banco National de Desenvolvimento Econômico e Social, the European Investment Bank and the Corporación Andina de Fomento (owned by 12 Andean and Caribbean countries).

33. *The Guardian*, "Bolivia's Left-Wing Upstart Alarms US," July 15, 2002.

34. Jeremy Bigwood and Eva Golinger, "USAID's Silent Invasion in Bolivia," North American Congress on Latin America, Washington, DC, May 2009.

35. Office of Transition Initiatives, "What We Do," Bureau for Democracy, Conflict, and Humanitarian Assistance, USAID, Washington, DC.

36. Roger Burbach, "Orchestrating a Civic Coup in Bolivia," CounterPunch, November 18, 2008.

37. Mark Weisbrot, "The United States and Bolivia: A New Beginning?," *Huffington Post*, May 25, 2011.

38. Goldberg was previously chief of mission in Kosovo, a statelet which NATO helped break away from Serbia.

39. UN News Centre, "Latin American Nations Voice Concerns to Ban over Rerouting of Bolivian Leader's Plane," New York, July 9, 2013.

40. The Guardian, "US Admits Contact with Other Countries over Potential Snowden Flights — as It Happened," July 4, 2013.

41. BBC News, "Spain 'told Edward Snowden Was on Bolivia President's Plane'," July 5, 2013.

42. Telesur, "Evo Morales Asks Citizens to Believe in Bolivia, Not US Rule," February 14, 2016.

43. WT Whitney, "Clouds Gather over Bolivia's Change Process as US Intervenes," *CounterPunch*, February 16, 2016.

44. Atilio Borón, "The Bolivian Vote for 'No' Is Born in Washington," *The Dawn*, February 11, 2016.

45. F. Jimenez, "Brazilian Government Announces Board of the State-owned Company that Will Manage Exploration of the Pre-salt," Pre-Salt, Brazil, October 15, 2013.

46. *The Guardian*, "Brazilian President Postpones Washington Visit over NSA Spying," Rio de Janeiro, September 17, 2013.

47. *The Globe and Mail*, "Charges that Canada Spied on Brazil Unveil CSEC's Inner Workings," Toronto, October 7, 2013.

48. Glenn Greenwald, "After Vote to Remove Brazil's President, Key Opposition Figure Holds Meetings in Washington," *The Intercept*, April 18, 2016.

49. *The Guardian*, "Brazil Minister Ousted after Secret Tape Reveals Plot to Topple President Rousseff," May 23, 2016.

50. *The New York Times*, "Brazil's Congress Has Approved a Measure to Give Private Companies a Larger Role in Exploring One of the World's Largest Oil and Gas Reserves." November 10, 2016.

51. *Financial Times*, "Shell Aims to Expand in Brazil's Deep Fields after Rules Shake-up," November 2016.

52. Glenn Greenwald, "Brazil's Right Wing Jailed Ex-President Lula Because They Couldn't Win at the Polls," *Democracy Now*, April 9, 2018.

53. Mark Weisbrot, "Brazil's Popular Ex-President Lula Ordered to Prison after Politically Motivated Trial & Conviction," *Democracy Now*, April 6, 2018.

54. Francisco R. Parra, *Oil Politics: a Modern History of Petroleum* (New York: I.B. Tauris, 2010).

55. Under operating services agreements, foreign companies operated oilfields for PDVSA, who paid them a fee and bought the oil. Under risk/profit-sharing agreements, foreign companies bore all exploration costs and, if oil were found, PDVSA could opt to buy a 35 per cent interest. Under strategic associations, foreign companies could produce extra-heavy oil with PDVSA in the Orinoco Oil Belt.

56. Herbert Smith Freehills, "ExxonMobil Is Awarded US$1.6 Billion in ICSID Claim against Venezuela — to Be Set off against Award in Parallel Contractual Arbitration," October 16, 2014.

57. Carles Muntaner, Joan Benach and Maria Paez Victor, "The Achievements of Hugo Chávez," CounterPunch, December 14, 2012.

58. Eva Golinger, "Coup and Countercoup, Revolution!," *VenezuelanAnalysis.com*, April 13, 2010.

59. Ed Vulliamy, "Venezuela Coup Linked to Bush Team," *The Observer*, London, April 21, 2002.

60. Eva Golinger, "The CIA Was Involved in the Coup against Venezuela's Chávez," VenezuelanAnalysis.com, November 22, 2004.

61. Bart Jones, *Hugo! The Hugo Chávez Story from Mud Hut to Perpetual Revolution* (London: The Bodley Head, 2008).
62. "Venezuela Decrees Nationalization of Last Foreign Controlled Oil Fields," VenezuelanAnalysis.com, February 27, 2007.
63. Telesur, "The Long War: Venezuela and ExxonMobil," November 18, 2015.
64. Caroline Simson, "A Cheat Sheet to Venezuela's ICSID Disputes," *Law360*, July 29, 2016.
65. Frank Murder, "Oil Giants Punish Venezuela through Dutch Treaty," *Eurasia Review*, January 7, 2016.
66. Mark Weisbrot, "The Truth about Venezuela: A Revolt of the Well-off, not a 'Terror Campaign'," *The Guardian*, March 20, 2014.
67. "Fact Sheet: Venezuela Executive Order," White House, Washington, DC, March 9, 2015.
68. Agencia EFE, "Obama: Policy Shift on Cuba 'Showing Results,' Silence on Venezuela Troubling," Madrid, April 9, 2015.
69. Gabriel Hetland, "The End of Chavismo? Why Venezuela's Ruling Party Lost Big, and What Comes Next," *The Nation*, December 10, 2015.
70. Andrew Buncombe, "CIA Chief Hints Agency Is Working to Change Venezuelan Government," *The Independent*, July 25, 2017.
71. Tyler Durden, "What Trump's Venezuela Sanctions Will Do to Oil Prices," *ZeroHedge*, July 26, 2017.
72. "Mercosur Bloc Rejects Use of Force in Venezuela," *Reuters*, August 12, 2017.
73. "Presidential Executive Order on Imposing Sanctions with Respect to the Situation in Venezuela,"White House, Washington, DC, August 25, 2017.
74. Joyce Nelson, "Canada vs. Venezuela: Have the Koch Brothers Captured Canada's Left?" CounterPunch.
75. "China Says Venezuela Can 'Appropriately' Handle Debt Load," Reuters, November 17, 2017.
76. Nick Cunningham, "Aggressive US Oil Sanctions Could Bankrupt Venezuela," OilPrice.com, July 23, 2017.
77. CBC, "Alberta and the National Energy Program."
78. Canadian Encyclopedia, "Economic Nationalism."

Chapter 10
1. Glenn Greenwald, "Wes Clark and the Neocon Dream," *Salon*, November 26, 2011.
2. "Remarks by President Trump at the Unleashing American Energy Event," White House, Washington, DC, June 29, 2017.
3. "An America First Energy Plan," White House, Washington, DC.
4. US Secretary of State Rex Tillerson, "US Engagement in the Western Hemisphere," University of Texas at Austin, February 1, 2018.
5. US Secretary of State Rex Tillerson, "Press Availability with Argentine Foreign Minister Jorge Faurie," State Department, Washington, DC, February 4, 2018.
6. Colonel (ret'd) Andrew Bacevich, *The Limits of Power: The End of American Exceptionalism* (New York: Holt, 2009).
7. Chalmers Johnson, *Blowback* (New York: Holt, 2004), p. 288.
8. Gen. Stanley McChrystal, "Former US General Warns of 'Tremendous Resentment' of Drones," Reprieve, January 21, 2014.
9. Linda J. Bilmes, "The Financial Legacy of Iraq and Afghanistan: How Wartime Spending Decisions Will Constrain Future National Security Budgets," Harvard Kennedy School, Faculty Research Working Paper Series RWP13-006, March 2013.
10. National Priorities Project, "Military Spending in the United States," Northampton, MA.
11. Conn Hallinan and Leon Wofsy, "The American Century Has Plunged the World into Crisis. What Happens Now?" Foreign Policy in Focus, June 22, 2015.

12. Natylie Baldwin, "The High Cost of American Hubris," *Consortium News*, August 26, 2016.
13. World Bank, "By the Numbers: The Cost of War & Peace in the Middle East," February 2016.
14. Michael T. Klare, "Resource Wars," blog.
15. Michael T. Klare, *Rising Powers Shrinking Planet: The New Geopolitics of Energy* (New York: Metropolitan Books, 2008).
16. Zbigniew Brzezinski, *The Grand Chessboard: American Primacy and Its Geostrategic Imperatives* (New York: Basic Books, 1997).
17. Chalmers Johnson wrote a trilogy on the consequences of empire: *Blowback, The Sorrows of Empire*, and *Nemesis: The Last Days of the American Republic*.
18. Congressional Budget Office, "Growth in DoD's Budget from 2000 to 2014," Washington, DC, November 20, 2014.
19. William Hartung, "Ignoring the Costs of War," *TomDispatch*, May 9, 2017.
20. Public Intelligence, "Strategic Communications: How NATO Shapes and Manipulates Public Opinion," November 28, 2012.
21. NATO Strategic Communications Centre of Excellence, "About Strategic Communications," Riga, 2016.
22. NBC News, "10 Companies Profiting Most from War," March 6, 2012.
23. *Democracy Now*, "Global Tensions Rising after U.S. Strike on Syrian Airbase," April 10, 2017.
24. *Washington Post*, "Russian Propaganda Effort Helped Spread 'Fake News' during Election, Experts Say," November 24, 2016.
25. Is It Propaganda Or Not? "An Initial Set of Sites That Reliably Echo Russian Propaganda," November 30, 2016.
26. News sites include Consortium News, Drudge Report, Mint Press, Moon of Alabama, The Duran, Truthdig, Truth-out, Zero Hedge — all thought-provoking journals.
27. European Parliament, "EU Strategic Communication to Counteract Anti-EU Propaganda by Third Parties," November 23, 2016.
28. "H.R.5181 - Countering Foreign Propaganda and Disinformation Act of 2016," House of Representatives, Washington, DC.
29. EurActiv, "European Parliament Adopts MEP Fotyga's Report on Stratcom," November 27, 2016.
30. Julian Borger, "Nuclear Watchdog Chief Accused of Pro-Western Bias over Iran," *The Guardian*, March 22, 2012.
31. NATO, "Defence Expenditure of NATO Countries (2009–2016)," March 13, 2017.
32. *The New York Times*, "Transcript: Donald Trump's Foreign Policy Speech," April 27, 2016.
33. "Remarks by President Trump at NATO Unveiling of the Article 5 and Berlin Wall Memorials," Brussels, May 25, 2017.
34. Prime Minister's Office, "Prime Minister Trudeau Attends NATO Leaders' Meeting," May 25, 2017.
35. Global Affairs Canada, "Address by Minister Freeland on Canada's Foreign Policy Priorities," Ottawa, June 6, 2017.
36. Ministry of National Defence, "Strong, Secure, Engaged — Canada's Defence Policy," Ottawa, June 7, 2017.
37. Murray Dobbin, "Is Trudeau Ready for a Middle East War?" blog, November 17, 2017.
38. NATO, press release, "New NATO Division to Deal with Emerging Security Challenges," Brussels, August 4, 2010.
39. NATO, press release, "Secretary General Opens NATO Energy Security Centre of Excellence in Vilnius," September 6, 2013.
40. NATO Energy Security Centre of Excellence website.
41. EU Climate Action and Energy Commissioner Miguel Arias Cañete, speech, "Europe's Energy Security Challenges: 'La Union have la fuerza'," Atlantic Council, Washington, DC, February 4, 2015.

42. Remarks by President Donald Tusk after the First Session of the European Council Meeting, March 19, 2015.
43. *Wall Street Journal*, "Hungary's Viktor Orban Looks for Fight over EU Energy Union," February 18, 2015.
44. *New York Times*, "Transcript: Donald Trump's Foreign Policy Speech."
45. Zbigniew Brzezinski, "Towards a Global Realignment," *The American Interest*, August 17, 2016.
46. *RT News*, "Tillerson Pits Beijing's 'Predatory' Africa Expansion against Washington's 'Responsible' Support," March 8, 2018.
47. Without US participation, the other 11 countries (including Canada) signed a modified version in March 2018, named the Comprehensive and Progressive Agreement for the Trans-Pacific Partnership.
48. "Russia's Rosneft to Take Control of Iraqi Kurdish Pipeline amid Crisis," *Reuters*, October 20, 2017.
49. "Russia's Rosneft, Iran's NIOC Agree to Team up on Oil and Gas Projects Worth $30 Billion," *Reuters*, November 1, 2017.
50. *RT News*, "Moscow Offers Saudis Stake in Arctic Energy Project," February 15, 2018.
51. *RT News*, "Russia Inks Huge Energy Deals with Saudi Arabia, Challenging US Dominance in Gulf Region," February 15, 2018.
52. President Trump substituted Mike Pompeo for Rex Tillerson as Secretary of State, John Bolton for H.R. McMaster as National Security Advisor, and selected Gina Haspel for Mike Pompeo as CIA Director.

SELECTED BIBLIOGRAPHY

BOOKS

Bacevich, Andrew J. *Washington Rules: America's Path to Permanent War*. New York: Metropolitan Books, 2010.

Bacevich, Andrew J. *America's War for the Greater Middle East*. New York: Random House, 2016.

Brzezinski, Zbigniew. *Grand Chessboard: American Primacy and Its Geostrategic Imperatives*. New York: Basic Books, 1997.

Chalabi, Fadhil J. *Oil Politics, Oil Myths: Observations of an OPEC Insider*. London & New York: I.B. Tauris, 2010.

Cooper, Andrew Scott. *Oil Kings*. New York: Simon & Schuster, 2011.

Engdahl, F. William. *Myths, Lies and Oil Wars*. Self-published, 2012.

Engler. *A Propaganda System: How Governments, Corporations, Media and Academia Sell War and Exploitation*. Halifax: Fernwood Publishing, 2016.

Hopkirk, Peter. *The Great Game: The Struggle for Empire in Central Asia*. New York: Kodansha Globe, 1994.

Johnson, Chalmers. *Nemesis: The Last Days of the American Republic*. New York: Metropolitan Books, 2007.

Klare, Michael T. *The Race for What's Left: The Global Scramble for the World's Last Resources*. New York: Metropolitan Books, 2012.

Klare, Michael T. *Rising Powers, Shrinking Planet: The New Geopolitics of Energy*. New York: Metropolitan Books, 2008.

Kowaluk, Lucia, and Steven Staples, editors. *Afghanistan and Canada: Is There an Alternative to War?* Montreal: Black Rose Books, 2009.

Longhurst, Henry. *Adventure in Oil. The Story of British Petroleum*. London: Sidgwick and Jackson, 1959.

McQuaig, Linda. *It's the Crude, Dude: War, Big Oil and the Fight for the Planet*. Toronto: Doubleday Canada, 2004.

Muttitt, Greg. *Fuel on the Fire: Oil and Politics in Occupied Iraq*. London: Bodley Head, 2011.

Parra, Francisco. *Oil Politics: A Modern History of Petroleum*. New York: I.B. Tauris, 2010.

Porter, Gareth. *Manufactured Crisis: The Untold Story of the Iran Nuclear Scare*. Just World Books, 2014.

Sampson, Anthony. *The Seven Sisters: The Great Oil Companies and the World They Shaped*. London: Viking Adult, 1975.

Stein, Janice, and Eugene Lang. *Unexpected War: Canada in Kandahar*. Toronto: Viking Canada, 2007.

Taft, Kevin. *Oil's Deep State*. Toronto: Lorimer, 2017.

Van Buren, Peter. *We Meant Well: How I Helped Lose the Battle for the Hearts and Minds of the Iraqi People*. New York: Metropolitan Books, 2012.

Warnock, John W. *Creating a Failed State: the US and Canada in Afghanistan*. Halifax and Winnipeg: Fernwood Publishing, 2008.

Welsh, Jennifer. *The Return of History: Conflict, Migration and Geopolitics in the 21st Century*. Toronto: Anansi Press, 2016.

Yergin, Daniel. *The Prize: The Epic Quest for Oil, Money & Power*. New York: Simon & Schuster, 1993.

ARTICLES

Foster, John. "The Petroleum Factor: Are Oil and Gas Being Left out of Current Conflict Narratives?" *Open Canada*, January 30, 2015.

Foster, John. "Afghanistan, the TAPI Pipeline, and Energy Geopolitics." *Journal of Energy Security*, March 23, 2010.

Foster, John. "A Pipeline through a Troubled Land: Afghanistan, Canada and the New Great Energy Game." Ottawa: Canadian Centre for Policy Alternatives, June 19, 2008.

INDEX

277